NATURE, H
STATE

NATURE, HISTORY, STATE

1933–1934

Martin Heidegger

Translated and edited by
Gregory Fried and Richard Polt

With essays by Robert Bernasconi, Peter E. Gordon,
Marion Heinz, Theodore Kisiel, and Slavoj Žižek

Athlone Contemporary European Thinkers

B L O O M S B U R Y

LONDON · NEW DELHI · NEW YORK · SYDNEY

Bloomsbury Academic

An imprint of Bloomsbury Publishing Plc

50 Bedford Square   1385 Broadway
London   New York
WC1B 3DP   NY 10018
UK   USA

www.bloomsbury.com

Bloomsbury is a registered trade mark of Bloomsbury Publishing Plc

"Über Wesen und Begriff von Natur, Geschichte und Staat". Übung aus dem
Wintersemester 1933/34 (pp. 53–88) taken from *Heidegger-Jahrbuch 4 –
Heidegger und der Nationalsozialismus I, Dokumente* edited by Alfred Denker
and Holger Zaborowski © 2009 Verlag Karl Alber part of Verlag Herder GmbH,
Freiburg im Breisgau

Marion Heinz, Volk und Führer. Untersuchungen zu Heideggers Seminar *Über
Wesen und Begriff von Natur, Geschichte und Staat* (1933/34) (pp. 55–75) taken from
Heidegger-Jahrbuch 5 – Heidegger und der Nationalsozialismus II, Interpretationen
edited by Alfred Denker and Holger Zaborowski © 2010 Verlag Karl Alber part of
Verlag Herder GmbH, Freiburg im Breisgau

'Heidegger in the Foursome of Struggle, Historicity, Will, and *Gelassenheit'* adapted
from Slavoj Žižek, *Less Than Nothing* (London: Verso, 2012),
pp. 878–903. Reproduced with permission from Verso.

This English translation and editorial material
© Gregory Fried and Richard Polt and contributors 2013, 2015
First published in paperback 2015

Gregory Fried and Richard Polt have asserted their rights under the Copyright,
Designs and Patents Act, 1988, to be identified as the Editors of this work.

British Library Cataloguing-in-Publication Data
A catalogue record for this book is available from the British Library.

ISBN: HB: 978-1-44117-638-7
       PB: 978-1-44111-617-8
     ePDF: 978-1-44116-852-8
     ePub: 978-1-44113-325-0

Library of Congress Cataloging-in-Publication Data
A catalogue record for this book is available from the Library of Congress.

Typeset by Newgen Imaging Systems Pvt Ltd, Chennai, India
Printed and bound in Great Britain

CONTENTS

ABOUT THE CONTRIBUTORS

Gregory Fried (Suffolk University) is the author of *Heidegger's Polemos: From Being to Politics* and (with Charles Fried) *Because It Is Wrong: Torture, Privacy and Presidential Power in the Age of Terror*.

Richard Polt (Xavier University, Cincinnati) is the author of *Heidegger: An Introduction* and *The Emergency of Being: On Heidegger's "Contributions to Philosophy."* Together, Fried and Polt have translated Heidegger's *Introduction to Metaphysics* and *Being and Truth* and edited *A Companion to Heidegger's "Introduction to Metaphysics."*

Robert Bernasconi is Edwin Erle Sparks Professor of Philosophy at Pennsylvania State University. He is the author of *The Question of Language in Heidegger's History of Being*, *Heidegger in Question: The Art of Existing*, and *How to Read Sartre*. The topics of his published essays include Kant, Hegel, Levinas, and critical philosophy of race.

Peter E. Gordon is Amabel B. James Professor of History at the Center for European Studies at Harvard University. His books include *Rosenzweig and Heidegger: Between Judaism and German Philosophy* and *Continental Divide: Heidegger, Cassirer, Davos*. He has also co-edited several books, including *The Cambridge Companion to Modern Jewish Philosophy*, *Weimar Thought: A Contested Legacy*, and *The Modernist Imagination*.

Marion Heinz (Universität Siegen) is the author of *Zeitlichkeit und Temporalität: die Konstitution der Existenz und die Grundlegung einer temporalen Ontologie im Frühwerk Martin Heideggers* and *Sensualistischer Idealismus: Untersuchungen zur Erkenntnistheorie des jungen Herder (1763–1778)*. She is the editor of volume 44 of the Heidegger *Gesamtausgabe* and has also edited and co-edited a variety of volumes on German philosophy, feminism, and gender theory.

Theodore Kisiel (Northern Illinois University) is the author of *The Genesis of Heidegger's "Being and Time"* and *Heidegger's Way of Thought: Critical and Interpretive Signposts*. He has translated Heidegger's *History of the Concept of Time* and published numerous articles on Heidegger.

Slavoj Žižek (University of Ljubljana) is the author of books on topics including Lacan, Marxism, and contemporary culture, including *The Sublime Object of Ideology*, *In Defense of Lost Causes*, *The Parallax View*, *Living in the End Times*, *Less Than Nothing*, and *The Year of Dreaming Dangerously*.

EDITORS' INTRODUCTION

Richard Polt and Gregory Fried

Martin Heidegger's support for the Nazi regime has long been a matter of public knowledge, but only recently have we gained a clearer picture of the details of his political activities and positions. Together with other documents from Heidegger's tenure as the first National Socialist rector of the University of Freiburg in 1933–4, the seminar in this volume is an essential piece of evidence for those who wish to assess the degree to which he was intellectually committed to Nazi ideology.[1] In the light of this text, Heidegger's postwar attempts to minimize the extent of his support for Nazism are no longer credible, and any interpretation that makes a simple distinction between his philosophy and his politics is no longer tenable—for in this seminar, Heidegger sketches a political philosophy, consistent with his views on the historicity of *Dasein* or human existence, that explicitly supports Hitlerian dictatorship and suggests justifications for German expansionism and persecution of the Jews.

This is not to say that the text necessarily renders Heidegger's thought as a whole bankrupt. We still must ask whether we can disentangle the truer or more promising aspects of his philosophy from the pernicious ones. We still must try to diagnose the errors in Heidegger's views and understand the merely ideological or culturally conditioned elements in them, while remaining open to the possibility that they can provide insights that transcend the dark circumstances of this seminar. We still must judge this text in the larger context of Heidegger's thought. The five essays by leading thinkers and scholars in this volume take up these philosophical challenges, offering us distinctive ways to read the seminar from appropriately critical, yet not dismissive perspectives.

The seminar

Heidegger held his seminar "On the Essence and Concept of Nature, History, and State" in ten sessions from October or November 1933 to February 1934. We do not have Heidegger's own notes or text for the seminar, if such existed; instead, the text consists of student protocols or reports on the seminar sessions. These protocols were reviewed by Heidegger himself, as confirmed by two interpolations he makes in the text. The protocols also generally sound like Heidegger; readers familiar with his lecture courses will recognize typical trains of thought and turns of phrase. The first protocol provides one student's perspective on the discussions that took place during the opening session of the seminar; it is valuable as a glimpse of the atmosphere in Heidegger's classroom and his practice as a teacher. To judge from the remaining protocols, the subsequent nine sessions must have proceeded more like a lecture course, for only Heidegger's voice is present, and he develops a fairly continuous line of argument. Thus, while we cannot rely on this text as a verbatim transcript of what Heidegger said, it is reasonable to take it as good evidence of the essential content of the views he developed during this seminar.

The text of the protocols forms part of Heidegger's papers in the Deutsches Literaturarchiv in Marbach (item DLA 75.7265). The text was generally unknown until Marion Heinz accidentally discovered it in 1999, as she explains in her essay in this volume. It then circulated among some scholars, and Emmanuel Faye relied on it in his controversial study of Heidegger's politics.[2] The seminar protocols were finally published in German in 2009.[3] With our translation, English-speaking readers have the opportunity to draw their own conclusions about this remarkable text.

In a retrospective on his teaching written around 1945, Heidegger refers to the seminar as developing a "critique of the biologistic view of history."[4] It is true that Heidegger consistently rejects the reduction of human beings to the biological, including biological racism, but Heidegger's most distinctive concern in the seminar, and its primary point of interest for most readers today, is the development of the rudiments of a communitarian and authoritarian political philosophy. For a detailed analysis of the seminar, we refer the reader to Marion Heinz's essay. It may be useful, however, to present a brief summary of each session here.

Session 1: This is the only protocol that gives us a sense of the personality of its author, Karl Siegel. Siegel blames both the students and the professor for the rather confusing and unproductive first session of the seminar, but he helpfully identifies Heidegger's general strategy of trying to undercut traditional concepts of nature, history, and state, along with scientific and epistemological prejudices, for the sake of a fresh encounter with the "essences" of these phenomena.

Session 2: Heidegger investigates the essence of nature and provides historical perspective on the concepts of *natura* and *physis*, emphasizing that *physis* originally referred not just to a particular domain of beings, but to all beings in their very way of Being.

Session 3: There is a deeper connection between history and time than there is between nature and time, even though all natural processes occur in time. Furthermore, time cannot be understood merely through quantitative measurements of the duration of events.

Session 4: The Kantian and Newtonian conceptions of time cannot do justice to historical, human time. These conceptions take time as an objective or subjective dimension with a uniform linear structure, but in human existence we must make decisions about which times are significant. In this sense, animals have no time, since they are not able to "decide both forwards and backwards."

Session 5: Time is the "authentic fundamental constitution of human beings" as the beings who "can have and make history." Heidegger now turns to the state, rejecting traditional ways of practicing political philosophy by asking about the state's origin or purpose; he seeks an ontological understanding of the connection between state and people.

Session 6: Heidegger seeks to restore the political to its rightful status as the unifying essence of a community. The state fulfills this essence, so that the state is "the way of Being of a people" while the people is "the ground that sustains" the state. A people can be understood in various ways, including through racial concepts, but perhaps most fundamentally it is "a kind of Being that has grown under a common fate and taken distinctive shape within a *single* state."

Session 7: A born leader can decisively affect the Being of the state and people. Such a leader must be supported by an educated elite or "band of guardians." Since a people without a state is unfulfilled and lacks its Being, the people properly loves its state and binds itself together with the leader to a single destiny, ready for sacrifice.

Session 8: The space of a people has two aspects. The immediately familiar homeland calls for rootedness in the soil. But there is another impulse, "working out into the wider expanse," that calls for "interaction." Germans who live outside the boundary of the Reich are denied the opportunity to participate in the extended space of state-governed interaction, while rootless people such as "Semitic nomads" may never understand "our German space."

Session 9: State and people are bound together through the "implementation" of the will of the leader. Heidegger raises the question of the essence of the will of the people, and of will in general, distinguishing will from wish, drive, and urge. "An animal cannot act, because it cannot will."

Session 10: A true leader will not use coercion, but will awaken a harmonious will in the led. This may require education as "the implementation of the will of the leader and the will of the state, that is, of the people." Heidegger ends by praising the "Führer-state" as the culmination of a historical development that has reconstructed community after the Middle Ages were dissolved by modernity.

Context

The seminar is distinctive as Heidegger's most concerted attempt to develop a political philosophy. But of course, it is not a self-contained work that can be understood purely on its own. It stands within the context of Heidegger's voluminous writings over many decades, the complex history of German political thought, and the violent struggles of the twentieth century. The contributors to this volume address these contexts in a variety of ways. Here we will simply draw attention to a few texts by Heidegger that are particularly important to forming a well-rounded judgment on his political thought, before we return to some distinctive concepts in the seminar and consider their implications.

Being and Time (1927) generally appears to operate on a level of ontological abstraction that rises above particular political views, and the text emphasizes individual more than communal existence. Still, the climactic section 74 sketches a communal authenticity that would involve a generation's discovery of the people's destiny through communication and struggle (*Kampf*).[5]

After assuming the rectorship of the University of Freiburg in April of 1933, Heidegger delivered his inaugural Rectoral Address, "The Self-Assertion of the German University," on May 27, 1933. In this speech, Heidegger delineated three forms of service to the state: military, labor, and knowledge service. He claimed that the traditional concept of academic freedom was only a negative form of freedom, and that true university life must involve a will to a self-assertion in which leader and follower, teacher and student, together forge a bond in the pursuit of knowledge in the service of the people's destiny. During this period, Heidegger made other pronouncements to both the university and the broader public in support of the National Socialist regime, including speeches in favor of the plebiscite of November 12, 1933, in which Hitler called on the German people to ratify his domestic and foreign policies.[6] For a discussion of the Rectoral Address, see Theodore Kisiel's essay in this volume.

Heidegger delivered two lecture courses during his year as rector, which are collected in the volume *Being and Truth*. Particularly striking is the introduction to the course "On the Essence of Truth," which appears to celebrate *polemos* or "struggle" as the essence of Being. In a particularly disturbing passage, Heidegger explains struggle as standing against the enemy, and comments that the internal enemies of the people have to be rooted out without mercy, "with the goal of total annihilation."[7] (For the full passage, see Slavoj Žižek's essay, p. 164.) In conjunction with the remark on "Semitic nomads" in the 1933–4 seminar, these thoughts seem to anticipate and endorse a possible Holocaust. The same lecture course notably includes a ferocious attack on Erwin Kolbenheyer, a novelist and Nazi ideologue who had presented a "biological" account of the purpose of art in a speech at Freiburg.[8] For Heidegger, the destiny of a people has to be understood in distinctively historical, not biological terms.

After stepping down as rector, Heidegger delivered a lecture course in 1934 on *Logic as the Question of the Essence of Language* that explores what it means to be a people.[9] While marked by its contemporary political context, the lecture course adopts a tone that is rather more questioning than the 1933–4 seminar and less dogmatic. For further discussion of this course we refer to the reader to Robert Bernasconi's essay in this volume.

Heidegger's 1934–5 seminar on Hegel's *Philosophy of Right* explores a variety of themes including sovereignty, law, and freedom, showing an attraction to a right-Hegelian point of view but also raising numerous questions, particularly in Heidegger's private notes for the seminar.[10]

With his 1934–5 lectures on Hölderlin's "Germania" and "The Rhine," Heidegger embarks on an exploration of this poet as a figure who recognizes the difficulty of "the free use of the national"[11] and points the way to a deeper, less immediate encounter with German destiny.

Introduction to Metaphysics (1935) develops a confrontational understanding of the relation between Being and human beings and criticizes various supposedly half-hearted political developments of the time for missing the "inner truth and greatness" of National Socialism.[12]

By studying Nietzsche and Ernst Jünger, Heidegger evidently hoped to come to grips with this "inner truth"—the metaphysical basis of the Nazi movement. Heidegger's various lectures and writings on Nietzsche

(1936–42) were revised and published after the war in two volumes, where Heidegger cut some of the more political passages.[13] These texts evolve from an initial fascination and enthusiasm to a rather negative view of Nietzsche as trapped in a metaphysics of the will to power and eternal recurrence. Through an intensive study of Jünger's 1932 work *Der Arbeiter* (*The Worker*), Heidegger concluded that Jünger was an exponent of a one-sided Nietzscheanism.[14]

The private writings of the late thirties and early forties offer evidence of Heidegger's disillusionment with Nazi ideology: drawing on his critique of Nietzschean will to power, he criticizes the Nazi celebration of violence and insists that Being transcends power and manipulation; he also denounces willful assertions of the primacy of the *Volk* that fail to understand that the people must look beyond itself to recognize its destiny within the history of Being. These critiques do not bring Heidegger any closer to liberal or leftist points of view, however; instead, he seems to distance himself from all political positions.[15] In a dialogue composed at the very end of the war, Heidegger rejects the moral judgments that are being passed on Germany and attributes evil to a nonmoral "devastation" at work in Being itself.[16]

The Bremen lectures of 1949 are an example of how Heidegger drew on his account of Western metaphysics to position himself in the postwar period as a critic of all modernity, including Nazism. The most famous passage here presents "the production of corpses in the gas chambers and extermination camps" as "in essence the same" as mechanized agriculture and nuclear bombs.[17] Readers must decide whether passages such as this point out deep roots of modern nihilism, whether they are reductive and pose false equivalencies, or whether the truth lies somewhere in between.

We can find anticipations of Heidegger's political engagement in the 1920s, and echoes of it in the 1940s and thereafter; the careful reader must determine whether those resonances are enough to condemn Heidegger's thought as a whole, or whether he succeeded in thinking through his own errors. In either case, his support for Nazism in the 1930s, and in 1933–4 in particular, is a critical point in his life and thought. The seminar on "Nature, History, and State" is essential reading if we are to form a judgment on this crucial episode.

The politics of the seminar

Let us return to the seminar itself and to what we take to be some of its most notable features as a study in political philosophy.

First, Heidegger assigns an ontological status to the relation between people and state: that is, what it means for a particular people to *be* must be established through its state. While he leaves open the question of what a people in general is, he claims that the state is not just "grounded on the Being of the people" (p. 46 below), but *is* the Being of the people (46, 52, 57). "The people that turns down a state, that is stateless, has just not found the gathering of its essence yet; it still lacks the composure and force to be committed to its fate as a people" (46). A people without a state *is not yet*, in the sense that it has not yet found its unique fulfillment as a community.

Heidegger elaborates on the people-state relation through an analogy to individuals. Because individuals' own Being is an issue for them, they have consciousness and conscience. They care about their own Being, they want to live, and they *love* their own existence. In just the same way, the people loves its state: "The people is ruled by the urge for the state, by *erōs* for the state" (48). This is why we care about the form of the state, or the constitution—which is not a contract or a legal arrangement, but "the actualization of our decision for the state; . . . constitution and law . . . are factical attestations of what we take to be our historical task as a people, the task that we are trying to live out" (48–9).

The erotic urge for the state is to be distinguished from "drive" as felt by lower animals; bees and termites are instinctively driven into cooperative formations, but this is a nonhuman phenomenon and not genuinely political (48; cf. Aristotle, *Politics*, 1.2, 1253a8–9). The vagueness of an urge also separates it from will, which is clearly focused on a particular goal (58).

Heidegger briefly distinguishes his concept of the political from two others. Carl Schmitt's view that the essence of the political is the friend-enemy relation comes in for some criticism when Heidegger emphasizes that in Schmitt's view, "the political unit does not have to be identical with state and people" (46). Heidegger implies that a group based on solidarity against an enemy is less fundamental than a *Volk*—whatever that may be. Heidegger also criticizes Bismarck's concept of politics as "the art of the possible," which depends too much on "the personal genius of the statesman" (46).

But this remark should not lead us to expect an anti-dictatorial point of view, and in fact, Heidegger's views as presented here easily lend themselves to a personality cult: he claims there can be a born leader, an individual who "must be a leader in accordance with the marked form of his Being." A born leader needs no political education, but he ought to be supported by an educated elite, a "band of guardians" who help to take responsibility for the state (45). Heidegger seems to envision something like Plato's "perfect guardians," the philosopher-rulers, but here they are in service to a creative leader who knows instinctively, not philosophically, what to do. This leader not only understands, but actually "brings about" what the people and the state are. It is noteworthy that these words were penciled in by Heidegger himself on the student protocol (45; cf. a similar insertion on 46). The born leader drafts the state and people, so to speak: he draws the line between who "we" are and who "we" are not. The focused will of the leader provides the clear identity that a vague urge cannot.

There is little room for debate and disagreement within Heidegger's complex of people, state, and leader. "Only where the leader and the led bind themselves together to *one* fate and fight to actualize *one* idea does true order arise" (49). He envisions "a deep dedication of all forces to the people, the state, as the most rigorous breeding, as engagement, endurance, solitude and love. Then the existence and superiority of the leader sinks into the Being, the soul of the people, and binds it in this way with originality and passion to the task." The citizens are ready to sacrifice themselves in order to defeat "death and the devil—that is, ruination and decline from their own essence" (49).

In the eighth and perhaps most original session of the seminar, Heidegger focuses on the political meaning of space. In all of Heidegger's thought, space is meaningful: it is not a geometrical abstraction, but a complex of places where things and human beings belong—or fail to belong. Here he develops two aspects of the space of a people: homeland (*Heimat*) and territory. (Heidegger indicates the latter with a variety of words: *Land, Herrschaftsgebiet, Territorium,* and *Vaterland.* The term "fatherland" is mentioned only one other time in the seminar, on p. 52, where Heidegger implies that it reflects an inadequate relationship to the people.) The immediately familiar homeland, the locality into which one is born, is small, not just in its measurements but in the coziness of its familiarity. The proper relation to it is *Bodenständigkeit:* groundedness, standing steadfast and rooted in the soil. But there is another impulse, which Heidegger calls *Auswirkung in die Weite,* working out into the wider expanse. The space of the state, the territory, requires this extended "interaction" (*Verkehr*). Only when rootedness in the soil is supplemented by interaction does a people come into its own. What is the most important element of this "interaction"—is it war? Commerce? Travel? Or something else?

While Heidegger does not answer this question, the passage could be seen as an example of a dialectic between home and homelessness that is at work in many of Heidegger's texts. In *Being and Time,* one must experience the uncanniness of anxiety before one can return authentically (*eigentlich,* "own"-ly) to one's familiar environment. If we were completely ensconced in our surroundings, they would be our habitat and we would be nothing but animals. But as Heidegger puts it in 1935, "we cannot wholly belong to any thing, not even to ourselves."[18] And yet we do belong partly, finitely, to our home. The key to authentic dwelling is precisely the recognition that this dwelling is finite and contingent. Accordingly, "When one is put out of the home . . . the home first discloses itself as such."[19] Admittedly, interaction with a wider territory is not the same as facing the abyss of anxiety, but both involve the readiness to step out beyond the immediately familiar.

What are the concrete implications of Heidegger's thoughts on political space? He makes two telling remarks. First, Germans who live outside the boundary of the Reich cannot participate in the extended space of state-governed interaction. And if the state is the very Being of the people, these groups are being "deprived of their authentic way of Being"—prevented from fulfilling themselves as Germans (56). Their politico-ontological *erōs* is being thwarted. Despite his reservations about the slogan *Volk ohne Raum*, "people without space"—a people necessarily has *some* space of its own (53)—Heidegger's comments fit all too easily with the Nazi call for *Lebensraum* and Hitler's evident ambitions to unify the German people under one state.

Secondly, different peoples have different relations to their spaces and affect the landscape in accordance with these relations. Heidegger contrasts a *bodenständig* people to a nomadic people that not only comes from deserts, but also tends to lay waste to every place it goes. He adds that perhaps "Semitic nomads" will never understand the character of "our German space" (56).[20] The implied characterization of Jews as aliens is obvious. We should also note that Heidegger does an injustice to nomads: nomadic people can be very much at home in the landscape through which they travel, and their practices may well be ecologically superior to those of settled agriculture.

When he returns to the relations among state, people, and leader, Heidegger raises the question of the nature of the will of the people, but does not resolve it, resorting instead to a disappointingly vague remark: it is "a complicated structure that is hard to grasp." He prefers to emphasize the inseparable, "single actuality" of people and leader (60). To be led is not to be oppressed: the true leader will show the path and the goals to those who are led, rather than coercing them (61). "The true implementation of the will [of the leader] is not based on coercion, but on awakening the same will in another, that is . . . a decision of the individual" (62).

But what about those who cannot recognize the path, or who disagree with the goals? Heidegger seems not to care what will become of these dissidents. Instead he looks to the glorious deeds that manifest "the soaring will of the leader" (62). Heidegger does briefly discuss resistance, or will that is contrary to the leader's, but he seems to see it purely as a negative phenomenon that requires reeducation. Education at all levels "is nothing but the implementation of the will of the leader and the will of the state, that is, of the people" (63). It seems that Heidegger envisions complete unanimity as the ideal. Even if community depends on individual decisions, any such decision that contradicts the will of the state, which is identical with the will of the leader, is out of order and amounts to a betrayal of the people.

The essays

It should be clear from this overview that in the seminar Heidegger was ready to put the ontological and existential concepts of *Being and Time* into the service of an authoritarian, expansionist, and exclusivist political program—in short, the program of National Socialism. How are we to judge this use or abuse of Heideggerian thought? How does the seminar relate to Heidegger's other work and to his way of pursuing philosophy? How does it relate to others' attempts to theorize Nazism? And does it contain any insights that might still be illuminating for us today? The five contributors to this volume offer a range of perspectives on such questions, from close readings to broad philosophical and historical contextualizations.

Marion Heinz's "*Volk* and *Führer*" investigates Heidegger's methodology in the seminar, compares his account of human existence there to the account in *Being and Time*, and explicates the connections among people, state, and leader according to the seminar. Reflecting on the philosophical basis for Heidegger's attraction to the Hitlerian dictatorship, Heinz points to his conception of historicity, his appropriation of Nietzsche, and his rejection of a politics based on rational principles.

In his essay "Heidegger in Purgatory," Peter E. Gordon argues that Heidegger's way of pursuing phenomenology through concrete illustrations leaves it highly susceptible to bathos and ideological contamination by the jargon Victor Klemperer called the *lingua tertii imperii* ("the language of the Third Reich"). Gordon directs our attention to crucial points in the seminar where Heidegger deploys a strategy of analogy to disguise political claims as ontological insights. This is especially true of Heidegger's anti-Semitic attack on the "nomad." Gordon ends with the suggestion that philosophy itself is nomadic and that even Heidegger's philosophy therefore remains open to new appropriations that escape the crude reductions of this text.

Robert Bernasconi's "Who Belongs? Heidegger's Philosophy of the *Volk* in 1933–34" juxtaposes the seminar with the *Logic* lecture course of the following semester in order to show how, in a complex political competition for intellectual leadership in the party, Heidegger takes a decisive turn in his own philosophical understanding of what constitutes belonging to the people, by connecting that belonging to historically situated, resolute decision rather than the pseudo-science of race.

Theodore Kisiel's essay emphasizes the broader evolution of Heidegger's political thought, which he interprets in terms of Heidegger's "three concepts of the political." For Kisiel, the seminar is typical of the middle phase of Heidegger's political thought, where Heidegger focuses on humans as beings who must collectively decide their own way of Being. Kisiel also points out Heidegger's indebtedness to the tradition of German conservative thought that sought a distinctive national mode of combining freedom and responsibility through proper education.

Slavoj Žižek's contribution, adapted from his book *Less Than Nothing*, reads the seminar and related texts in terms of class struggle, will, and drive and regrets Heidegger's later turn away from will to *Gelassenheit*. Žižek admires Heidegger the revolutionary activist, although not the particular direction that his political engagement took. For Žižek, Heidegger was right to seek authenticity by engaging in the historical tangle of attachments and interests that constitute us.

The translation

In translating the protocols we have aimed at a readable text that also provides consistent renderings of key concepts. The reader may therefore trace how Heidegger employs salient words and phrases throughout the seminar. As compared to Heidegger's more intricate texts, the seminar is couched in relatively accessible terms and uses little specialized or experimental language, as is appropriate for a teaching situation that does not presuppose any familiarity with Heidegger's publications or private writings. We have endeavored to reproduce the extemporaneous quality of the seminar protocols, without sacrificing rigor.

Readers may find the German words that correspond to major English terms by consulting the index. The senses of the central terms "beings" (*das Seiende* or *Seiendes*), "Being" (*das Sein*), and "Dasein" emerge naturally in Heidegger's discussions. A few other words call for some commentary here.

The term *bodenständig*, which features prominently in Session 8, literally means "standing on the soil," and echoes the nationalist cliché *Blut und Boden*, "blood and soil." Heidegger uses the term in a variety of texts to connote a well-grounded attitude, an attitude that is not "free-floating" but remembers its roots in concrete experience. We render the word here as "rooted in the soil." For further discussion of the concept, see the end of Theodore Kisiel's essay.

The same session refers to the need for *Verkehr*, which we translate as "interaction." The term is built on the root *kehren*, "to turn," and could thus be rendered most literally as "circulation." It is the common German term for traffic, both in the narrow sense of vehicular traffic and in the broader sense of exchange, interchange, or intercourse.

When seeing the terms "leader" and *Führer*, readers should remember that *Führer* is the ordinary German word for "leader," which of course became the title for Hitler as Germany's supreme leader.

The term *Volk*, related to our "folk," is translated as "people." All National Socialists focused their efforts on promoting the *Volk*, which they often but not always understood in racial terms. As Robert Bernasconi explains in his essay, Heidegger attempted to stake out a distinctive philosophical position on what constitutes a people.

Bracketed numbers in the seminar refer to the printed German edition of the text in *Heidegger-Jahrbuch* IV. In the interpretive essays, parenthesized page numbers refer to pages of this translation unless otherwise indicated.

The dates on the protocols are reproduced here as they stand in the manuscript. The third protocol is undated. The fourth protocol is dated one day later than the fifth, and the ninth and tenth protocols both bear the same date. All dates provided are Fridays, except the date on the fourth protocol, which is a Saturday. The discrepancies may be due to the fact that some protocols bear the date of the seminar session, while others bear the date of the composition or delivery of the protocol itself. The preposition *am* (on) that is to be found before some dates suggests that these are the dates of actual seminar sessions. This is the case for the fifth, sixth, and tenth protocols.

Marion Heinz provided us with detailed criticisms and suggestions for our translation, and we have gratefully adopted many of them. We would also like to thank Theodore Kisiel for his characteristically generous assistance; his expertise with Heidegger's texts, as well as his acumen for solving particularly difficult translation problems, has been a great help to us. In addition to helping us improve our word choices at many points, Profs. Heinz and Kisiel were able to resolve some uncertain readings in the printed version of the text by comparing it to the original manuscript and to a transcription prepared by Klaus Stichweh.

PART ONE

ON THE ESSENCE AND CONCEPT OF NATURE, HISTORY, AND STATE

SEMINAR, WINTER SEMESTER 1933–4

SESSION 1[1]
November 3, 1933

I. Our seminar director began by drawing our attention to the two sides of the question that we will consider: the theme of the seminar is the *essence and concept* of nature, history, and state.

He explained the relation between the two questions—the question of the essence of a thing or domain, and the question of its concept—as follows:

1 the two questions should not be confused, and

2 we must get acquainted with the essence of the domain in question before we think about its concept.

For it is not absolutely necessary to grasp the essence of a domain such as nature in a concept, and it may even turn out to be impossible in the end.

This simple reminder of the difference between the question of the essence of a domain and the task of grasping it conceptually—a task that should be taken up only later—was explained no further. As the session went on, this reminder proved too weak to force our discussion in the direction of the question of essence and keep it there. So for most of the first session of the seminar, an older natural scientist and an older student of philosophy began with number two—the concept—after all. These two older gentlemen first had to be drawn in, so to speak, to the primary question that faced us, and brought back to it. But the available time was too short to really lead the two "advanced" minds back to the simple, prescientific beginning of the question of the essence of the domains at hand, which consists in the plain, uncomplicated, quite naive expression of how nature, history, [54] and state are given to us; there was not enough time for the two gentlemen not only to be convinced that it was fair for them to be stopped and turned back in their thinking, but also to take active steps in the other direction. So that the first session would not end in confusion, Professor Heidegger himself then had to give us a simple presentation of two basic differences in the way nature is given to us (the difference between the material and the formal concept of nature—see below). This may have surprised some participants who no longer clearly remembered the course of the seminar from its beginning.

This was *how the seminar as such took place.* As it seems to the author of this protocol, our director could not have been very happy about this development, since the watchword he had set for our questioning was not taken up and followed at all, or only very poorly. The two main speakers could not have been satisfied, since at the end they may well have had the feeling that the seminar had passed over them, and that something had been coerced from them that they could not understand so quickly and whose implications they could not anticipate. And above all, the real and proper "beginners" among the seminar participants, and all who prefer a slow, considered, and truly step-by-step approach to the question, must have been very unsatisfied, if not completely confused.

Now, on this point one must make an observation that is obvious in an experienced and cooperative philosophical circle, where everyone has the sure feeling that he can rely on the others and can really speak openly without any worries—but here, in a freshly convened beginners' seminar, the point may need to be made explicitly. Obviously, negative judgments such as the ones the author of this protocol has had to make about the far too rash and hasty speculations of the two main speakers are meant neither "morally" nor pedantically. For surely there were more students in the room who had just the same attitude as these two gentlemen and would have said the same thing—if they had been able to speak so readily. So in this regard, the way our first session went was simply typical, and the obstinacy of the two gentlemen was fully in order. Nevertheless, I would again like to point out and emphasize the strangeness of the situation: it was the director of this philosophical seminar, who was a professor of philosophy, for whom the two gentlemen were speaking too "philosophically," too "theoretically," too deeply, too exaltedly, and not naively and naturally enough—and it was the students who began with the second part, whereas usually this would have been the right and customary thing to do, and many may well have expected it from a seminar in philosophy.

[55] II. But this course of our first session, which has been sketched in its general character, took place on the basis of a particular question, and we now have to specify and draw out this point more precisely.

After the reminder and warning, reported above, about the difference between the question of essence and the "later" task of grasping a concept, which presupposes that the question of essence has been carried through, the director took up the second part of the announced theme of the seminar and drew our attention to the triad of nature, history, and state, what they are for us, and whether the sequence in which they are listed is arbitrary.

1 On the first question: the expression with which a participant tried to sum up all three, "life domain," was rejected as a term, and it was stipulated that in the context of the seminar, in order to avoid confusions, we should restrict the word "life" to the Being of plants and animals, and reserve the word "Dasein"[2] for human Being. We must say, then, that nature, history, and state belong in the domain of our Dasein, and that they are essentially fields (the only ones? the most important ones?) in which our Dasein plays itself out and maintains itself.

2 The result of the short, preliminary discussion of the sequence in which they are listed was that the order must not be arbitrary. Instead, the three fields have been ordered consciously and intentionally so that each successive one is narrower: history and state are incorporated in nature, and the state in turn belongs within history—it is a historical actuality. Here, as an aside, Professor Heidegger also asked the opposite question: whether every historical actuality involves a state just as much as the state belongs to history or is historical.

As brief as this first stage of the interpretation was, our reflections on nature, history, and state, understood together in their essence, got underway in an easy and relaxed manner. When Professor Heidegger finished this stage with the remark that we "now" had a certain idea of each of the three fields, this seemed to me to indicate that we should now turn to one of the three fields in particular, in the same calmly focused spirit and with a view to the two topics of inquiry that we had established in the first phase: (1) the question of nature's relation to our Dasein, what nature has to do with our human Dasein, and (2) the problem of sequence, that is, the question of how nature is connected to the other two domains, history and state, so that at the end of the seminar we could turn back to the unified essence that encompasses all three fields.

But instead of the cheerful progress that we were expecting along the indicated path, we suddenly got stuck in our discussions. A certain artificiality and affectation came over the speakers, while a certain lack of restraint and individualistic self-indulgence came over some others, [56] and everything that was brought up by the different sides from then on no longer fit together properly, but ran off in different directions. The seminar director reacted primarily in two ways: first, he tried using humor to bring certain speakers who had fallen into such linguistic artificiality and narrowness back to reason, so to speak; secondly, he took the other group, which was speculating all too freely, blithely and loosely and starting to ramble, and, by interrogating them sharply, forced them to take a stand and formulate things more precisely. They will all still remember vividly, for example, how the professor forced the gentleman who wanted to insist that everything was interior to him to accept even the lectern into his interior; but then the gentleman did not take the bait and admitted that he had the lectern *before* him, not within him (if he was not to falsify the sense of his representation of the lectern). Nevertheless, our discussion kept wavering up to the end of the session and did not get over the disturbance that has left our discussion at the point where we now stand.

In a philosophical conversation there are no accidents, and there should be none. This is why the main question for the author of this protocol was how this blockage, artificiality, and affectation could suddenly have arisen, after the discussion had started off in such a flexible way.

To begin with, *in what did the disturbance consist?* In the rise and domination of a certain principled reflectiveness, or maybe it would be better to call it a reflective adherence to principle, which, once it had had its say, got mixed into nearly all the assertions and brought a hasty impatience into the speaking and thinking of the participants in the seminar—or it brought conflict into our thought and speech by destroying the innocence and naiveté of the plain, "simple" expression of what is given to us and how it is given. Above all, in our reflections it hindered thought itself—the process of slowly pacing off and pacing around the domain in question and then exploring it carefully, step by step.

Now, this reflective adherence to principle was not somehow generated within the seminar itself or awakened by it; it was already there, and it simply took control when it got the first opportunity to have a word. *But how could this happen?* If I may express my personal view, the door through which it burst into our discussion was the seminar director's instructions for questioning, which were somewhat too indefinite in their formulation and left too many possibilities open. After he briefly presented nature, history, and state in their unitary meaning for human Dasein and indicated the problem of how the three fields are to be ordered, he asked what we should do next; this was probably just meant to rouse us, so to speak, so that we might make a new, greater effort and proceed along the path we had begun, in the same way—but not that we should put the path itself into question "in principle." But he posed the question in such a strong tone that [57] the author of this protocol himself was startled for a moment and had the feeling that now something quite new would follow, namely, that we should first reflect on *how* we were to proceed in principle in our philosophizing.

The seminar director's later question about how nature is given could also be taken wrongly in this sense, and in fact it was: it was *not* understood as a challenge to take up a concrete and actual reflection on the essence of nature, starting with one of the factually accepted attitudes and relations to nature, but instead it was misunderstood as bringing up the epistemological problem of the givenness *of such a thing* as nature, history, or state.

The first to reply to the seminar leader's question of what we should do next was the natural scientist, and the second was the gentleman with the interiority that generated everything and had everything inside it.

Both gentlemen began with number two (if we distinguish between essence and concept), that is, they took as their point of departure certain preexisting and preconceived concepts and theories. The other possible way in which one could have begun with number two, namely by starting right away to construct the concepts, was not proposed or even considered by any participant in the seminar.

The natural scientist began with the concept of nature as an exact lawfulness, and then immediately emphasized without further argument that the three domains of nature, history, and state "must" have a common *principle*. He imagined that the philosophical seminar should proceed in such a way that its only goal was to exhibit the common laws that, so to speak, ran through all three domains.

It was conceded to him that one can find and produce a connection between the question of the essence of nature and the exhibition of laws in the natural sciences. But this is a very difficult undertaking. And in no case is it a matter of merely coming up with some imprecisely conceived, indefinite, preexisting, and preconceived scientific concepts, and then without testing them, carrying them over to the domains of history and the state—and in this way leaping over the fundamental fact that nature, history, and state are *given to us as fields of Dasein*.

Then, using a concrete object available in the classroom (the chalk), we briefly explored how difficult it is to find the exact character of the givenness of even such a small and inconspicuous thing as a piece of chalk and to come really close to it in language.—Regarding our question of the essence of nature, history, and state, the seminar director also brought our attention especially to the fact that, in this little example of the chalk, we could already see how things stand with nature, history, and state in general. It is not just humanity that is related to nature, history, and state; even the simple chalk stands in relation to them.

[58] But now it must be said, regarding this interlude in the seminar, that the participants were not aware of it as such. No one, as it seems to the author of this protocol, caught onto it and was in a position—after the course of the seminar to this point, and particularly after the reflective adherence to principle had been expressed so strongly—to pay attention to the very concrete How of a thing such as a piece of chalk in the way that was desired (although we were not directly challenged and instructed to do this).

The effect of this conflict was then that all the formulations that had been introduced were taken too far and, although they did not lose their grip on what stood nearby and was at hand, as it were, they became forced and artificial. After what had happened, we were all making a more or less conscious effort to turn our formulations and even our simple statements in the direction of the universal and first principles, which was precisely what we were supposed to set aside.

So, after two attempts at dialogue had failed to break through to the simple question of essence and to the necessary reflection this question first requires on what is given to us and how, the seminar director erased everything that had been said so far, so to speak, and set out once again from the beginning. He alerted us again to the question of essence and to the fact we had ascertained that nature is given to us; then he asked clearly and unambiguously *how* nature is given to us.

The question had hardly been asked, and there was no chance for anyone to proceed from the question to reflection, before—one must say— the second main speaker let fly with his theory to which, as he said, he had resigned himself after extensive thought, his theory of the interiority that generates everything and has everything inside it (nature and the lectern).

He was finally forced to concede that before all "philosophizing," he had to ascertain the actual state of affairs, what is given and how, and that he must hold on to this state of affairs quite independently of epistemology if he wished to approach the essence of a thing and say something correct and significant about it. — This was without doubt the strongest point in the session, and there could be no doubt anymore about what the seminar director wanted.

Now, then, the discussion slowly went in the right direction, and a whole series of important points about actual natural givens, their ways of givenness, and ways in which we relate to nature were introduced. But, as I have said, the time was too short to develop them all properly and fully, to collect them, and to gather them together into their decisive, fundamental possibilities.

So in conclusion, the seminar director offered his own clarification, which pointed to the difference between the material and formal concepts of nature.

[59] The material concept of nature takes nature, logically speaking, as the sum total of all the things that have the characteristics of natural things; that is, it takes nature as a whole, *as a domain.*

The formal concept of nature, in contrast, aims at the Being of things that belong to the domain of nature, and more precisely at what their kind of Being highlights as nature. — If we bring this difference back to our initial distinction between essence and concept, it means that I can conceive of the whole as nature only if I already have a formal concept of nature, a deeper knowledge of nature's kind of Being. The distinction between domain and kind of Being should also apply to history and the state, and we should pay attention to it there.

SESSION 2[1]
November 17, 1933

We closed our first session with the distinction between the formal and material concepts of nature. We did not want to run the risk of *talking* about such a split and division of nature without clearly knowing the meaning of this word. It is not a coinage of the moment, but stands at the end of a historical sequence.

So what does *natura* mean? "Getting born." Birth occurs in the realm of living things; getting born indicates a relation to what is alive. But what about heaven and earth, mountain and valley, which are nature for us just as plants and animals are? What made the word *natura* capable of undergoing such an extension of its reference that today we can encompass as nature not only what gets born, but what does *not* get born?

The Latin word gives us no solution. It is not the beginning of the Western conception of nature. Before it there stands the Greek word *physis*, growth. What does that mean? Does it get us any further?

Both the Latin "getting born" and the Greek "growth" indicate a *process*. What is going on when something grows? A *development*, we think, since something is getting bigger. But how so? Getting bigger is not the essence of development. Maybe something is *altering* in growth. How does alteration happen? When the light goes out in the classroom, has it altered? No, a *change* has taken place. So what is *that*? Does the chalk lit by the light change if, losing its whiteness, it turns blue? No, it is altered, because its color has become—*other*.

We have not yet experienced whether, in growth, there is alteration or change, development or becoming other. But the processes that we [60] believe we see in growth are ultimately *motions*. So growth, too, is ultimately a motion. This cannot be some *arbitrary* motion. There must be something *special* that distinguishes the motion of *physis*. For the concept of "growth" has undergone that *extension* whose origin we are seeking. What is special about the motion of growth that lets us include the "*non*-living," such as storm and clouds, in the sphere of nature?

In order to find what is distinctive about this motion, we will consider its *opposite* so that it can come into relief. What is it that, as such, opposes the motion of growth? Is it death, since death is rest and not the movement of the living? What is *rest*? The condition of being unmoved is not rest; a triangle is unmoved, but does it *rest*? Only what can be moved can rest. Rest is a limit case of motion, and death perhaps a limit case of life. Movement is exhausted in rest, and rest gives birth to motion.

In this way we *cannot* find what is distinctive about the movement in growth. We distance ourselves from it in a conceptual construct, and the essence of growth slips away from us. How do we *stand*, then, in front of something that is growing? How does the tenderness of a blossom originally touch us? How does the flower by the fence affect us? We say that it has "grown naturally," whereas the wire fence is "man*made*." What is the flower's having grown naturally? It too is something made, but something *that created itself*. Being-from-itself; coming-forth-from-itself; being-moved-by-itself; this by-itself is the essence of growth. The Greek *physis* is what, without human intervention, coming from itself, streams around human beings, gives them rest or unrest, calms or threatens them.

Now we know the origin of the conceptual extension. For *physis* is everything that creates itself. The blowing winds come from themselves, and so does the roaring sea. Man too comes from himself, as do his works and his history. For the *inception* of Greek philosophy does not distinguish between "nature" and non-natural "growth." It sees all beings creating themselves; for it, the *whole of Being* presents itself as By-Itself. This is why *physis* is the totality of Being for the first Greek philosophers, whom Aristotle calls the *physiologoi*: those who seek the *logos* of *physis* as the whole of Being. We should not call them "nature philosophers"; they do not distinguish between what we call "nature," "history," and so forth.

Now, what about the "nature" that we divide conceptually into the material and the formal? How is it that we managed to determine the material domain of things that have a natural character?—We must know about a thing's *kind of Being*, that is, the sort of way in which it is, if we want to assign it to some domain. The material concept thus *presupposes* the formal; it encompasses what satisfies the formal concept. How does nature relate to these two concepts?

The formal and material concepts of nature are *grasped as one* through [61] *physis—natura*—nature, which is what creates itself. Nothing can produce itself without being a something; nothing grows that is not a thing. Nature tells us something both about what its things are and about how they are. The miracle of language harbors such a doubling that comes together as one.

Now if we ask about the "nature" of a human being, we want to get behind the "nature" of a thing, and we mean the "essence." What does that mean? What does it mean that "nature" has yet a *third* sense when we seek *what a thing is—to ti esti*? If *physis—natura*—nature grasps as one:

the *what-Being* of a being, as
something that belongs to a domain, and
the *Being-such* of a being,
then it says what a being is: *to ti esti*, the what-Being of a being as a whole.

If we follow the historical development of *physis* as the whole of Being, we will notice its *restriction* as a concept. *Physis* finds its counterpart in *thesis*—what is posited, positing, *making* in accordance with positive law. "Nature" is opposed to what is made, or "art"; nature now signifies only what produces *itself*. As such, it is revealed most strikingly where it creates itself in the realm of the "living." But the interpretation of nature's characteristics has shifted to the "nonliving": Today, atomic physics believes it can yield knowledge of the miracle of living Being.

After considering nature, we will try to grasp history in a similar way.

What does "history" mean? The past, we think, what *has* happened. But is history only the past? No. *History is everything that happens at all:* history is what happened, but also what is happening and will happen.

The triad of what happened, what is happening, and what will happen is encompassed by the *material* concept of history. It means the realm of all things that have the characteristic of happening. But thanks to the unifying doubleness of language, "history" also contains this *formal* concept: happening as such, which expresses the *Being-such* of a being. What is the formal happening as such related to? *Which* being is determined by it in its kind? Only currently happening activity? Is history only what *is happening*? No, because what has happened and what will happen in the future are a "happening" to the same degree. So the formal concept of history grasps the three realms of the material *as one*, relating itself equally to each. But "history" means happening in its totality, in general. The happening of what has happened "is" no less than the happening of what is happening now and of future happening. Historians for whom history is not such a *totality of happening* must fail.

[62] This consideration of history brings us to a concept of Being that is essentially distinct from that of nature. We must sketch the difference between the two.

SESSION 3[1]

First we supplemented what we had said about *physis*. How could it be possible that *physis*, for the Greeks, meant beings as a whole—*physis*, which in our language means what grows, what comes from itself? Why does the word originally mean *what is*, for the Greeks?

In order to answer this question we must clarify what the Greek *einai* and *on* mean. They always mean a Being-present, Being-in-the-light-of-day, *pareinai*. What is absent has no Being, it is concealed. But *kryptesthai*, being concealed, is the concept that the Greeks oppose not only to Being or *ousia*, but also to *physis*; for *physis*, as what grows and emerges, is at the same time what comes to light, what offers itself. Here we can clearly see the common meaning of *physis* and *ousia*. It consists of growing, coming up, taking form. What is, is what is unconcealed. Heraclitus speaks of this connection between *physis* and unconcealment when he says *hē physis kryptesthai philei*, that is, beings endeavor to conceal themselves, or more clearly: not to be there. Thus, for the Greeks, growth, Being, and Being-unconcealed are bound together in a unity. With this knowledge we have gained something essential for the understanding of Greek Being.

Now let us briefly review the course of our questioning, so that we can stay aware of the point where we stand in our consideration of the essence and concept of nature, history, and state. We had first established that nature, history, and state are in some way domains of our Dasein, and that they are connected somehow. In order to know this connection, we must first try to get clear on what nature, history, and state are. We grasped nature on the basis of *physis* as what produces itself by itself, and here we showed the two ways the word *physis* can be interpreted—formally and materially. Then we explained history as happening—in present, past, and future—and we also clarified the material and formal concepts of history.

[63] This is where our investigation began last time. According to the usual way of speaking, history means something past: one says, "That belongs to history." History can also mean something that comes from somewhere and has developed, as when we say, "Something has a long history." When we assert that history includes not only what has happened, and not only (as contemporary history) what is happening now, but also what will happen in the future, we have expanded the usual concept of history in a certain respect, namely, with regard to time. We can grasp the essence of history only on the basis of time, but we completely ignored time when we were determining the essence of nature. Do we have a right to such a procedure?

Does not time have something to do with nature, then? After all, a plant that develops between spring and fall needs time to do so. The *times* of the year, the seasons, are important for natural life, and we also speak of an incubation *time* or period. All growth occurs in time. How is it then, that we can leave time out of the picture when we determine the essence of nature? Let us look more closely at the role that time plays in nature.

The modern conception of nature is determined by men such as Galileo who believed that they could come closer to what nature is by using mathematical methods. We call this the mathematization of the concept of nature—when one thinks that mathematical laws provide access to the understanding of nature. Natural processes are simply explained mechanically as changes of position of a particular material element in time. In this way, they can be calculated. But with the calculation of a process, do we really get an understanding of its essence, or of the essence of nature? Motion is a change of place in time. Changing place means traversing a path. What is a path? A path is not just any arbitrary distance, but one that actually is or should be measured. This requires time. Time must, therefore, be included in the definition of a path, and in fact it has a particular function: with the help of time, the path is divided. The definition of the path is d = vt, distance = velocity × time. That is how simply time in nature is conceived mathematically. The path is taken only as an example; every fundamental definition of nature includes time—time conceived in this manner. One considers natural processes only as something mathematical, and fails to see much of what constitutes the essence of natural process, or sees it inadequately.

From all this there follows—and this is important at the moment for our investigation—that all natural processes are somehow in time and linked to time. How? The mechanical conception of nature does not clarify this issue in a way that satisfies our question. Instead, our question arises once again: if time is really everywhere in nature, in some way, then why is it not expressed in our definition of the essence of nature, as it is in our definition of the essence of history? Does not time have the function, [64] in nature as well as in history, that we calculate and count with it? So it must seem, after all, that we have been on the wrong path. No—it is just that, when we ask about the *essence* of nature and history, our way of posing the question must relate time, too, to this essence. Our question is now: how far does time determine every being as a being, in the realms of nature and history?

To answer this question, we must first solve two preliminary questions. How do we grasp time in natural and historical processes? And what is time? Within a certain time, I achieve a certain goal. Where is time there? I can measure it with a clock. But even if my clock is not running, time is still there. Is it a part of motion? Maybe it is true that it has something to do with motion, if we also include rest as a limit case of motion—but this is not what concerns us at the moment. Is it perhaps something that we think up, with whose help we can put processes in order? A measure, in other words? How about that—is time actually the measure? Do we not measure, instead, with the help of the sun?

Finally, one claims that "time is the duration of natural processes"—but that too, in the end, brings us back to time as measure. This does not get us any further with our question. We keep taking time as a mathematical quantity, as in physics, where one operates with time as something measurable and calculable.

Now someone answers the question of the essence of time by pointing out that time is a differential, that is, a limit value of the present. This opens new possibilities for knowledge. Time is only in the moment, so right away, time no longer is; and what will come is not yet. So time is constricted to the point of the present now-Being. Everything earlier and later is excluded. We must see that on this path, although we have come farther, we will not find what we are seeking. For in this way we cannot grasp and hold time, since it always no longer is anymore. In general, when we are asking about time, we cannot answer—as we do with other things, such as a tree, a house, and so forth—what it is, where it is, and how it is. Time is, in principle, something completely different from the other things we ask about. On the one hand it is only the current now, but on the other hand, as we rightly believe we can assert, it comprises past, present, and future.

Now we have to take what we have discovered about time into our posing of the question. What evidence justifies us in grounding the historical as such through time in particular? We must bring this together with the other question: why is time of fundamental significance for the essence of history, quite otherwise than for the essence of nature?
[65]

SESSION 4[1]
January 13, 1934

In the last session we occupied ourselves with time. So that we could reveal over the course of our further sessions just how untenable it is to bifurcate the world into subjectivity and objectivity, and so that we could adopt the right fundamental orientation to time, we first examined the two most important theories of time, the Newtonian and the Kantian, both of which proceed on the basis of a partition of the world into the subjective and objective.

Newton, known along with Leibniz as the great inventor of differential calculus, conceived of time in the way his calculus required: as a temporal stream continuously flowing in one direction, in whose intervals all events in space can be unambiguously ordered. This Newtonian time was supposed to be an independent occurrence outside of our subjective understanding and therefore was supposed to become, like all other objects, the content of our experience. This concept of time is objective, in contrast to the Kantian one, which is known to us as the subjective concept of time.

For Kant, time is no longer a content of experience; rather, time is the form of sensory intuition. Time is form, because it is the subjective condition "by which alone intuitions can take place in us."[2] Time is a form of intuition and not of the understanding, because I can think of only a single time, never different times at once. But what one can represent only singly is an intuition. And furthermore, time is the form of inner intuition, because time is the manner in which the mind intuits itself. Time, as our intuition, is therefore characterized as the faculty by which the mind looks inwards and is distinguished from appearance in space, which is not oriented inwards and is therefore called external intuition. But should the fact that spatial intuition does not point inwards in the same sense as time provide a reason to distinguish between inner and outer intuition? Least of all can we draw such a distinction merely because with the help of spatial intuition we go forth into space and understand the juxtaposition of things. If we were entirely cut off from the outer world, we would still have an experience of space, presumably: the feeling of having a body. Space, understood as an intuition, becomes one-sidedly geometrical and is therefore treated too one-sidedly. We must not ask: how must space be constituted so that it satisfies the axioms of geometry? Rather, we must ask: how is space constituted so that a science such as geometry is possible? A response to the philosophical question about space and time should not proceed according to the standpoint of science, and especially not according to mathematical physics [66], as has been attempted. A theory in physics, such as the theory of relativity, should not presume the right to refute or confirm a philosophical doctrine of space-time. So when, on the basis of purely physical relationships, time is treated as the fourth dimension of space, we can take this seriously as a mathematical theory, but not philosophically.

To come to grips with the essence of time, we have to free ourselves from every theoretical presupposition, place ourselves into the world, and ask ourselves how we relate to time.

We are familiar with expressions from everyday life that have to do with time, such as: we need time; we gain time; we lose time; and so on. From such manners of speaking, it is clear how seriously we take time: after all, the time that we have at our disposal is bounded by death. We therefore see ourselves as compelled to divide up our time in a precise way.

The necessity of dividing time leads us to the question of the reckoning of time. Our time is oriented to the sun. That we measure our time by the sun in particular is not a matter of necessity but rather depends upon an agreement. In order to carry out a division of the day into hours, minutes, and seconds, we have built ourselves our clocks. We coordinate particular positions of the sun with particular positions of the clock. The connection between sun and time is the We. We coordinate them because we have to deal with time. With this coordination, we make the tacit assumption that the sun obeys the same mechanical rules (acceleration, etc.) as the gears of our clock, for if this were not the case, then any coordination would be absurd.

But let us look away from the reckoning of time and turn to the question of how it stands with time itself. Where is time when we look at a clock and say it is such-and-such o'clock? When we say, "It is seven o'clock," why is there something more to this than the naming of a number? For not just any statement can say this, but we are saying it in this particular way, and we emphasize the "now" that appears in the sentence, "Now it is seven o'clock." In the Now time gets its meaning for us. This is why the Now has precedence over the After and the Before, and from the perspective of the Now, Before and After even appear to be nothing. For only the Now really is; the Before is no longer and the After is not yet. We cannot hold on to the Now, because in every moment another Now is the Now. The Now thus seems to have fundamental significance for calculus as the limit transition or infinitesimal that dissolves the contradiction that lies in the essence of the continuum. For one has to view the ordered Nows as a continuum, that is, as a region in which no one point is exceptional. But we have just seen that one now, *the* now, is in fact exceptional. Only through the limit function inherent to the differential calculus does this contradiction get resolved. Through the infinitesimal, one Now becomes distinguished and every other Now becomes subordinated to it.

This Now is there and does not necessarily need to be oriented to another occurrence. But since no occurrence is a Now, every Now can be oriented to something else. Our time is specified by the date. Time must be datable. This means that it must be possible for something to be given to which our now may be oriented.

The Now requires the We. For it is we who say, "Now it is seven o'clock." The Now obliges us to decide both forwards and backwards. The animal does not stand under this obligation to decide, because otherwise it would have to be able to order things, as we know from the lecture course.[3] The animal therefore has no time.

Because of this, we already see that the Kantian–Newtonian concept of time must lead into error and is a violent abstraction. In the subsequent sessions we plan to examine how this concept is inadequate for the time of nature and history.

[67]

SESSION 5[1]
January 12, 1934

At the beginning of the session, we returned to the Kantian understanding of time in order to expand on what we had said on this topic.

We had said that time, for Kant, was the form of inner intuition, that is, intuition directed inwards.— But what does "form" mean?

The essential character of form is grasped as "determination." Form thus determines the content, or what can be determined; time as form determines the experiential contents of inner intuition.

Now, how do we determine intuition? The protocol said that intuition was something singular, in contrast to a concept. This did not satisfy us.

We realized that intuition and concept have something in common: both are modes of representation. — Nevertheless, in intuition I represent a singular This, while in a concept I represent something that applies to many things, something that is nonintuitive and universal. Intuition is further characterized by the fact that in it I sense or perceive, while in a concept I think and construct creatively and spontaneously.

For the Kantian way of discussing time, this means that every individual thing given to me in my mental processes is determined by time. I perceive the processes of my thinking, feeling, and speaking only in the succession of time.

In contrast, space as the form of outer intuition means that everything external presents itself to me in the spatial order of the next to each other, behind, and in front.

[68] But now, how are we to understand that for Newton, time appears as a determining factor in *space*?

We do not grasp occurrences in space as such; rather, *we* grasp them. The cognitions of physics, as cognitions, as psychological processes in our consciousness, stand within the form of time, and thus so do the contents that are thought in them. This answer of Kant's is an artificial theory—so it was said—and is contradicted by the fact that we immediately sense temporal succession and do not first get it through reflection.

After these supplemental thoughts on time in Kant, we reconstructed the context in which we are asking about time, so that we might be completely clear about how we are proceeding.

To begin with, we were speaking about nature, but then we distinguished history from it because we essentially understand history on the basis of time. On the basis of some suggestions, we understood history, naturally enough, as the past, but then we moved beyond these preliminary stages. In any case, time immediately played an essential role in our discussion of history, whereas we had neglected it in nature, even though the "t" does not play an unessential role in nature either.

Why do we speak in this way about nature and history? This question drove us to further questions about time.

In asking about time, we began with particular theories in order then to understand time in contrast to them, apart from every theory. We then determined that we grasp time in the "here and now" and that the presupposition for this is that we have something like time in the first place.

But if we say "now," and try to comprehend this "now," we experience that it has always already disappeared. What has happened to the "now," where has it gone? It is gone as the "now" and yet it is still there, as a past "now." I still have it. As it slips away, what character does this disappearing "now" have on its way? Is it a "then, when," a "previously"?—Only insofar as I am already reflecting on this. Neither is it something general such as "not-now." It is a "just happened." The singular "now" is now always already a "just happened," and as having such a structure, it has a relationship that reaches into the present, although it is flowing away into the past. Likewise, every "now" has a relation to the next "now": the "*about to happen*." Thus— it was said—there is basically no "now" anymore, no present; instead, we stand between "just happened" and "about to happen," in a double relation to future and past.

Now, how is it possible for me to stand in this temporal horizon? How is it possible that "just happened" and "about to happen," as horizon, give me the immediate knowledge of the "now"?

What makes it possible for me to grasp the vanishing "now" as what just happened? An experience?—A representation?

No, a *retention*. I retain the "now" in its change because I go along with it into the "just happened," I live in the "just happened." This past that does not slip away is what makes it possible for me to remember.

[69] In turn, the relation to the "about to happen" is *expectation.* Thus, human beings stand in their distinctive way of waiting and retaining that makes it possible for them to reflect, to free themselves from being delivered over in an eternal "now" to what faces them in each case. Insofar as we are presencing in expecting and retaining, we can speak of a "now," a "just happened," an "about to happen," an "at that time," a "right away," and a succession of time.

We refer to this fundamental constitution of human beings as authentic time. As human temporality, it is the condition for the time of which we commonly speak.

So there are two things that we understand as "time":

First there is the time with which we are used to reckoning, that time between 5 and 7 o'clock, *the* time in which the processes of nature and history occur. But then there is a temporality in which man himself is.

This is why in our consideration of history we "quite spontaneously" introduced time. This does not mean the time that the historian can use to determine (and test) that in AD 800, Charlemagne was crowned emperor. No, we are talking about history as *our* past, as what was the fate of our ancestors and thus is our own. We do not understand time as a framework, but as the authentic fundamental constitution of human beings. And only an entity whose Being is time can have and make history. An animal has no history.

With this understanding, we emerged from our perspective so far, in which we were taking nature and history as equally objective processes. Instead, history is now the distinctive "term" for human Being.

Now, we have to say regarding this reflection that it was spoken from our own historical Dasein in this moment and thus must be subject to a certain intelligibility, like all statements and truths about human beings, which always have to be attained in one's own decision. We must keep this in mind as we now ask about the nature of the state.

The state

We had begun by saying that the domains of nature, history, and state are progressively narrower—that history is embedded in nature, and the state as a historical phenomenon is embedded in history. Now we want to see whether this characterization is in fact correct; for now, we simply asked whether there is any history without a state.

If we now ask about the state, we are asking about ourselves.

[70] Now, how can we tackle this issue with our questioning, in order to display the essence of the state?

One can ask about the purpose of the state. This approach assumes that the state is a human institution and that there was a condition of man before a state, a condition that forced him to found a state. It was remarked that this sort of question is asked at a particular time, in a state in some particular condition. This was meant to help us see how important it is to get clear on where we have to stand.

At bottom, the question of the purpose of the state is also the question of its origin, and it is in this form that the question of its essence usually appears. But the question of origin is not at all an original questioning about the state, for I can construct a theory of the beginnings of the state or interpret available sources informing me about its beginnings only if I know what a state is. But behind this knowledge there already stands yet another very particular decision.

State—what does this "term" express?

As we did when we considered nature, we can take the state (1) materially: just as substances and living things belong in the realm of nature, citizens, officials, tax offices and the like belong in the realm of the state. (2) We can take the state formally: then we ask how, in what way, something is. We then understand by "state" a way of Being in which humans are.—It is in this way, then, that we primarily want to grasp the essence of the state, and not as an area of history.

Now, which being belongs to this state?—"The people" [*das Volk*]. We must then ask what we understand by "people," for in the French Revolution they gave the same answer: the people.

This answer is possible only on the basis of a decision for a state. The definition of the people depends on how it is in its state.

To begin with, we established formally that the people is the being that *is* in the manner of a state, the being that is or can be a state. We then asked the further formal question: what character and form does the people give itself in the state, and what character and form does the state give to the people?

The form of an organism? Impossible, because when we ask about the state we are asking about the essence of man, and not about the essence of an organism.

The form of order? That is too general, since I can order everything—stones, books, and so on. But what hits the mark is an order in the sense of mastery, rank, leadership, and following. This leaves open the question of who is master. In Aristotle and Plato, the question of the essence of the state begins with the question: who rules, who is permitted to rule?

But we should strive to gain a genuine knowledge of the state, so that the state may form our essence and thus come to power.

[71]

SESSION 6
January 19, 1934

At the beginning we noted in regards to our conception of *temporality* that we see the future as the fundamental characteristic of time and that for us the future is connected directly with the past. We persist from the past into the future, and only in this way do we persist in the present. This conception is contrasted to the first presentation of the concept of time in Aristotle's physics, where the Now is considered the fundamental phenomenon of time, the present, while past and future are understood as no–longer–now or not–yet–now.

Then we turned to the concept of the *state* and clarified the meaning of the word: *status* means condition, it means a mode of Being, and so state, that is, *status rei publicae*, literally means the mode of Being of a people.

One customarily describes *politics* as every practical and theoretical occupation in the state and having to do with the state. Now, this word "politics" comes from the Greek *polis*, which means the state as *community*, which, in Greece, was the sole site where all the state's Being took place— it was where everything happened that we characterize as the state. If Aristotle then coined the well-known expression that the human being is a *zōon politikon*, that does not therefore mean that we must be communal beings—or, as the Romans translated it, an *animal sociale*—simply because we cannot survive alone or because, for better or worse, from our first day of life onwards we are naturally surrounded by other people. Rather, quite apart from such biological considerations, human beings are truly the *zōon politikon* because to be human means: in a community, to carry in oneself the possibility and the necessity of giving form to and fulfilling one's own Being and the Being of the community. Human beings are a *zōon politikon* because they have the strength and the capacity for the *polis*, and here the *polis* is not conceived as something already subsisting in advance, but rather as something to which human beings can and must give form. But in this sense, the human being certainly "belongs to the polis" or is *politikos*—as the living being, that is, which has the possibility and the necessity of existing in the polis.

But state *and politics* in this genuine sense are related in such a way that a state is possible at all only on the grounds of the fact that the Being of human beings is political. And if it is widely believed that it is the reverse, that the state is the precondition for politics, then that is due to the ascendancy of a false and vulgar concept that there is nothing more to politics than the business of the state, according to which politics certainly depends on the existence of a state.

[72] But to proceed, the word *politics* was subjected to still further narrowing:[2] it was made into a circumscribed[3] domain, one among many others, such as private life, the economy, technology, science, religion. Politics was set next to all these others as one area within culture, as one said. And one even believed it possible to establish this philosophically by assigning the values of the true, the good, and the beautiful to each and every one of these cultural areas. And so the realm of the political became a markedly inferior one: it went so far that "political" could be equated with "slippery," and a politician meant someone who knew how to twist things with parliamentary tricks.[4]

The development began in the Renaissance, when the individual human being, as the person, was raised up as the goal of all Being—the great man as the two ideals: *homo universalis* and the specialist. It was this new will to the development of the personality that brought about the complete transformation according to which, from then on, everything was supposed to exist purely for the sake of the great individual. Everything, and therefore politics too, now gets shifted into a sphere within which the human being[5] is willing and able to live to the fullest. Thus politics, art, science and all the others degenerate into domains of the individual will to development, and this all the more as they were expanded through gigantic accomplishments and thus became specialized. In the times that followed, all the domains of culture were allowed to grow ever farther apart until they could not be kept in view as a whole,[6] up to our own day, where the danger of such behavior displayed itself with elemental clarity in the collapse of our state.

We therefore recognized it as an urgent task of our time to counter this danger in order to attempt to give back to *politics* its proper rank, to learn to see politics again as the fundamental characteristic of human beings who philosophize within history, and as the Being in which the *state* fully develops, so that the state can truly be called the way of Being of a people.

And with this we come to the entity that belongs to the state, its substance, its supporting ground: *the people* [*das Volk*]. Here too, we began with the question of what the word *Volk* means, and we found that with this word we shed light on the most diverse sides of what the people comprises. If, for example, we say "folk song," "folk customs," then we say the word *Volk* in a way that alludes to the life of sentiments and feelings; by this we mean a certain naive,[7] unspoiled, fresh originality of mores. This is different from turns of phrase such as "the crowd of people scattered": here we see an aggregation of subordinates, of the uneducated "rabble," which is supposed to be numerically superior and shut off from so-called "higher" goods; this way of speaking, then, emphasizes the social differentiation of the people.

By contrast, an expression such as "taking the census of the people" [*Volkszählung*] certainly means neither counting the "unspoiled" people as described above, nor something like the counting of a rabble; rather, it encompasses those who belong as citizens to a *single* state. So here we are selecting as the boundary and definition of the people [73] the characteristic of belonging to the state. But closely related to this is a term such as "public health" [*Volksgesundheit*], in which one also now feels the tie of the unity of blood and stock, the race. But in the most comprehensive sense, we use the term *Volk* when we speak of something like "the people in arms": with this we mean nothing merely like those who receive draft notices, and also something other than the mere sum[8] of the citizens of the state. We mean something even more strongly binding than race and a community of the same stock: namely, the nation, and that means a kind of Being that has grown under a common fate and taken distinctive shape within a *single* state.

SESSION 7[1]
February 2, 1934

The political as the fundamental possibility and distinctive way of Being of human beings is, as we said, the foundation on which the state has its Being. The Being of the state is anchored in the political Being of the human beings who, as a people, support this state—who decide for it. This political, that is, historically fateful decision requires us to clarify the original, essential connection between people and state. An understanding and knowledge of the essence of the state and people is needful for every human being. This knowledge, the concepts and cognition, belong to political education, that is, what leads us into our own political Being; but this does not mean that everyone who gains this knowledge can or may now act politically as a statesman or leader. For the origin of all state action and leadership does not lie in knowledge; it lies in Being. Every leader *is* a leader; he must be a leader in accordance with the marked form of his Being; and he understands, considers, and brings about[2] what people and state are, in the living development of his own essence.

A leader does not need to be educated politically—but a band of guardians in the people does, a band that helps to bear responsibility for the state. For every state and all knowledge about the state grows within a political tradition. Where this nourishing, securing soil is lacking, even the best idea for a state cannot take root, grow from the sustaining womb of the people, and develop. Otto the Great based his empire on the prince–bishops by obliging them to service and knowledge in political and military matters. And Frederick the Great educated the Prussian nobility into guardians of his state. Bismarck oversaw this process of rooting his idea of the state in the firm, strong soil of political nobility, and when his sustaining arm let go, the Second Reich collapsed without any support. We may not overlook the founding of a political tradition [74] and the education of a political nobility. Every individual must now reflect in order to arrive at knowledge of the people and state and his own responsibility. The state depends on our alertness, our readiness, and our life. The manner of our Being marks the Being of our state. In this way, every people takes a position with regard to the state, and no people lacks the urge for the state. The people that turns down a state, that is stateless, has just not found the gathering of its essence yet; it still lacks the composure and force to be committed to its fate as a people.

This is why we have to be especially ready to try to clarify further the essence of people and state. We begin, again, by clarifying the political as a way of Being of human beings and what makes the state possible. There are other concepts of the political that oppose this approach, such as the concept of the friend-enemy relation that stems from Carl Schmitt. This concept of politics as the friend-enemy relation is grounded in the view that struggle, that is, the real possibility of war, is the presupposition of political behavior; that the possibility of the struggle for decision, which can also be fought out without military means, sharpens present oppositions—be they moral, religious, or economic—into radical unity as friend and enemy. The unity and totality of this opposition of friend and enemy is the basis for all political existence. But a decisive aspect of this view is that the political unit does not have to be identical with state and people.

Another conception of the political is expressed in Bismarck's saying, "Politics is the art of the possible." Possibility here does not mean an arbitrary possibility that can be dreamed up accidentally, but what is solely possible, the only thing possible. Politics, for Bismarck, is the ability to see this and to bring it about [?],[3] which must essentially and necessarily arise from a historical situation, and at the same time the *technē*, the skill, to make actual what one knows. With this, politics becomes the creative project of the great statesman who can survey the whole happening of history, and not just the present—who, in his idea of the state, sets a goal that he keeps firmly in view despite all accidental changes in the situation. This view of politics and the state is tied closely to the personal genius of the statesman upon whose essential vision, strength, and attitude the Being of the state depends; when his power and life stop, the state begins to lose its power.

Again we see that a state that is to endure and mature must be grounded in the Being of the people. The people, the being, has a very particular relation to its Being, the state. We now have to consider how these relations between people and state, and beings and Being, are essentially linked. We should follow two paths here: first we should draw a distinction between beings and Being in general, [75] and then we want to ask about the distinction between state and people, starting with our own state and people.

Is there a difference between Being and beings? If so, in what does it consist and how far can it be clarified? The distinction between Being and beings has often been explained by saying that beings are the content, or what can be determined, and Being is the form, which determines. This does not capture the essence. On the other hand, there seems to be a close connection between Being and beings. One does not seem thinkable— much less distinguishable—without the other. Being is the condition for beings, and beings in turn are the condition for Being. Here we cannot get a clear view. Maybe we are already asking wrongly when we ask about the difference. In any case, our failure must at least then show us why we cannot ask in this way, and how a genuine question would have to get started here. But for now, let us ask concretely: What is a being? What is Being?

The chalk is a present-at-hand being. We see it and assert something about it: the chalk is white. When we do so, we can detect the chalk and the whiteness of the chalk in experience, with our own eyes. But where is the "is," the form of the auxiliary verb "to be" that we constantly use in our assertions? We cannot see "is." What is the "is"? We use "is" in various senses. In the sentence "The chalk is white," the "is" expresses a quality, a property, a how-Being. The "is" means something else in the sentence "The chalk is present at hand," for presence at hand is not a property but rather a kind of Being, what-Being. But with this distinction we really have not yet clarified what the essence of the "is" and Being is. Being is in no way visible, we cannot have any image of it. And still, we constantly say "is" and understand right away, without any theory, this "is"—but we cannot say what we mean by it. As self-evident as this "is" seems to be, it becomes just as obscure, difficult, and puzzling when we ask about it. We cannot ask about Being with the question: what is Being? Are we supposed to recognize the "is" only if it "is *not*," that is, on the basis of the Nothing? If this were so, would not the whole world, we ourselves, and everything become null? This is outrageous and confusing. Within the self-evident there suddenly opens an abyss, unsurveyable and dangerous, but unavoidable for whoever truly *questions.* Human beings, who in accordance with their essence have to question, must expose themselves to the danger of the Nothing, of nihilism, in order to grasp the meaning of their Being by overcoming nihilism.

We cannot explain the question of Being further here; we simply see that there is an essential difference between Being and beings, and that this difference is completely other than the difference between one being and another, such as the book and the chalk.

But we must still indicate the ambiguity that Being has: the chalk is; a dog is; a human is. In all three assertions we specify that [76] *something* is, something that is not nothing. But in each of these three situations, Being is something different: chalk as chalk is an object, while to be a dog is to be an animal, and thus, as living, to have a different kind of Being from present-at-hand objects. And Being-human is quite different and distinct in its way of Being. How so? What is it that distinguishes human Being?

We say that humans are conscious of their Being and of the Being of other beings; they have consciousness. This human consciousness is not only something knowable, which one can either know or not, but is a fundamental capacity of human Dasein. Human beings' own Being is an issue for them, and thanks to consciousness they can concern themselves with it. The height of human consciousness harbors in it the possibility of the deep fall into unconsciousness. In the constant powerlessness of unconsciousness and lack of conscience, man sinks beneath beast. The animal has no relation to Being; it cannot be unconscious, derelict, or indifferent. But when human beings lose their consciousness and conscience, they lose their most proper worth. Without consciousness, the knowing and caring about the height and depth, greatness, and powerlessness of their Being in the whole of the world, they are no longer human beings, and since they cannot be animals or plants or objects, at bottom they are nothing at all. With the loss of consciousness, human Being becomes null.

Just as human beings are conscious of their Being-human—they relate to it, they are concerned with it—in the same way, the people as a being has a knowing fundamental relation to its state. The people, the being, that actualizes the state in its Being, knows of the state, cares about it, and wills it. Just as every human being wants to live, wills to *be here* as a human being, just as he keeps holding on to this and loves his Dasein [Being-here] in the world, the people wills the state as its way to be as a people. The people is ruled by the urge for the state, by *erōs* for the state. But inasmuch as *erōs* is something distinctly human, this will to a state cannot be conceived biologically, or even compared to the drive of bees and termites to their "state." For the life (*zōē*) of animals is fundamentally different from human life.

The people's love for the state, its wish and will for it, expresses itself as taking a position, rejection, dedication—in short, as concern for the essence and form of the state. So the form or constitution of the state is then also an essential expression of what the people takes to be the meaning of its own Being. The constitution is not a rational contract, a legal order, political logic, or anything else arbitrary and absolute; constitution and law are the actualization of our decision for the state—they are factical attestations of what we take to be our historical task as a people, the task that we are trying to live out. Accordingly, knowledge of the constitution and law is not just the province of so-called "politicians" and jurists, but as thinking and consciousness of the state, it belongs to the Dasein of every individual human being who takes upon himself the struggle and responsibility for his people. Our task at this [77] historical moment involves the clear development and transformation of thinking about the state. Each and every man and woman must learn to know, even if only in a vague and unclear way, that their individual life decides the fate of the people and state—either supports it or rejects it.

This knowledge also includes commitment to the order of the state. Order is the human way of Being, and thus also the way of Being of the people. The order of the state expresses itself in the delimited field of tasks of human individuals and groups. This order is not merely organic, as one could suppose and has supposed on the basis of the fable of Menenius Agrippa,[4] but is something spiritual and human, which also means something voluntary. It is based on the relations of human beings in ruling and serving each other. Like the medieval order of life, the order of the state today is sustained by the free, pure will to following and leadership, that is, to struggle and loyalty. For if we ask, "What is rule? What is it based on?" then if we give a true and essential answer, we experience no power, enslavement, oppression, or compulsion. Instead what we experience is that rule and authority together with service and subordination are grounded in a common task. Only where the leader and the led bind themselves together to *one* fate and fight to actualize *one* idea does true order arise. Then spiritual superiority and freedom develop as a deep dedication of all forces to the people, the state, as the most rigorous breeding, as engagement, endurance, solitude, and love. Then the existence and superiority of the leader sinks into the Being, the soul of the people, and binds it in this way with originality and passion to the task. And if the people feels this dedication, it will let itself be led into struggle, and it will love struggle and will it. It will develop and persist in its forces, be faithful and sacrifice itself. In every new moment, the leader and the people will join more closely in order to bring about the essence of their state, that is, their Being; growing with each other, they will set their meaningful historical Being and will against the two threatening powers of death and the devil—that is, ruination and decline from their own essence.

SESSION 8[1]
February 16, 1934

Last time, before we got into our main topic, we still had to add some supplemental points to the session before last.

The Greeks had two words for what we call life: *bios* and *zōē*. They used *bios* in a twofold sense. First, in the sense of [78] biology, the science of life. Here we think of the organic growth of the body, glandular activity, sexual difference, and the like. For most of our scientists today, biology seems suspicious from the start, because beyond the experimental table and the microscope, it seeks a direct relation to life—and to human life in particular, our life, which to these scientists often seems less important as a research topic than the physiology of the frog. This is why we do not find any real biology, even in our universities. If we wanted to occupy ourselves with it anyway, we would need just one thing: we would have to make use of the relevant findings of zoology, botany, and physiology while staying open to biological ways of posing problems. Biology is the name for a natural science in the broadest and most universal sense.

Another sense of *bios* for the Greeks is the course of a life, the history of a life, more or less in the sense that the word "biography" still has for us today. *Bios* here means human history and existence—so there can be no *bios* of animals. *Bios*, as human *bios*, has the peculiar distinction of being able either to stand above the animal or to sink beneath it. In the *Nicomachean Ethics* ([Book I] Chapter 3, 1095b), three *bioi*, three fundamental forms of human existence, are distinguished: the *bios apolaustikos*, the life of enjoyment, whose standard for things is enjoyment, pleasure, *hēdonē*; the *bios politikos*, in which everything is decided on the basis of ambition, repute, and renown; and the *bios theōretikos*, the highest fundamental form of human existence, the life of one who authentically contemplates—the philosopher. Of course, this does not refer to people like our scientists today.

In addition to *bios*, the Greek language also has the word *zōē*. To begin with, it is life as a purely physiological process; yet the meanings of *bios* and *zōē* are intermingled. In the New Testament, *zōē* means the life of blessedness, the life bound to God. But when the Greeks say that the human being is a *zōon logon echon*, they mean a living being (in the sense of zoology) that can speak.

We also had to add something about the inner reasons for the failure of Bismarck's politics. We heard that a people, in addition to needing a leader, also needs a tradition that is carried on by a political nobility. The Second Reich fell prey to an irreparable collapse after Bismarck's death, and not only because Bismarck failed to create this political nobility. He was also incapable of regarding the proletariat as a phenomenon that was justified in itself, and of leading it back into the state by reaching out to it with understanding. But the main reason is probably that the *Volk*-based character of the Second Reich was exhausted in what we call patriotism and fatherland. These elements of the union of 1870–1 are not [79] to be judged negatively in themselves, but they are completely inadequate for a truly *Volk*-based state. They also lacked an ultimate rootedness in the *Volk*, the people.

Before we got into our main topic, we briefly connected it to what came before. We saw that the question of the state cannot be posed in isolation, that the state cannot be projected by a political theorist, but that it is a way of Being and a kind of Being of the people. The people is the entity whose Being is the state. So we can consider things in two ways. The first point of view, which we have already considered, comes from above, in a certain sense—from the universal, from Being, and what is. Now, this universal point of view should not be confused with the attempts to deduce the state in the seventeenth and eighteenth centuries. Rousseau, for instance, believed that the state was a *contrat social* that was based only on each individual's striving for his own welfare. This state would no longer be the state in the sense of the political as the fundamental character of Western man, who exists on the basis of philosophy; it would be a subordinate means to an end, in service to the development of the personality in the liberal sense, one domain among many.

The second possible point of view comes from below, in a certain sense, from the people and the state, from us ourselves. This procedure forces us to distinguish two paths we can take. We want to feel our way forwards first by considering the people in isolation, and then by considering the state in isolation. This distinction, of course, can only be methodological, since it is after all impossible to consider the people without a state—the entity without its Being, in a certain sense. The first question, the question of the people, which is the first topic that concerns us, must be directed in such a way that we will reach the state.

Now, we might put forward the following line of thought: since the state, as the Being of the people, is evidently historical, we could ask about the people and its historical character on this basis. But since at this point we have not yet decided whether or not every activity of the people has something to do with the state from the start, we want to take another tack in our work for now.

We already saw earlier that natural processes and the happening of history occur in space and time. Now we want to try to comprehend the people on this basis as well. Space and time have long been [understood as] aspects that determine beings in their singularity, uniqueness, individuality. They are *principia individuationis*, principles of determination. Through these principles, one can determine beings or realities in their concretion, or at least help to determine them—and the people too, in particular.

If we ask about the people in space, we must fend off two misconceptions from the start. When we hear these two words, we think to begin with of a contemporary slogan: "a people without space." If by this we mean living space [*Lebensraum*], then without a doubt we have said too much. Perhaps one could say: a people without adequate living space, without sufficient [80] living space for its positive development. We must always know that space necessarily belongs to the people in its concrete Being, that there is no such thing as a "people without space" in the most literal sense. — The second error consists in taking the space of the people or the state, following geography or geopolitics, as a bounded geometrical surface that we can measure precisely in terms of square kilometers—that is, as a measurable, extended area. Even if we just consider this notion from a purely geometrical point of view, it contradicts the sense of the word "space," which is, after all, three-dimensional and as such is measured not with plane measures, but cubically.

Now, since we at least know what "space" does not mean—this measurable, extended area—we can question further. We do not want to simply count up and arrange what we know about the relations between a people and space, but we want to continue our reflections by comparing the way human beings and a people relate to space and the way dead matter, plants, and animals relate to space.

To begin with, we will ask about matter in space. The science that concerns itself with the relationship of merely material beings to space is physics. In the latest results of its research, concerning atoms, atomic nuclei, and electrons, physics has shown that bodies do not simply stand in space in a purely geometrical way, that space is not an indifferent medium that surrounds the bodies in question, but that these bodies are oriented into space in a very particular way. The position of a body in space is fundamentally non-arbitrary; it stands in a completely definite reciprocal relation to its surroundings. This linkage of things to space and to fields is part of their essence and their kind of Being. Quite new possibilities for scientific method are provided by this atomic or field physics. Today there are already physicists who, in principle, are expressing the idea of solving biological problems with the help of field physics. True, this attempt would be a regression to materialism, but all the same, it indicates a possibility of taking up the question in a fundamentally new way. — By the way, these thoughts are not at all as new as they may seem to us. Aristotle, in his theory of the spheres, already sees cosmic space as something that is not indifferently empty. He assigns every matter to its appropriate place.

Now let us ask how the relation of dead matter to space differs from that of living things. Is it that animals can move around in space, and mountains apparently cannot? (Actually, they do move, and in fact move constantly, but their way of moving is different.) The difference in the manner of moving does not yet change anything in the relationship to space. The decisive difference is that the animal somehow has to deal with space, that it operates in space and is in turn marked by it. For instance, for a fish, dwelling in water is not an arbitrary condition, but a necessity; it is precisely what gives the fish living space and the possibility of life. It is also a fact that [81] crabs that live in pools grow when they are put into a larger body of water. They orient themselves to the space in which they find themselves at the time. Zoology and botany decline to investigate such things; they consider them frivolous. In most cases, these sciences are not open to such questions and have no feel for them. The questions are alive, in a very broad sense, in ecology, the theory of the locale of individuals. But so far, ecologists have simply determined where plants and animals live; they have not asked in a fundamental way about locale. Biology is more open to this particular problem. It calls the relation between living being and space the "environment." This word is meant to indicate that the limit between space and living being is not the surface of the living body, that the living being does not simply take up a section of indifferent space; the living being rules space over and above the body, it possesses a Being that is oriented beyond the body.

Since human Being, as we have already seen, is essentially different from animal Being, presumably human Being in space is also completely different from that of the animal. For the Being of the people, as a human way of Being, space is not simply surroundings, or an indifferent container. When we investigate the people's Being-in-space, we see that every people has a space that belongs to it. Persons who live by the sea, in the mountains, and on the plains are different. History teaches us that nomads have not only been made nomadic by the desolation of wastelands and steppes, but they have also often left wastelands behind them where they found fruitful and cultivated land—and that human beings who are rooted in the soil have known how to make a home for themselves even in the wilderness. Relatedness to space, that is, the mastering of space and becoming marked by space, belong together with the essence and the kind of Being of a people. So it is not right to see the sole ideal for a people in rootedness in the soil, in attachment, in settledness, which find their cultivation and realization in farming and which give the people a special endurance in its propagation, in its growth, in its health. It is no less necessary to rule over the soil and space, to work outwards into the wider expanse, to interact with the outside world. The concrete way in which a people effectively works in space and forms space necessarily includes both: rootedness in the soil and interaction.

Only on this basis can we start moving in the direction of the state. The people and the state have a space that belongs to them. But it has not been decided whether the space of the people coincides with the space of the state. So the state cannot be an intellectual construct, or a sum of legal principles, or a constitution. It is essentially related to space and formed by space. Its space is, to a certain extent, the space of the people rooted in the soil, insofar as it is grasped in terms of the will to work out into the expanse, in terms of interaction, in terms of power. This space we call land, sovereign dominion, territory; in a certain sense, it is the fatherland. The homeland is not to be confused with the fatherland. The homeland will in [82] most cases, from a purely external point of view, be a narrower region of the space of the state. But it is never this in principle; it need not have anything to do with the state. There are completely different relations at work in the two. We can speak of the state only when rootedness in the soil is combined with the will to expansion, or generally speaking, interaction. A homeland is something I have on the basis of my birth. There are quite particular relations between me and it in the sense of nature, in the sense of natural forces. Homeland expresses itself in rootedness in the soil and being bound to the earth. But nature works on the human being, roots him in the soil, only when nature belongs as an environment, so to speak, to the people whose member that human being is. The homeland becomes the way of Being of a people only when the homeland becomes expansive, when it interacts with the outside—when it becomes a state. For this reason, peoples or their subgroups who do not step out beyond their connection to the homeland into their authentic way of Being—into the state—are in constant danger of losing their peoplehood and perishing. This is also the great problem of those Germans who live outside the borders of the Reich: they do have a German homeland, but they do not belong to the state of the Germans, the Reich, so they are deprived of their authentic way of Being.— In summary, then, we can say that the space of a people, the soil of a people, reaches as far as members of this people have found a homeland and have become rooted in the soil; and that the space of the state, the territory, finds its borders by interacting, by working out into the wider expanse.

In this connection, at the end of our last session we still made a few brief remarks on the significance of folklore for the life of a people. We heard that people and space mutually belong to each other. From the specific knowledge of a people about the nature of its space, we first experience how nature is revealed in this people. For a Slavic people, the nature of our German space would definitely be revealed differently from the way it is revealed to us; to Semitic nomads, it will perhaps never be revealed at all. This way of being embedded in a people, situated in a people, this original participation in the knowledge of the people, cannot be taught; at most, it can be awakened from its slumber. One poor means of doing this is folklore. It is a peculiar mishmash of objects that have often been taken from the customs of a particular people. But it often also investigates customs, mores, or magic which no longer have anything to do with a specific people in its historical Being. It investigates forces that are at work everywhere among primitive and magical human beings. So folklore is not suited to ask about what belongs specifically to a people; often it even does the very opposite. This is why it is a misunderstanding and an error to believe that one can awaken the consciousness of the *Volk* with the help of folklore [*Volkskunde*]. We must above all guard ourselves against being overly impressed by the word "folk."
[83]

SESSION 9[1]
February 23, 1934

Looking back over the previous sessions, we keep this firmly in view: people and state are not two realities that we might observe isolated, as it were, from one another. The state is the preeminent Being of the people; we will leave open the question of whether and how a people is also possible in a condition before it has a state. But at the same time, the people in its Being is not bound to the state insofar as the state appears in this or that form, the people can outlast the state in a certain way—although this point should not be misunderstood. So the Being of the people and the Being of the state are in a certain sense separable.

What is a people? This question about the essence of the people *per se* is one we simply cannot pose, because the people is always already seen from the perspective of a particular Being of a state, and so is always already politically determined. We can never clearly establish the Being of a people in itself because in such an undertaking a particular state-consciousness always already plays a role. The same is the case if we want to get clear about the concept of "the state." For this reason, one cannot establish a theory of the state that is not already built upon particular ties to the Being of a people. Thus political-philosophical questioning about one or the other [i.e. people or state] is always played out within a certain polarity, within the difference between people and state as a being and its Being.

Once again we ask, what is the state? As we have already said earlier, a general characteristic of the state is "order." On the face of it, this is a purely formal category that in itself does not yet have any connection to a definite region of Being. We see order everywhere; I can put stones and the like in order. This abstract concept of order as a purely formal direction for thinking easily leads reflection about the state astray, as is proven by nineteenth-century theories of the state.— For this reason we ask more pointedly: what is being claimed about this order in the state? How is order meant here? Order in the sense of the order of rule, of superordination and subordination, of leadership and following. And yet, what does order of mastery, order of power, mean?—The will of one gets implemented in the will of others, who thereby become the ruled. But this tells us nothing about how this implementation happens. Nor is anything said about whether and to what extent the will of those ruled coincides with the will of the ruler, which surely is of fundamental importance for the relation of the one to the other and above all for the relation as a whole. And yet already this notion of ruler and ruled suggests the view that necessarily and from the start takes the people as "the mastered" in the real sense of the word, thereby in principle denying to the people a will of its own.

[84] Here we have a mastery that recognizes nothing higher than itself; here mastery becomes sovereignty, where the supreme force is taken as the essence and expression of the state. This condition, in which the state as this supreme power pertains to only one or a few, explains the tendency to assign this sovereignty to the other partner, the people, which then necessarily leads to the other extreme. Only on the basis of the notion of sovereignty as absolutism can we really understand and explain the essence of the French Revolution as an opposing phenomenon.

Therefore we said that mastery is power in the sense of implementation of the will. But this presumes a certain powerfulness and governing force that first guarantee an implementation. Because mastery and sovereignty are modes of Being of the people, the question of the origin and the foundation of power can always be raised only on the basis of a particular way in which the people has its Being in a state, and so the question is always already politically defined. The will of the state implements itself in various definite ways, for example, in administration. Through its various intermediaries, this implementation of the will is admittedly attenuated and no longer fully manifest to us as what it is, especially after we have gotten used to seeing the state as one region among many, one reality among many, and in this way we have lost a direct, living relation to the state.

But what is will?—We distinguish willing from wishing. Both are a certain kind of striving. This tells us nothing yet, though; animals also strive, if only by following a drive. By contrast to wish, will is the striving that engages in action; wish lacks engagement. But will is more than mere urge. Urge does indeed aim at something, but this "something" is, in contrast to willful striving, not sharply delineated, not clearly seen and recognized. Will aims at an individual thing, urge aims at a whole complex of possibilities. We cannot declare absolutely that will aims at the definite and important, and wish at the indefinite and unimportant. Otherwise we could not say, on the one hand, "He does not know what he wills to do," while on the other hand, one could not wish a sick person "health," which surely is a particular good, and a high one. We will not get into the question of well-wishing. What is characteristic for the distinction [between willing and wishing] and thereby for the essence of willing is therefore engaged striving on the one hand and, on the other, disengaged longing.

Will aims at a goal. But the one who is striving willfully does not recognize and grasp this goal blindly and on its own; rather—and this is essential—it is seen in connection and in combination with the ways and means. So the goal is always already grasped together with the possibility of its actualization. Will grasps the situation, the whole fullness of time; in the will works the *kairos* that demands resoluteness and action. This involves deliberation, in which I run through the field in which particular laws are at play.

[85] Now, what should I call this willful striving? Initiative? —No, initiative does not pertain to every willing, or, to put it better, to everyone who wills. Initiative pertains only to someone who makes a beginning of something. Energy? —Not this either. Energy is a particular heightened and sustained activity of the will. What, then? "Action." An animal cannot act, because it cannot will. This activity determined by the will is what Aristotle named *praxis*, and he distinguished it according to the properties of what the will strives for and according to the modes of its realization in technical-practical and moral-practical activity.

The first mode has to do with the actualization of an object. For example, "It is my will to build a house." What I am willing here is an object that is related to nature. The accomplishment and ordering of this actuality "house" is essentially determined by nature; it happens through technology in the widest sense. What is willed is a being that is based on particular natural relations and laws. The architect must already accommodate himself to certain factors in making his plan, and even more so in making it actual: when he digs the foundation and comes across this or that unanticipated obstacle, and then when in his handling of the building materials he is entirely dependent on their laws and must also take this or that possibility into consideration.

Things are different with the activity that is directed to the will of an individual or a whole group in order to elicit this or that action or attitude in them. Here we have a community of will. What the one who acts wills is a willing Being among others. Kant calls this activity moral-practical.

Moral, because it is related to human beings, who are free according to their essence and therefore moral.

So much for a clarification of the concept of "will." We should never equate the will of an individual with the will of a people. Both display entirely specific structural relations. The will of a people is not free in the sense of the freedom of the individual will, and this fact is of great importance for the implementation of the will. The will of the people is a complicated structure that is hard to grasp. The leader has to deal with this structure, not with free individuals. The will of the people is not the sum of individual wills but rather a whole that has its own, originary characteristics.

The question of the consciousness of the will of the community is a problem in all democracies, a question that can really become fruitful only when the will of the leader and the will of the people are recognized in their essence. Our task today is to direct the fundamental attitude of our communal Being toward this actuality of people and leader in which both as a single actuality are not to be separated. Only when this fundamental schema is achieved by way of essential transformation is a true leader-education possible.

[86]

SESSION 10[1]

Report on the last session of the seminar of Winter Semester 1933–34, on February 23, 1934

Following up on the previous session of the seminar, we again spoke about the fact that a people always outlasts its form of state. But this point is not to be understood to mean that a people can alter its current form of state arbitrarily; the change of a state and the form of a state in general are connected to a people's disposition and will, either to decline or to build itself up.

The character of the state as an order of rule led us to explain the relation between rulers and ruled. First we had to reject the simple equation of the ruled and the oppressed. Ruling involves power, which creates a rank order through the implementation of the ruler's will, inasmuch as he is actually powerful—that is, he shows paths and goals to the ruled. Under this true rule, there are ruled people who are not oppressed.

We then added to the argument over the essence of the will. In contrast to wish, it was said, will characterizes engagement on behalf of a particular goal. It became clear that this definition was insufficient, since there can be engagement in some arbitrary goal, as in the case of adventurers. There is a further form of behavior in which one "knows" the goal without being engaged at all—but true knowledge this cannot be. True knowledge involves both an understanding of the goal and engagement—that is, a leap into the accomplishment of the goal—along with persistence, which makes the engaged person develop.

But now—and with this question, we reached back to where we got started in our question about the will—what is going on when one implements one's own powerful will that is directed at the whole?

Before we actually asked the question, we got to talking about the form of implementation. One can distinguish two forms or ways: first persuasion, and then coercion.

Persuasion can happen (1) through speech, and (2) through action. For the Greeks, speech was a preeminent means to political power. Their political instinct recognized the persuasive force of speech in an exemplary manner; we know this unforgettably from Thucydides. It is an unconscious recognition of the power of speech that in our own day, the speeches of the Führer made an impression that came to be expressed by the term "the drummer."[2]

However, the effective will is most urgently "persuasive" in acts. The great effective actor is at the same time the "powerful" one, the "ruler," whose Dasein and will becomes determinative—through "persuasion," that is, when one knows and recognizes the soaring will of the leader.

[87] But the will can also be implemented by coercion, where commands are a form of carrying out the will. This form is not creative. Still, a command can trigger conviction, as in 1914.

This point led us to ask whether coercion can generate a will, and what the attitude of the "coerced" is in an action that is performed under coercion. It became apparent that mere compliance is inadequate, and this helped us reach a more precise definition of the unwillingness that comes into play here: unwillingness is a particular form of willing (not a not-willing, but itself a kind of willing). This willing-in-unwillingness is the privative relation here, a distinctive negative relation. This was clarified by contrasting the examples of a blind man and the supposed idea of a blind stone: while a blind man lacks something that belongs to being human, seeing does not belong to the stone as stone, so we cannot speak privatively of a blind stone, as if it lacked some part of its particular Being as a stone.

The true implementation of the will is not based on coercion, but on awakening the same will in another, that is, the same goal and engagement or accomplishment. The implementation of the will, in this sense, transforms people in proportion to the greatness of the effective will. This implementation is not a matter of a momentary yes-saying, but a decision of the individual. The crucial factor here cannot be the sum, as precise as it may be, but only the qualitative value of the individual decision, the degree of comprehension and penetration. It is in this sense that we must understand the current demands for "political education": not a memorization of sentences and opinions and forms, but the creation of a new fundamental attitude of the will.

The will of the leader first transforms the others into a following, and from the following arises a community. Their sacrifice and service comes from this living connection, not from mere obedience and the force of institutions.

A particular and distinctive form of the implementation of the will is education (and school education, as the education of knowledge, is part of this): at bottom it is nothing but the implementation of the will of the leader and the will of the state, that is, of the people. We merely alluded in this connection to other forms of implementation of the will of the state, such as governmental administration and the justice system.

Finally, we emphasized the characteristic form of our current state formation as a coming-to-be of the people, and with this we explained one of the essential concepts of the modern theory and formation of the state: the concept of sovereignty. Johannes Bodinus[3] first recognized and formulated this concept with great precision in his *Republica* (1576), defining it as *summa in cives ac subditos legibusque soluta potestas* [supreme and absolute power over the citizens and over those subject to the laws]. For Bodinus, this power stands [88] only under the higher bond to God. Today one often says "people" where formerly one said God, and defines this ultimate bond accordingly. The higher bond creates the highest freedom, whereas lack of commitment is negative freedom. One has sometimes understood political freedom in this latter sense, and thus misunderstood it—a phenomenon that is supposed to have led to the sovereignty of the people, just as the *omnipotentia Dei* was secularized into the sovereignty of the state.

This train of thought led us to discuss three great disintegrations that have occurred many times since the dissolution of the universal commitments and obligations of the Middle Ages:

1 The collapse of dogmatic-ecclesiastical faith, of the concept of creation, occurred in the wake of the first dissolution of a great bond: man became a self-legislating being that wills to, and must, found his own Being himself. This is the source of Descartes' search for a *fundamentum absolutum*, which he found in the conviction *ego cogito, ergo sum*. The Being of man is based on reason, that is, mathematical *ratio*, which is elevated to the decisive power of the world.

2 The second disintegration consists in the disintegration of the community—the fact that the individual in himself is the final court of appeal.

3 Descartes carries out the sharp separation between mind and body.

The concept of sovereignty developed in the context of this movement.

Of the three domains that we touched upon in the course of our explanations and questions—nature, history, and state—the state is the narrowest, but it is the most actual actuality that must give all Being new meaning, in a new and original sense. The highest actualization of human Being happens in the state.

The Führer state, as we have it, means the completion of the historical development: the actualization of the people in the leader. The Prussian state, as it was completed with the cultivation of the Prussian nobility, is the precursor of today's state. This relation testifies to the elective affinity between Prussianism and the Führer. From this tradition stems the saying of the great royal elector, spoken in the spirit of Luther—and we too stand in this tradition, if we acknowledge its meaning: *Sic gesturus sum principatum, ut rem populi esse sciam, non meam privatam.*[4] [I will exercise leadership knowing that it is an affair of the people, not my private matter.]

PART TWO

INTERPRETIVE ESSAYS

1 *VOLK* AND *FÜHRER*

Investigations of Heidegger's Seminar *On the Essence and Concept of Nature, History, and State*

Marion Heinz

Heidegger's seminars *On the Essence and Concept of Nature, History, and State* from Winter Semester 1933–4 and *Hegel on the State* from Winter Semester 1934–5 have provided the fuel for the debate that Emmanuel Faye has rekindled on the question of the nature and extent of the infection of Heidegger's thinking by National Socialism. As one can already gather from the title of Faye's book—*Heidegger: The Introduction of Nazism into Philosophy in Light of the Unpublished Seminars of 1933–35*[1]—the author wants to fortify the widespread (though very controversial) thesis that it was not only in 1933 that "Heidegger devoted himself to putting philosophy at the service of legitimizing and diffusing the very bases of Nazism and Hitlerism."[2] There are good reasons why Faye places the seminars of 1933–4 and 1934–5 in the center of his investigations: these are texts—or more precisely, student transcripts of seminar sessions from the period of Heidegger's rectorate, with corrections by his own hand—which were accessible to only a few Heidegger scholars until 1995 and that were published only recently.[3] Thus an analysis of these texts can be brought to bear in a project of unmasking the true form of Heideggerian thought, a project that might even manage to persuade the not inconsiderable number of apologists for Heidegger. For the content of these seminars provides nearly seamless support for Faye's central thesis that the substance of Heidegger's philosophy consists in justifying and politically and propagandistically validating the *Führer* state, the ideology of blood and soil, and other core elements of the Nazi worldview.[4]

For Faye, the seminar of 1933–4 ranks as "the main text: the one in which we see the total identification of Heidegger's teaching with the principle of Hitlerism itself."[5] While Faye claims these transcripts as the decisive evidence for the propagandistic use of thought, we should keep in mind that the texts were not published by Heidegger himself. This does not mean that the content of the transcripts does not in a general way reflect what transpired in these seminars—after all, they were corrected by Heidegger and thus, in a certain sense, authorized. Nonetheless, they do not have the same status as published texts as regards the trustworthiness of their wording and the exact patterns of argumentation. For instance, these transcripts are not free of contradictions and self-corrections of greater or lesser significance. But this also means that they constitute important documentation of Heidegger's academic instruction during his rectorate and should be valued as such. So even if there are good reasons not to approach these pieces of evidence by means of classic textual analysis, one should at least review and interpret the course of the seminars and their essential contents, in order to then, in a second phase, consider the relevance of these new discoveries for the assessment of Heidegger's thinking as regards his support for National Socialism. In what follows I will concentrate on the Winter Semester 1933–4 seminar *On the Essence and Concept of Nature, History, and State*.

As traditional as the title of the seminar may seem at first, the protocol for the first session already makes it clear that Heidegger's discussions are devoted completely to his own philosophical approach. Here nature, history, and the state are understood as the essential domains "in which our Dasein plays itself out and maintains itself" (17). Their order in the title of the seminar corresponds to their objective order, in which nature is the inclusive domain in which history has its place, and the state in turn belongs within history—so that we are dealing with successively narrower domains of Dasein. This order in which one domain is included in another, or belongs within another, is not a logical and conceptual order, even if the title speaks explicitly of "essence and concept." As domains of existence, their characteristics are not to be developed from epistemological points of view. Instead, they must be conceived in their essence on the basis of the factual positions and attitudes of Dasein toward them (cf. Session 1). What is at stake, then, is a phenomenological investigation that must ascertain what is given and how it is given. In other words, the essence is nothing other than the thing in the How of its original givenness; here, since we are beginning with Dasein, it is clear in advance that the primary access to the essence of a thing is not made possible by the logical functions of the concept or judgment, or by cognitions determined by these logical forms. The protocols are full of indications by the "seminar leader" that we must avoid theoretical and epistemological prejudices. Nevertheless, Heidegger uses the term "concept." But the "concept" named in the title of the seminar is never defined here in its general meaning (as, say, existential concepts are defined as a type in *Being and Time*). No general phenomenological concept of the concept is developed, but kinds of the concept are introduced: with regard to all three domains, a formal and a material concept are to be distinguished. By formal concept, Heidegger understands the "way of Being" of something, and by material concept, the totality of what belongs to a certain domain in accordance with this formal concept. Heidegger gives an ontological intepretation to the conceptual relation between intension and extension, in such a way that the formal concept of a thing means the way of Being that determines the thing, a way of Being that is to be exhibited in its own sense and distinguished from others; this way of Being permits us to understand beings as having a certain Being (Session 2). The sum total of the beings that are determined by a particular way of Being is what Heidegger wants to understand in this seminar as a domain or realm. This ontological interpretation of the concept of concept goes hand in hand with a depreciation of logic as the basis of knowledge and an appreciation of language. For according to Heidegger, language is responsible for the connection between way of Being and domain, that is, the formal and material concepts. Here the ontic-ontological function of articulative discourse in *Being and Time*, which is manifested in the hermeneutic "as," returns in a new form.

Nature cannot be understood adequately in terms of the meaning of the Latin word *natura* (being born), a meaning that has been sedimented in the German *Natur* and English *nature*. Instead, we have to go back to the inception of the Western conception of nature, which is manifest in the Greek word *physis*. The Greek understanding of nature does not yet treat nature as a special domain separate from art; nature, understood formally as a special kind of movement—a "coming-forth-from-itself," a "being-moved-by-itself," or a "growth" in the broadest sense—is seen materially in Greek thought as the whole of beings, included in this "conceptual extension" (24). Accordingly, beings as what grows and emerges have the sense of "Being-present," "Being-in-the-light-of-day"; as such, they are opposed to what is concealed. "Thus, for the Greeks, growth, Being, and Being-unconcealed are bound together in a unity" (27).

History is understood analogously to nature, with regard to its material and formal concept. Materially, history is the entire domain of past, present, and future happening. Formally, Heidegger defines history as happening, in order to make a transition to the theme of temporality as the phenomenon that comes to expression in the essence of history (25–6). Here too, theory interferes with our access to the phenomena. The Newtonian and Kantian theories of time, which grew on the soil of modern philosophy, must be irrelevant to defining time; instead, we must determine the essence of time on the basis of our relation to time. Unlike *Being and Time*, the seminar begins with the now-time that is accessible in our use of clocks in order to display the original phenomenon of time—temporality as the fundamental constitution of human beings, which in turn is the condition for the everyday experience of time (cf. Session 4). This authentic time is what is decisive for the understanding of history: "we are talking about history as *our* past, as what was the fate of our ancestors and thus is our own" (37). In accordance with *Being and Time*, Heidegger explains the priority of the future in authentic temporality, but draws a conclusion that emphasizes the past: "We persist from the past into the future, and only in this way do we persist in the present" (42). It is decisive for all of Heidegger's further remarks that this definition of happening is itself indebted to human historical self-understanding—that is, it is "spoken from our own historical Dasein in this moment" and, like all propositions and truths about human beings, "which always have to be attained in one's own decision," it is "subject to a certain intelligibility" (37).

These preliminary considerations on the status of the claim to truth of philosophical statements, such as statements on the concept of history, prepare for the explication of the state as the third and narrowest domain of existence. Methodologically, the preliminary considerations serve to legitimate the procedure that Heidegger observed in what follows—namely, to derive the truth about the essence of people and state from historical considerations. For Heidegger, this is justified because knowledge of the state arises from historically motivated decisions (cf. Session 5). As we will see in detail below, Heidegger's appeals to historical circumstances are fundamental elements of what he conceives as political education. Heidegger categorically rejects the attempts to found the state rationally as a structure of sovereignty by means of the figure of the social contract, which are definitive for modern theories of the state: for Heidegger, the state is not to be understood as an arrangement created by human beings for a particular end (cf. Sessions 5 and 8). Applying the distinction between the formal and material concept to the conception of the state, Heidegger defines the state, as regards its material concept, as *Volk*: "the people is the being that *is* in the manner of a state" (38). Thus the state can be approached formally as "the way of Being of a people" (43).

Nevertheless, it is apparent that Heidegger's method of defining the state departs significantly from his definition of the other domains of existence: because with the disclosure of authentic temporality and historicity we have reached the foundation of the historical truth that is definitive here, the state cannot be treated using the procedure that has been employed so far to define the essence of a domain—namely, using the formal concept to yield the material concept. The phenomenon under consideration demands the opposite procedure, that is, by reflecting historically on one's own present, one should bring the definition of the essence of the state into the decisive situation of the moment. In other words, if the concept of the state is approached as a human way of Being, then it is the historically existing human being who puts his own historical truth up for decision with the formal definition of the state. Because the domain of the state is materially the people, and because human beings who have been unified into a people must define themselves on the basis of their particular historical truth, the essence of the state must be derived from its material concept, that is, from historically existing human beings; in contrast, a theory of the state cannot be used to define the entity that has this way of Being. Accordingly, Heidegger embarks on a historical reflection on how the Renaissance and its guiding idea of great men could eventuate in a decline of the political, so that politics could end up as one domain of the will to individual development, alongside other domains such as science and art. The dynamic of specialization of activities and dissociation of the domains of life, set in motion by the will to individual achievement, culminates in the collapse of "our state" that we can ascertain today (42). Heidegger interprets the Renaissance as the beginning of a distortion that extends to the present: the individual human being now becomes the end of Being, and this defines the meaning of all the domains of human life. In Heidegger's perspective, the liberation of the individual that occurred in the Renaissance corresponds to the liberal concept of the state, which conceives of the state as a means to the end of "the development of the personality in the liberal sense" (52). Like Carl Schmitt, Heidegger sees liberalism as the cause of the decline of the state (although his understanding of liberalism differs from Schmitt's). The liberal picture of the world and humanity, and the inherent dangers of this picture, must be opposed by philosophy today inasmuch as philosophy seeks to win back the proper rank of politics, understood as the "practical and theoretical occupation . . . having to do with the state" (41). Politics must be enabled to take its place as "the fundamental characteristic of human beings who philosophize within history, and as the Being in which the *state* fully develops, so that the state can truly be called the way of Being of a people" (42–3).

This requires us to take up the Aristotelian doctrine of the human being as *zōon politikon*. With this return to Aristotle, Heidegger initially rejects a purely biologistic foundation of people and state through the theory of race, yet at the same time he presents his own attempt to found the antidemocratic *Führer* state in terms of existential ontology as the legitimate continuation of the Greek inception. Heidegger interprets the Aristotelian definition of the human being as the political animal as meaning that human beings have the possibility and necessity of forming and completing their individual and communal Being in a community (Session 6). He thus lays out a path to authorizing his own position: for Heidegger, grounding the Being of the state in human Being means founding it in a "historically fateful decision" (45). This appeal to Aristotle, which is decisive for everything that follows, is hardly as innocuous as it may seem at first. Aristotle's definition of the human being as a political animal is undergirded by a conception of the human being as a rational, speaking animal whose telos, *eudaimonia*, is to be realized in the common deliberative praxis of free and equal citizens; but this conception plays no role in Heidegger's thought. He simply adopts the formal notion of the teleological orientation of human beings to life in a community, but founds it on his own concept of temporal Dasein.[6] This philosophical amalgam interprets the essence of the political in a completely new way, which is incompatible with Aristotle, as "historically fateful decision"; furthermore, the state is now newly defined as the human way of Being that springs from this decision, a way of Being that is to be founded and formed by the historical essence of humanity. Heidegger also introduces the concept of the *Volk* on this basis: the people is "something other than the mere sum of the citizens of the state. We mean something even more strongly binding than race and a community of the same stock: namely, the nation, and that means a kind of Being that has grown under a common fate and taken distinctive shape within a *single* state" (43). So what is constitutive for the people is not its natural Being, nor is it a political community that emerges from a social contract among the citizens. Instead, "the Being of the state is anchored in the political Being of the human beings who, as a people, support this state—who decide for it" (45). Accordingly, people and state are based on the historical Being of humanity, whose fundamental possibility and distinctive way of Being is the political.

With this definition of the human being as a political animal, the fundamental traits of existence in *Being and Time*, as well as the relation between individual existence and people in that text, are fundamentally transformed.

For the existential ontology of *Being and Time*, the happening of Dasein is "defined as *destiny*. With this we designate the happening of the community, of the people" (*Sein und Zeit*, 384). These statements from §74 of *Being and Time*, which remain unclarified in their ontological conditions of possibility, namely their temporal sense, but which have been repeatedly identified as the point of departure for Heidegger's adoption of National Socialism, are taken up and transformed in this 1933–4 seminar. In *Being and Time*, the happening of the people is grounded in the happening of the particular, individual Dasein, which is essentially a happening-with as a consequence of Dasein's Being-in-the-world, which is determined as a Being-with; but in this seminar, Heidegger implements the political as a central ontological determination of human beings. The conception of the essential relatedness of the particular existing individual to beings that lack Dasein's type of Being and to beings as Being-with—in such a way that the entirety of these meanings of beings disclosed by one's own individual Dasein is the world—is now narrowed down to care for Being within the community of the *Volk* and for this community itself. We could sharpen this point by saying that while in *Being and Time* the measure of existing consists solely in whether the particular Dasein grasps itself in its "essence" as a finite domain of projection, in order as such to take decisions on particular matters, Dasein is now conceived as directed teleologically in advance to a particular possibility: existing in the political community. The way in which this highest end is realized now decides how Dasein is. The state as telos of Dasein's Being now becomes the authentic founder of the meaning of Being: the state is "the most actual actuality that must give all Being new meaning, in a new and original sense. The highest actualization of human Being happens in the state" (64).

This also means a shift in the temporal foundations of existing: who Dasein is, is not based on the way in which temporality temporalizes, but instead, a historical reflection on the situation of the people leads to a sort of appeal to the particular Dasein; in response, the individual Dasein can either show that it is fit for the appeal, or fail. Otherwise than in *Being and Time*, philosophy no longer has the role of calling the particular Dasein to authentic, finite existing by means of existential projections; the task of philosophy is now to interpret the historical moment and to bring Dasein before its historical decision as a political being.

The formation of the political as a fundamental possibility of Dasein cannot, then, simply be left to the existentiell resolve of the particular Dasein. Instead, it needs "political education, that is, what leads us into our own political Being" (45), or in other words, "the creation of a new fundamental attitude of the will" (63). The task of philosophy is to prepare a knowledge of the essence of the state and people that is intrinsically oriented to praxis, or as Heidegger says, to the "leap into the accomplishment of the goal" (61). This knowledge—which is also communicated concretely in the situation of this seminar—can "now" address itself only to individuals: "Every individual must now reflect in order to arrive at knowledge of the people and state and his own responsibility" (46). It is not accidental that Heidegger presents this imperative, as well as the essential contents of this knowledge, as the result of reflections on the present political situation as the moment in which a Third Reich is being founded. In a new historical reflection that now concentrates on the fate of the Reich, Heidegger considers the continuities and ruptures between the first and second German Empires and tries to define the present situation as marked by the collapse of the Second Reich, a collapse partly due to Bismarck.[7] In accordance with the insight into the essential historicity of truth, it is in such a historical consideration of the fate of the German Reich that the fundamental insights into the construction and structure of the state are to be gained—insights that are supposed to be definitive for philosophical education in the present, which is understood as a moment of decision. As befits the historicity of the truth of the knowledge that Heidegger is seeking here, after critically evaluating the subjectivism that is set free in the Renaissance, he reflects historically on the concrete situation of human beings existing here and now; the function of this reflection is to determine the contents and the addressees of philosophical education, in order to prepare the historical moment of decision for the new Third Reich.

We can sum up Heidegger's philosophical reflections on the state in the following sketch:

Unlike in Plato's *Republic*, the educators, the philosophers, should not also be the rulers of the state. "For the origin of all state action and leadership does not lie in knowledge; it lies in Being. Every leader *is* a leader; he must be a leader in accordance with the marked form of his Being; and he understands, considers, and brings about what people and state are, in the living development of his own essence" (45). "A leader does not need to be educated politically—but a band of guardians in the people does, a band that helps to bear responsibility for the state. For every state and all knowledge about the state grows within a political tradition. Where this nourishing, securing soil is lacking, even the best idea for a state cannot take root, grow from the sustaining womb of the people, and develop" (45). So according to Heidegger, the state is constituted in such a way that it is led by a *Führer*, a leader qualified by his own Being, who must rely on a political nobility as the guardians of the political tradition. But because the Second Reich under Bismarck, unlike the First Reich under

Otto the Great and Prussia under Frederick the Great, "overlooked" the need to root the state in a political nobility, this tradition was cut off with the collapse of the Second Reich, a collapse that was due in no small part to this neglect. And this break is the reason why "now" every individual is challenged to develop knowledge about the state and take responsibility for the state. "The state depends on our alertness, our readiness, and our life. The manner of our Being marks the Being of our state" (46). So according to Heidegger, philosophy must reflect historically on the "fate" of the German Reich and thus disclose its own present as a historical moment in which philosophy can carry out this "development and transformation of thinking about the state"; this development will put individuals in a position to learn "that their individual life decides the fate of the people and state—either supports it or rejects it" (49). Accordingly, philosophy itself must ground itself historically on a "reflection" on the fate of the German Reich, for its task of developing thought about the state is determined by the historical moment (Session 7). And the philosophy that thus grasps itself in its own momentaneity prepares the ground for individuals to be in the moment, in the sense that they will decide the Being of the people.

Even the temporal ontology of Dasein in *Being and Time* did not understand itself as having the task of ascertaining facts about Dasein, but of bringing Dasein before the truth of its existing so that it might decide on its own whether it corresponded as an entity to this way of Being (*Sein und Zeit*, 315). Now this evocative understanding of truth is decisively transformed: on the basis of the temporal conception of Dasein, Heidegger develops a sort of meta-reflection on political history whose intention it is to bring Dasein, understood as a political being, into the situation of deciding for a particular form of community-building. The temporal determination of Dasein is saddled with these considerations on political history as a second level of temporal interpretation. Now philosophy is put into the position of identifying particular, concrete possibilities of existing—which according to *Being and Time* can arise only from the individual Dasein that grasps itself within the limits of its Being; these possibilities are to be identified as decisive for a particular historical-political human situation and elevated to the rank of the tribunal that should decide on the momentaneity of existing. The existential characteristics of individual Dasein lose their formal character and are instituted as concretely determined, philosophically authorized standards for the political situation of Heidegger's time when he demands that the present be determined on the basis of the future, so that by taking over the fate of the German Reich, one should grasp the founding of a Third Reich that overcomes the collapse of the Second Reich but preserves its essence.

These preliminary clarifications of the addressees and contents of political education are carried forward with an explicit explanation of the relation between people and state. This relation is defined more precisely as a reciprocal one: the people forms and characterizes [prägt] itself in the state, and the state gives the people its form and character (Session 5). If it is furthermore the case that the people is the entity that relates to its state as to its own Being (Session 7), we must explicate the relation between people and state further by way of the relation between entity and Being. Being is said in many ways, and what is distinctive of human Being consists, as Heidegger says here, in that the human being has consciouness of his own Being and the Being of other beings; consequently, he can be concerned with his own Being (cf. Session 7). But with this, human beings—unlike animals—are also in danger of becoming "unconscious, derelict, or indifferent" in relation to their own Being, and thus losing "their most proper worth" (48). Through their knowing and caring relation to Being, human beings are confronted with the Nothing in a twofold way: they can themselves become null through lack of consciousness, and they have to "expose themselves to the danger of the Nothing, of nihilism, in order to grasp the meaning of their Being by overcoming nihilism" (47). Obviously two different thoughts are linked here.

On the one hand, Heidegger refers to the initially trivial state of affairs that the human being, as Dasein, understands Being—and thus is confronted with the Nothing inasmuch as Being is a nonentity, and so in a certain sense a Nothing. Only on the basis of the analysis of anxiety does the condition that we are held out into the Nothing—a condition that is intrinsic to the understanding of Being—gain a voice: the relations to beings that we rely on become null so that we can experience the uncanniness of the world as world. "Within the self-evident there suddenly opens an abyss, unsurveyable and dangerous, but unavoidable for whoever truly *questions*" (47). The meaninglessness of beings at the same time opens up the possibility and necessity of Dasein for it to project itself in its own Being. This bold move [Zumutung] is decisive for understanding Heidegger's decisionism: without an orientation to rational principles, Dasein is resolved upon itself as an entity that understands Being and decides upon particular, concrete possibilities of existence. The choice of these possibilities is based solely on the undisguised realization [Vollzug] of Dasein's finite, temporal existing.

On the other hand, nihilism here is also probably to be understood in Nietzsche's sense, as a historical movement that brings to light the nullity of all values. It is not accidental, then, that there are echoes of the last man, from the prologue to Nietzsche's *Zarathustra*, when Heidegger speaks of a lack of consciousness that makes man himself null. Only if man is defined as Dasein—as Heidegger will openly say—can this half-hearted nihilism be countered, for Dasein cannot have recourse to values or rational principles. In its understanding of Being, Dasein exposes itself to nihilism and at the same time overcomes it by taking itself over in its own nullity. Thus, the connection between politics and philosophy that has already been articulated in the definition of the political essence of the human being is now invoked again. Only the philosophically existing human being who faces the abyss of the understanding of Being can escape the danger of his own nullity by grasping the meaning of Being in the overcoming of nihilism.

To further clarify the relation between people and state, Heidegger repeatedly draws an analogy to the relation between an individual and his own Being. Just as the individual has a caring, knowing relation to his Being, "the people as a being has a knowing fundamental relation to its state"; just as the individual "loves his Dasein in the world, the people wills the state as its way to be as a people" (48). The existential-ontological grounding of the state by way of this analogy culminates in the interpretation of constitution and law as the actualization of "our decision for the state," as "factical attestations of what we take to be our historical task as a people, the task that we are trying to live out" (48–9). The "constitution of the state is . . . an essential expression of what the people takes to be the meaning of its own Being (48). It is superfluous to say that every form of a rational grounding of the state, or a rational system of law, is eliminated here: Without being able to indicate more precisely what we are to understand by the will of the people (cf. Session 9), Heidegger surrenders state and law to a collective decisionism that can hardly be concealed by the appeal to historical roots. The desperate pathos of this decisionism as the founding of meaning in the confrontation with nihilism is nothing but embarrassing.

The modern idea of the state fundamentally conceives of it as an order of rule grounded contractually by free and equal citizens; for Rousseau and Kant this is an order of freedom, so that the state must preserve the freedom and equality of those who submit to the social contract. Heidegger abandons this idea in favor of the medieval idea of a state order grounded in the relations of rule and service among human beings. "Like the medieval order of life, the order of the state today is sustained by the free, pure will to following and leadership, that is, to struggle and loyalty" (49). According to Heidegger, rule (*Herrschaft*) has nothing to do with "power, enslavement, oppression, or compulsion"; here rule is defined positively as subordination to a "common task":

> Only where the leader and the led bind themselves together to *one* fate and fight to actualize *one* idea does true order arise. Then spiritual superiority and freedom develop as a deep dedication of all forces to the people, the state, as the most rigorous breeding, as engagement, endurance, solitude, and love. Then the existence and superiority of the leader sinks into the Being, the soul of the people, and binds it in this way with originality and passion to the task. And if the people feels this dedication, it will let itself be led into struggle, and it will love struggle and will it. It will develop and persist in its forces, be faithful and sacrifice itself. In every new moment, the leader and the people will join more closely in order to bring about the essence of their state, that is, their Being; growing with each other, they will set their meaningful historical Being and will against the two threatening powers of death and the devil—that is, ruination and decline from their own essence. [49]

This harmonizing interpretation of the relation between the people and the individual to the state, and of the leader to the people, depends on affirming a common fate and serves all the clichés of heroic nihilism. The harmony he depicts does not restrain Heidegger at all from taking the further step, when he clarifies the nature of ruling, to answer the question of power wholeheartedly in favor of the leader. "Mastery is power in the sense of implementation of the will" (58). What distinguishes willing from wishing is that will always grasps the end with a view to the means and ways of its realization. "Will grasps the situation, the whole fullness of time; in the will works the *kairos* that demands resoluteness and action" (59). the will of the *Führer* is directed to the will of the *Volk*, "in order to elicit this or that action or attitude" in this community of wills (59). Heidegger has no qualms about misusing Kant to characterize this action of the leader as moral-practical action, rather than instrumental action, because of its relation to human beings as free and moral; he goes on to describe those who are subject to this will euphemistically as the ruled, but will not qualify them as oppressed (61). The philosopher Martin Heidegger teaches, in February 1934, that it is time to establish such an order of rule, that "our task today is to direct the fundamental attitude of our communal Being toward this actuality of people and leader" (60). His account of the state in general, in terms of Being and beings, is finally supplemented by a view "from below, in a certain sense, from the people and the state, from us ourselves" (52).

From this perspective, the spatiality of the people is understood as a leading principle of individuation. Reacting critically to Hans Grimm's slogan "people without space," Heidegger explicates his own notions of "people in space":

> Relatedness to space, that is, the mastering of space and becoming marked by space, belong together with the essence and the kind of Being of a people. So it is not right to see the sole ideal for a people in rootedness in the soil, in attachment, in settledness, which find their cultivation and realization in farming and which give the people a special endurance in its propagation, in its growth, in its health. It is no less necessary to rule over the soil and space, to work outwards into the wider expanse, to interact with the outside world. The concrete way in which a people effectively works in space and forms space necessarily includes both: rootedness in the soil and interaction. [55]

Heidegger defines the relation between the two aspects of a people's relation to space by explaining that rootedness as the expression of the homeland determined by birth can become the way of Being of a people only if it is supplemented by working out into the expanse, by interaction. Thus he distinguishes between the space of a people and the space of its state. "In summary, then, we can say that the space of a people, the soil of a people, reaches as far as members of this people have found a homeland and have become rooted in the soil; and that the space of the state, the territory, finds its borders by interacting, by working out into the wider expanse." (56). The political implications of these existential-ontological interpretations of "people in space" become manifest, first, as regards so-called nomads, and secondly, as regards Germans living outside the borders of the Reich. History teaches us about nomads in general that they "have not only been made nomadic by the desolation of wastelands and steppes, but they have also often left wastelands behind them where they found fruitful and cultivated land" (55). This means, then, that the specific living-space of a people marks it with a sort of essence that it also displays in quite different spaces. This sets up a criterion of exclusion in accordance with which certain peoples do not fit into, or belong to, certain living-spaces. Thus Heidegger not only adopts the Nazi ideology of blood and soil (even if it is transformed in terms of existential ontology), he also links it ideologically to an overt antisemitism when he says that "the nature of our German space . . . will perhaps never be revealed at all" to Semitic nomads (56). In plain language, the Jews as nomads are a danger to the German people in that they tend to devastate the living-space of this people. And they stand outside the possibility of experiencing the kind of revelation of nature that belongs to this space, for "this original participation in the knowledge of the people cannot be taught" (56); thus they are essentially marked as non-Germans. In the place of biologistic theories of the worthlessness of the Jewish people, Heidegger affirms a racism founded on existential ontology with his theory of the Jews as aliens and enemies of the life of the German people.

By way of the second aspect of a people's relation to space, working into the expanse, Heidegger tries to explain why the ethnic Germans who live outside German territory are suffering from a sort of essential lack: they do have a German homeland, but because they do not belong to the German state, the Reich, they are deprived of "their authentic way of Being" (55). Every participant in the seminar can easily infer in what way such an essential lack should be remedied.

In this consideration of people and state "from below," the relation of the three domains of nature, history, and state presents itself as follows: "nature works on the human being, roots him in the soil, only when nature belongs as an environment, so to speak, to the people whose member that human being is. The homeland becomes the way of Being of a people only when the homeland becomes expansive, when it interacts with the outside—when it becomes a state" (55).

This means that the natural influences on human beings become a way of Being that determines them as historical beings only through the state. If the Being of man as a political entity is fulfilled in the state, every domain of Dasein is also teleologically oriented to the state; that is, as domains of Dasein they must be defined in their sense on the basis of the state.

As the narrowest domain of human Dasein, the state is also the "most actual actuality," "the highest actualization of human Being" (64). In his reflections based on the concrete spatiality of people and state, Heidegger goes so far as to identify the state as the most actual actuality, in the sense of the essential completion of the human being, with the really existing *Führer* state of National Socialism: "Our task today is to direct the fundamental attitude of our communal Being toward this actuality of people and leader in which both as a single actuality are not to be separated" (60). But what is the justification for this Hegelianizing notion of the unification of essence and actuality in the recognition of the actual state as the essential fulfillment of the German people? The definition of the state in general must evidently be brought together with the concrete characterization if we are to bring the justifying connections into view: the leader has the most powerful at his disposal—a will that comprehends "the situation, the whole fullness of time" (59); the "implementation of the will [means] awakening the same will in another, that is, the same goal and engagement or accomplishment. The implementation of the will, in this sense, transforms people in proportion to the greatness of the effective will" (62). Thus, "The Führer state, as we have it, means the completion of the historical development: the actualization of the people in the leader" (64). The *Volk*, which has already been constituted by its relation to space as homeland, is first formed into a people in the highest and authentic sense, as a community of will, by the *Führer* and his powerful will. If the state is not to be understood as a contractually established arrangement for the securing of law, but as a destined community, then the community of the state can be founded only by the will of the leader. The leader's will—bound to nothing, freed of all values and rational principles, exposed to the pure Nothing—is what creates the political community by transforming the will of the individual. In resolute obedience to the leader, Dasein can complete itself both as a being that understands Being and as a being that belongs to a community. Heidegger's Being-historical legitimation of the Hitler state thus depends decisively on the thought that in the Being of the *Führer* the historical truth of Being is grasped in such a way that by the transformation of individual will a political community can arise in which "all Being" can receive a new meaning (64). With the affirmation of the will of the leader, the individual does not subordinate himself to an alien will, but finds the highest actualization of his essence, insofar as his historical and political Being are brought into convergence: Dasein brings itself into the historical truth of its existence, so that from this truth there simultaneously springs the true form of political community. Being political in this way, as historical existence, and existing historically as a political being, means being involved in the truth-happening of the creation of a new meaning of Being. And with this, the true rank of politics as the "fundamental characteristic of human beings who philosophize within history" (42) is restored.

Thus, the characterization of historicity as the fundamental constitution of the Being of Dasein has proved to be the basis of Heidegger's political doctrines. This justifies the historicity of all truth, so that it becomes imperative to prepare a moment in which the political future will be decided, and to reveal by means of historical considerations which tasks and particular contents are the issues that must be decided at this moment. This philosophy of history does not just define the role and task of philosophy in general as an authority that evokes historical decisions, it also defines the particular task of philosophy in this historical situation— philosophy must work against the decline of the political that is evident in the present, as a result of individualization, specialization, and dissociation, by winning back the rank of politics. At the end of his seminar Heidegger names three great "disintegrations" that have determined modernity: the disintegration of Christian faith and the self-grounding of humanity in reason; the disintegration of community and the elevation of the individual as the final court of appeal; and finally, the separation of mind and body (63–4). Heidegger sees the distinctive character of the historical situation of his time—again, in a Hegelianizing perspective—in the fact that we must supersede these modern oppositions. But this is to be achieved not by reason, but on the basis of Dasein as defined by its understanding of Being. The truth of existing that consists in grasping the meaning of Being by overcoming nihilism is to be brought into effect as the principle of constitution for all human relationships. Only in this way does Heidegger think that any future can be secured for Western man, who exists on the basis of philosophy (Session 8). In the National Socialist *Führer* state, Heidegger recognizes the actuality that fulfills or can fulfill this demand, if it can successfully be transformed into the essential (Session 9).

There is no doubt that this seminar proves that Heidegger used his philosophy from *Being and Time* to legitimate National Socialism, the *Führer* state, obedience, sacrifice, and struggle—as well as antisemitism and the particular mission of the German people in the ideologically invoked history of the West. He rejects law and democracy and declares that reason and criticism are obsolete, by appealing to existence and its historicity. The Third Reich, which he proclaims as the salvation from all the dangers of modernity, is grounded both as a whole and in all its elements on existential ontology and the history of Being: The *Führer* legitimates himself as such through his Being; the *Volk* has an existentiell relation of care to its state and its *Führer*; rule is a community of fate under the will of the *Führer*. All these relations are carried by decisions whose end is established by analysis of the factical—of history or the actual *Führer* state.

This seminar also validates the clear-sighted diagnosis of Heidegger's student Herbert Marcuse from 1934. Marcuse recognized existentialism as the philosophical basis for the totalitarian concept of the state.[8] Marcuse relied on Carl Schmitt to demonstrate the intrinsic connection between the totalitarian concept of the state and existentialism, but the text of this 1933–4 seminar now proves that Heidegger himself transferred his philosophy of *Being and Time* into a political existentialism whose points of agreement with Carl Schmitt would need to be investigated in a separate study.[9]

Marcuse sees Heidegger as a thinker who betrayed his own origins and ended in existentiell opportunism, while Faye interprets Heideggerian thought as the "deliberate introduction of the foundations of Nazism and Hitlerism into philosophy and it teaching."[10] We must raise the question of whether Marcuse's interpretation of the doctrine of *Being and Time* is too conciliatory. Marcuse blames Heidegger's deviation on a subjective error, and Marcuse himself initially took up *Being and Time* as a promising attempt to develop a conception of the concrete subject. In my own view, neither this occasionalist view nor Faye's notion of a seamless continuity between *Being and Time* and the political philosophy and propaganda of the Nazi period is correct. Under the influence of Nietzsche's philosophy, which Heidegger confronted intensively starting in 1929, the doctrines of *Being and Time* are put into the perspective of the history of Being; in this perspective, they are built up into the philosophical potential of overcoming nihilism, and only then do they become serviceable for a justification of National Socialism.[11] The confrontation with the breaks and losses of modernity and with Nietzsche's radical diagnosis of nihilism forces Heidegger to stop emphasizing only the meaning-potential of individual Dasein. Only the ambition to give Being as a whole a new meaning, which develops from his intensive engagement with Nietzsche beginning in 1929 and which cannot even be formulated in terms of *Being and Time*, promises the possibility of overcoming the epochal crisis. Against the disappearance of all greatness, against the anxiety in the face of the collapse of philosophizing Western man into unconsciousness, Heidegger deploys the doctrines of *Being and Time* as a decisive reservoir of salvation.

Heidegger's approach in terms of man understood as Dasein allows him a twofold connection to Nietzsche. First, by establishing pre-rational structures of understanding of Being as the human essence, Heidegger satisfies Nietzsche's critique of reason. Heidegger agrees with Nietzsche that reason is in no position to get a grip on the epochal crisis of meaning. Secondly, the understanding of Being as such is qualified in such a way that it both exposes itself to nihilism and in itself offers the possibility of overcoming nihilism. The understanding of man as Dasein thus proves to be the only philosophical position that is up to the level and radicality of Nietzsche's thought and is to be developed on the basis of a different conception of the overcoming of nihilism than the one offered by Nietzsche—the self-affirmation of will in knowledge and the greatest burden, the doctrine of the eternal recurrence of the same.[12] If the understanding of Being as such is thought as nihilistic yet at the same time as a capacity that can overcome nihilism, everything depends on directing human relations as a whole toward founding a new meaning of Being. The historical crisis of meaning cannot be brought under control by an appeal to the individual to exist authentically; for it requires a collective to be directed toward a new meaning of Being—and this means, for Heidegger, toward the leader as the highest potency of the understanding of Being and of the implementation of a new meaning of Being that originates in his own Being. The *Führer* as the figure that links Nietzsche's overman and the resolute Dasein of *Being and Time* is a creator in a double sense: he projects a new meaning of Being and also makes this meaning dominant by transforming human will. A turning of need,[13] in the sense I have sketched, is thus possible only when philosophy becomes political and politics is brought by philosophy into its true essence as the destinal founding of Being. The presumption of a *salto mortale* that perverts the "autonomy" of individual existence into following the *Führer* must be understood as the *ultima ratio* of a thinking that believes it can counter the abyss of world history only by implementing a new, supra-individual way to establish meaning, which renounces rational principles. The complete disempowerment of reason forces this philosophy to resort to the factical, to elevate the actual charismatic leader himself as the "principle" that promises the turning of need. Heidegger's affirmation of the "*Führer* principle" arises neither from some banal political opportunism nor from mere decisionism, but from the philosophical conviction that only a philosophy based on the concepts of temporality and historicity can offer an adequate answer to the challenge of nihilism by setting free the *kairos* in the shape of Adolf Hitler. The notion of demanding submission to the *Führer's* will and using philosophy for its legitimation is revealed as the paradoxical figure of thought, which bears Christian features, of winning oneself by giving oneself up—an *auto-da-fé* of philosophy in decline, staged as an ultimate rescue and revolt. In an unparalleled perversion, while displaying the pathos of extreme radicality, Heidegger makes his thinking abet the fulfillment of the factical.

2 HEIDEGGER IN PURGATORY

Peter E. Gordon

"History is always written from the sedentary point of view [. . .].
What is lacking is a Nomadology, the opposite of a history."
GILLES DELEUZE AND FÉLIX GUATTARI, *A Thousand Plateaus*

At this late date, it may seem there is little more that could be said
concerning *l'affaire Heidegger*. That Heidegger was not merely a political
naïf but an ideologically committed partisan of the Third Reich can no
longer count as scandalous news but should be obvious to anyone who
confronts the documentary evidence with open eyes. Nor can we take
comfort in drawing a clean line between his politics and his philosophy.
All too often in the early 1930s Heidegger mobilized the intrinsic terms of
his own philosophy (Dasein, Being, and so forth) to express his political
support for the regime. No less troubling, however, is that even in the
postwar era Heidegger never offered an unambiguous explanation for
either his actions or his readiness to justify his Nazi commitments with
philosophical appeals.[1] Even sympathetic readers have felt troubled at the
possibility of a "positive implication" between Heidegger's politics and his
philosophy.[2]

For many years, the response of critics to this situation could be
located on a spectrum, from totalizing condemnation to apologetic
containment. At one pole lie the critics who find the evidence so
damning they no longer feel Heidegger's works merit inclusion in the
philosophical canon at all. At the other pole are readers who wish to

salvage whatever they can and thus cleave to a prophylactic distinction between Heidegger's philosophical ideas (in which they see enduring value) and the ideological deployment of those ideas (which they are free to condemn). For more than half a century scholars have staked out a variety of political-interpretative stances between these two extremes, their contributions ranging across all the possible genres: the stubborn defense, the paradoxical deconstruction, the detective story, the manifesto, the *exposé*. The irony of our current impasse is that the more we know concerning the facts of the case the less we can hope that scholars will ever come to an agreement as to what these facts mean. Those baby-with-the-bathwater critics who already condemn Heidegger as a Nazi ideologue *tout court* will surely welcome this book as further evidence for the prosecution. Those who are still faithful devotees of Heidegger the philosopher will persist in appealing to the distinction between thought and history, even if this demands allegiance to a metaphysical dualism the philosopher wished to dismantle.[3] What remains unclear is whether additional documentation could ever suffice to prompt those who have written about this matter to modify their views. At issue, in other words, is a question of interpretative schemes: not the fact that Heidegger was a Nazi but the meaning we assign to this fact.

I will return to this question toward the end of my essay. As a preliminary matter, however, it is important to recognize just how difficult it is to sustain a strong distinction between thought and history when we consider the transcripts and protocols of Heidegger's seminars from the early 1930s. The difficulty is chiefly due to what we might call a mutual entwinement of philosophy and ideology. Any reader of these seminars who possesses even the most rudimentary knowledge of National Socialism cannot help but notice how the conversations participate in the barbarous linguistico-metaphoric structure that Victor Klemperer called the LTI, his own acronym for *Lingua Tertii Imperii,* or the language of the Third Reich.[4] The protocols of the winter 1933–4 seminar are especially distressing in this respect insofar as they demonstrate a readiness to traverse the imaginary line that should have separated genuine questions of philosophy from crude affirmations of National Socialist doctrine. In the protocols of the seminar this line is not only broken, it is utterly erased. Our task here is to understand the nature of the transgression. The following essay is divided into three sections. First, I offer a brief summary of some of the more salient facts concerning Heidegger's political activities during the period 1933–4; second, I examine the seminar protocols themselves to determine the strategies by which philosophy and the LTI become mutually entwined;

finally, I return to the more urgent question: Does this seminar reveal anything essential about Heideggerian philosophy, or will the conflicts of scholarly interpretation proceed as they did before?

Historical background

Heidegger offered his advanced seminar, "On the Essence and Concept of Nature, History, and State" at the University of Freiburg during the winter semester of 1933–4.[5] It convened for the first time on November 3, 1933 and concluded for its tenth and final session on February 23, 1934. Before turning to the contents of the seminar itself, we should recall that it was during precisely this period that Heidegger's political activity in support of the Third Reich reached its zenith. He was elected *Rector Magnificus* at Freiburg University on April 21 (assuming the actual post the next day) and he officially joined the Nazi party on May 3. He delivered his inaugural address as rector, "The Self-Assertion of the German University," on May 27 before an assembly of university faculty and students. Even in private gatherings he let his ideological assent be known. On June 30, at the home of Karl Jaspers, he warned of a "dangerous international alliance of Jews," taking little care to moderate his opinion even though he knew Jaspers' wife was Jewish. In more public venues he confirmed his administrative and ideological commitment to the new regime. On July 12 he wrote to the Ministry of Education indicating his support for anti-Semitic policies (identified in the rhetoric of the time as "cleansing" or *Säuberung*) that were designed to expel Jews from the civil service. It is also reported that in conformity with these policies he discontinued his official role as director for all dissertations of students of Jewish descent.[6] On November 3, Heidegger issued an official statement as rector that ratified the "cleansing" legislation specifically for students enrolled at Freiburg: economic aid would be forthcoming for student members of the SA and SS (or other such groups) but would be withheld from "Jewish or Marxist students" and anyone who according to regime classification was identified as "non-Aryan."[7]

Long after the war Heidegger sought to explain his official acts as rector as attempts to preserve the relative autonomy of the university against more zealous colleagues who would have been far more aggressive in the application of Nazi policy.[8] But the evidence suggests that Heidegger's posture during his term as rector was not merely defensive but rather bespoke a readiness to reinforce the ideological aims of the regime even beyond what was officially required. On December 16, 1933, he wrote a letter, unprompted, to Dr. Vogel, the director of a National Socialist professors' association at Göttingen University, in an effort to prevent the appointment of Eduard Baumgarten because of his apparent connections with the "liberal-democratic" circle in Heidelberg and his associations with "the Jew Fraenkel." He also warned that because Baumgarten had spent some time in the United States he had grown "Americanized." Four days later, on December 20, Heidegger wrote a colleague that "from the very first day of my assumption of the 'office'" he had striven for a "fundamental change of scientific education *in accordance with the strengths and the demands of the National Socialist State.*"[9] His zeal for denouncing suspected enemies of the regime is evidenced perhaps most of all by the case of the Freiburg professor of chemistry Hermann Staudiger (later a Nobel recipient): on September 29, 1933 Heidegger told the regional minister of education that during the Great War Staudiger had been a pacifist, and on February 10 1934, he recommended Staudiger's dismissal without pension.

It is not possible to interpret such behavior as the merely public conformity of a scholar who feared for his safety and career. On the contrary, Heidegger's record of official calumny and secret denunciation demonstrates that throughout his tenure as rector he was not merely a passive witness to Nazi seizure of power but an active participant in the process of *Gleichschaltung* that brought the universities into administrative and ideological alignment with the regime. Indeed, certain sessions of the seminar convened during weeks when Heidegger offered his most unambiguous statements of support for the NS-State. On November 10, 1933, he issued a statement in the Freiburg student newspaper ("German Men and Women") in anticipation of the November 12 plebiscite that was meant to affirm Hitler's unlimited authority. In this text Heidegger explains that the Führer is "*giving* the people the possibility of making, directly, the highest free decision of all: whether it—the entire people—wants its own existence or whether it does *not* want it." The following day (November 11, 1933) Heidegger repeated these words at a meeting of university professors in Leipzig.[10]

But if Heidegger showed a commitment to the Third Reich in both word and deed during the early 1930s, then it is permissible to ask whether this commitment also revealed itself in his philosophical instruction. One coincidence of dates should not escape our notice: Heidegger issued his official statement as rector to ratify the policy of "cleansing" amongst the Freiburg student body on November 3, 1933. That same day he also delivered a speech to "German Students," published in the *Freiburger Studenten Zeitung*, that ended with an explicit endorsement of the *Führerprinzip*: "Let not propositions and 'ideas' be the rules of your being (*Sein*). The Führer alone *is* the present and future German reality and its law. Learn to know ever more deeply: that from now on every single thing demands decision, and every action responsibility." He concluded with the customary exhortation: "Heil Hitler!"[11] As it happens, Professor Heidegger issued the ratification of cleansing policies and gave the address to the German Students on the very same day that he met with students for the first session of the advanced seminar on "Nature, History and the State."

The ideological saturation of the winter 1933–4 seminar

It would be gratifying to imagine that Heidegger's seminar remained a space for intellectual inquiry free from ideological contamination; but any such hope would be wildly counterfactual. Instead we confront a near-total saturation of what was supposed to be a philosophical exercise by a political language consonant with the new regime. When one considers the enormous prestige Heidegger enjoys in the canon of Continental philosophy what is perhaps most stunning is the thoroughgoing *unoriginality* of this language. This should be stated clearly and without decorum: much of the content of the seminar is vacuous and is only interesting because of the association *with Heidegger*. How it is transfigured into "serious" and ostensibly "philosophical" language as found elsewhere in his corpus is one of the mysteries we need to explain.

So infused is the seminar with the *Lingua Tertii Imperii* that it is tempting to characterize the ten-week protocols as evidence of a political indoctrination rather than as transcripts of a course in philosophy. We could speculate that among the students following the seminar some might have been already *more* committed to the objectives of the Nazi state than the professor who was their guide. But even this circumstance would hardly diminish the overall impression that Heidegger approved of the language and themes of the seminar. The general manner of inquiry in the seminar bears many of the familiar characteristics of seminars and lectures that Heidegger had offered, both at Freiburg and Marburg, since the early 1920s (a resemblance in method to which we will ultimately return). To this we must add that Heidegger apparently read the protocols his students had prepared, and in a few minor cases he penciled in his own corrections. This practice suggests, at the very least, that he did not find the contents of the seminar objectionable. The question of indoctrination is indeed worrisome. The fact that at the time Heidegger was not merely a professor but also rector of Freiburg should prompt us to ask whether students would have felt at liberty to offer objections or critical alternatives to the language in which they were being trained.

To appreciate the extent of the seminar's saturation with the LTI we might isolate three major facets for analysis: politics, prejudice, and method. These move progressively, from the self-evident to the speculative, and from the concrete to the highly abstract.

Politics

When we consider the seminar only at its most explicit and straight-forwardly *political* level, its proximity to the official language of the Third Reich is self-evident. For a seminar that presents itself as a purely philosophical inquiry into "the state," it poorly disguises the thorough-going banality of its ideological affirmations with the illusion that they have emerged only from the laborious search for "essence" and "ground." The seminar obeys the Heideggerian custom of historical philology but injects its linguistic discoveries with the ideology it wants to find.

The word "politics" comes from the Greek *polis*, "which means the state as *community* [*Staatsgemeinschaft*]" (41). This definition already turns politics towards an expression of communal unity (*Gemeinschaft*) and silences questions of modern society (*Gesellschaft*) or the liberal-legislative idea of the *polis* as a *Rechtsstaat*. The community gains its unity and "substance" only because it enjoys the *people* (*das Volk*) as "its supporting ground" (43). We are informed of this political lesson as if it were a neutral truth of ontological insight: ". . . the people [*Volk*] is the being that *is* in the manner of a state, the being that is or can be a state" (38). In place of philosophical argument we are told that this ontological truth extends back to the Greeks, for whom the *Staatsgemeinschaft* was "the sole site where all the state's Being took place." But why the *sole* site? This already implies a favorable view of the *total* state, since it was *there*, in the *polis*, that "*everything* happened that we characterize as the state" (41, my emphasis). This is ostensibly a truth not only in ancient Greece but also for the present, a point affirmed in a later session: "The highest actualization of human Being happens in the state [*Die höchste Verwirklichung menschlichen Seins geschieht im Staat*]" (64).

Also familiar is the Heideggerian narrative of historical decline, which here gains *ontologico-political* density: since the time of the Greeks, we are told, the very term "politics" suffered a deterioration when "it was made into a circumscribed domain, one among many others, such as private life, the economy, technology, science, religion." This is the well-worn narrative of *Seinsvergessenheit*, which now takes on a political meaning correlative to the rise of liberalism, which robbed politics of its *total* and communitarian role and made it merely "one area within culture" (42). The ninth session of the seminar (February 23, 1934) will make this anti-liberal polemic explicit as a rejection of individualism: "The will of a people is not free in the sense of the freedom of the individual will." The people's will "is not the sum of individual wills but rather a whole that has its own, originary characteristics" (60). As an historical illustration the protocols mention Rousseau, whose *contrat social* "was based only on each individual's striving for his own welfare" (52) (a statement that openly conflicts with Rousseau's view that the *volonté générale* is *not* merely the aggregate of individual wills).

The genuine state as theorized in the protocols should not have been a "subordinate means to an end [dedicated to] the development of the personality in the liberal sense" (52). But it is this atomistic and liberal-instrumentalist state that is apparently responsible for the crisis of German modernity:

The development began in the Renaissance, when the individual human being, as the person, was raised up as the goal of all Being—the great man as the two ideals: *homo universalis* and the specialist. It was this new will to the development of the personality that brought about the complete transformation according to which, from then on, everything was supposed to exist purely for the sake of the great individual. Everything, and therefore politics too, now gets shifted into a sphere within which the human being is willing and able to live to the fullest. Thus politics, art, science and all the others degenerate into domains of the individual will to development, and this all the more they were expanded through gigantic accomplishments and became specialized. In the time that followed, all the domains of culture were allowed to grow ever farther apart until they could not be kept in view as a whole, up to our own day, where the danger of such behavior displayed itself with elemental clarity in the collapse of our state [*Zerfall unseres Staates*]. (42)

The significance of the above passage, in sum, is to read liberalism as the final stage in a political-metaphysical crisis: the disintegrating forces of individualism first emerge in the Renaissance and give birth to the "specialist" whose corrosive effects terminate in the fall of the Wilhelmine Reich.

But we should not rest content with exposing merely the most obvious political references that are scattered throughout these protocols. The political meaning of this ostensibly "philosophical" inquiry begins at a far deeper level of argumentative strategy, where the relation of politics to Being is established through *analogy*. The relation appeals to the formal principles of fundamental ontology as laid down at the very opening of *Being and Time*, where the human being is said to have *always and already* (as a matter of "ontical priority") a certain understanding of Being: "*Understanding of Being is itself a definite characteristic of Dasein's Being.*"[12] This ontological understanding (or *Seinsverständnis*) belongs to the very Being of the human being as a constitutive mode of existence itself, and it is the task of the existential analytic to take up this preliminary or provisional grasp (*Vorgriff*) for thematic exposition.[13] In the Winter 1933–4 seminar this antecedent feature of Dasein's ontological constitution becomes the occasion for analogy: "*Just as* [*So wie*] human beings are conscious of their Being-human—they relate to it, they are concerned with it—*in the same way* [*so hat auch*], the people as a being has a knowing fundamental relation to its state" (48, my emphasis). The analogy extends well beyond the ontological relation itself into the broader field of existential comportments—care, decision (even, and this is interesting: *eros*)—all of which taken together give the bond between people and state a certain solidity and affective *depth*: "The people, the being, that actualizes the state in its Being, knows of the state, cares about it, and wills it." This is justified through analogy: "*Just as* every human being wants to live, wills to *be here* as a human being, just as he keeps holding on to this and loves his Dasein [Being-here] in the world, the people wills the state as its way to be as a people. The people is ruled by the urge for the state, by *erōs* for the state" (48, my emphasis on "just as").

The analogical gesture evident in such a passage is repeated countless times throughout the seminar: through an illicit anchoring of political facts in existential conditions, determinate ideological positions take on a profundity that resists criticism or revision insofar as these facts ostensibly have their roots in the *a priori* terrain of Being: "The political as the fundamental possibility and distinctive way of Being of human beings is, as we said, the foundation on which the state has its Being" (45). Such phrases have a superficial *appearance* of plausibility. With noteworthy echoes of Carl Schmitt (whose concept of the political receives an explicit acknowledgement in Session 7) the seminar awards "the political" an ontological status that is presumably distinct from the business of actual politics. One might have been tempted to say that politics is *ontologized*, except that this appearance of ontological priority is actually an illusion: it is only thanks to an arbitrary and ideological decision that any set of political arrangements gains the ontological prestige of ontological priority (as "the political") over and against the rest of politics. Heidegger disguises this decision as a foundational step in the ontological drama of "political being." What he calls a *decision* for the state is merely the result of an ideological *preference* that has been mystified with an ontological aura.

The result is a rather unimpressive repetition of nationalist and statist truisms, all of which assume merely the illusion of philosophical sophistication thanks to a series of political analogies: *just as* an individual Dasein in *Being and Time* always confronts the possibility of persisting in its average-everyday condition of inauthenticity (leveling, ambiguity, idle talk) or *modifying* this everydayness for the sake of its ownmost (*eigenste*) or authentic manner of existence, *so too* in the seminar the collective Dasein of the people is faced with a *decision* as to whether and how it will embrace the state for which it furnishes the ontological ground. "The Being of the state is anchored in the political Being of the human beings who, as a people, support this state—who decide for it" (45). The entire flow of analogy aims to reinforce "the original, essential connection between people and state." This connection is both realized and fortified in a "historically fateful decision [*geschichtlich schicksalhaften Entscheidung*]": the decision *for* a political existence (45). Such language resembles Heidegger's public statements of November 10 and 11, 1933, when he indicated that the plebiscite on Hitler's rule would be an occasion for "the highest free decision of all: whether it—the entire people—wants its own existence or whether it does *not* want it."[14]

Perhaps the most revealing statement of political authoritarianism occurs in Session 7 (February 2, 1934) when the student protocol adopts language of nearly erotic fusion between *Führer* and *Volk*, a unity that allows the people to be led into a "struggle" it will both "will and love" (*Kampf wollen und lieben*). The people "will develop and persist in its forces, be faithful and sacrifice itself. In every new moment, the leader and the people will join more closely in order to bring about the essence of their state, that is, their Being; growing with each other, they will set their meaningful historical Being and will against the two threatening powers of death and the devil—that is, ruination and decline from their own essence" (49).

As the seminar proceeds, the fateful analogy between ontology and politics initiates a movement from ostensibly neutral affirmations of the human "way of Being" to specific affirmations of the *Führer*, whose style of leadership becomes a major theme for exposition. Invoking a quasi-Aristotelian polemic against the fruitless politics of mere *theoria*, the protocols describe the *Führer* as a man of practical virtue, of worldly-ontological *phronesis*: for true leadership "does not lie in knowledge; it lies in Being" ["*nicht im Wissen, sondern im Sein.*"] (45). The distinction bears a close resemblance to the exhortation from Heidegger's November 3 rectoral speech to German Students: "Let not propositions and 'ideas' be the rules of your being (*Sein*). The Führer alone *is* the present and future German reality and its law." Animating all of these remarks is what we might characterize as a specific antipathy to politics as conceived as a *technique* (the instrumental-rational or administrative-managerial style associated with the modern-liberal state). In place of technique the protocols celebrate the leader as a man gifted with a mystified species of political understanding that is grounded in nothing other than ontological intuition: "For the origin of all state action and leadership does not lie in knowledge; it lies in Being. Every leader *is* a leader; he must be a leader in accordance with the marked form of his Being; and he understands, considers, and brings about what people and state are, in the living development of his own essence" (45).[15]

This species of ontological-political understanding also serves as the groundwork for a kind of *political education*. It is a noteworthy sign of candor that the protocols are ready to acknowledge leader's limitations in formal education. But what may seem a deficit turns out to be an advantage: "A leader does not need to be educated politically" (45). What the leader lacks in official learning he receives as a gift of ontological constitution or "essence." The emptiness of this category is evidenced in the ritual affirmation of an analytic truth: "Every leader *is* a leader" and every leader "must be a leader" because this identity conforms to "his Being" and "the living development of his own essence." All of these truisms adopt the familiar strategy of silencing any complaints regarding the leader's lack of intelligence or education by appealing instead to qualities such as "gut" or "charisma" that resist analysis.

If all of this has a familiar ring for readers today it is not only because the strategy remains a commonplace of authoritarian legitimation. We also know from Jaspers' memoirs that during Heidegger's visit to the Jaspers' home (the previous May, 1933) the host had asked how someone as uneducated (*ungebildet*) as Hitler could rule Germany: "It's not a question of education," Heidegger responded. "Just look at his marvelous hands."[16] At issue is a gesture of anti-intellectualism that inverts the conventional relation between theory and practice: the preeminence of the mind gives way to the body and more specifically to the artisanal, embodied mode of skilful coping with entities that appear in *Being and Time* under the name of the "ready-to-hand" (*zuhanden*).[17]

But even if the protocols acknowledge the leader's intellectual deficiencies, these are counterbalanced by a mysterious "band of guardians" who (like the guardians in Plato's *Republic*) possess the higher knowledge prerequisite for directing affairs of state, presumably alongside of or possibly behind the leader (45).[18] It is this band that will be entrusted with the task of "political education" which will involve "not memorization of sentences and opinions and forms" but instead "the creation of a new fundamental attitude of the will" (63). This notion of the guardian-class may reflect Heidegger's own ambitions at the time to "educate the leader" (*den Führer erziehen*), a phrase Karl Jaspers used to characterize the philosopher (often quoted as "*den Führer führen*," although this is not what Jaspers wrote).[19] We might speculate that Heidegger was entrusting the members of his seminar with a sacred responsibility of sharing in his *ex officio* role of political theorist or philosopher-king to the new regime. In his inaugural address as rector Heidegger anticipates this argument when he recommends that members of the academic community consider themselves responsible for "knowledge service" (*Wissensdienst*) as one of the three modes of service to the state, alongside labor-service (*Arbeitsdienst*) and military service (*Wehrdienst*). The German university would be recreated into "a place of spiritual legislation" and "the center of the most disciplined preparation for the highest service to the people."[20] The closing lines of the seminar's penultimate session on February 23, 1934 make an explicit reference to "leader-education" (*Führerschulung*), which suggests that Heidegger wished to prepare students for assuming this "knowledge-service" at the highest level (60).[21]

Prejudice

This entire discourse of political authoritarianism devolves into manifest absurdity when the seminar turns to the conventional phenomenological topic of space. Any reader who has devoted careful attention to Heidegger's existential analytic, (whether in *Being and Time*, or *Basic Problems of Phenomenology*, or other works from the 1920s) will know that the phenomenology of space plays a crucial role in the broader analysis of Dasein.[22] To be human is to find oneself always-already situated in an *environment* or *Umwelt*. To this existential space there corresponds a mode of englobed or contextual vision (*Umsicht*) which attends the engaged understanding of Dasein as being-in-the-world. Neither the Newtonian model of space as a mere container nor the Cartesian model of space as mathematized *extensio* will prove adequate for thematizing the embedded spatiality that is constitutive of Dasein's world. The Kantian theory of space (as a pure form of intuition alongside time) must also be deemed insufficient since it resides only on the side of the transcendental subject and cannot explain the ontologically *prior* phenomenon of the environment (*Umwelt*).[23]

All of this is familiar terrain for Heideggerian philosophy. What is perhaps most distressing in the protocols is the way this phenomenological inquiry into "primordial space" is transformed via analogy into a fairytale about natives and nomads: "For the Being of the people, as a human way of Being, space is not simply surroundings, or an indifferent container. When we investigate the people's Being-in-space, we see that every people has a space that belongs to it [*zugehörigen Raum hat*]" (54–5). Lurking in this somewhat anodyne formulation is a political verdict that a given people either "belongs" to a certain space or it does not. But this is already a shift in register and it involves a misunderstanding or an abuse of what should have been a phenomenological insight. After all, the claim that a certain kind of spatiality is *constitutive* of human existence has no obvious bearing on the factual question of whether a *specific* human group enjoys a proprietary attachment to a distinctive piece of land. The protocols record this shift in argumentation—from phenomenology to politics—as if it were wholly uncontroversial. More distressing still is the way the protocols seek to ratify the misunderstanding with a vacuous piece of anthropology: "Persons who live by the sea, in the mountains, and on the plains are different" (55).

With this observation we have passed well beyond philosophy into a region where any piece of absurdity is permissible. Enter the nomads:

> History teaches us that nomads have not only been made nomadic by the desolation of wastelands and steppes, but they have also often left wastelands behind them where they found fruitful and cultivated land— and that human beings who are rooted in the soil have known how to make a home for themselves even in the wilderness. (55)

Should there be any doubt as to the identity of these "nomads," the protocol soon takes care to note that they are "*Semitic nomads*" (56). It is a chilling phrase and all the more so when we recall that the previous spring Heidegger had indicated his official support for policies leading to the expulsion of Jews from Freiburg University. But the language is not unfamiliar: already in October, 1929 Heidegger had warned in a letter that "we are faced with a choice, either to provide our German intellectual life once more with real talents and educators rooted in our own soil [*bodenständige*], or to hand over that intellectual life once and for all to the growing *Verjudung* [literally, 'Jewification'] in the broad and narrow sense."[24]

Indeed, it is worth noting that the nomad was a frequent visitor in the LTI bestiary. Although Hitler and Goebbels typically preferred to expatiate upon the sins of "the Jew" (a creature who usually made his entrance after an unflattering adjective such as cunning, wily, deceitful, cowardly, etc.), Klemperer reminds us that other descriptions such as "parasitic" and "nomadic" were available "for the more educated palate."[25] The reference to *Semitic nomads* is especially convenient insofar as it delivers a poisonous caricature in the guise of academic erudition. But Dr. Goebbels (Ph.D, Heidelberg, 1921, for work on nineteenth-century drama) took great pride in his own academic credentials. In January of 1945 he published an essay in the *Reich* newspaper entitled "The Authors of All the Misfortune in the World" that inveighed against the Jews, who *"are driving millions of people to their death out of repulsion at our culture which they sense is far superior to their own nomadic conception of the world."*[26] The nomads who (in the language of the seminar protocol) had "left wastelands behind them" were the very same creatures who were kind enough to reappear a decade later when Goebbels needed a scapegoat for Germany's impending military defeat.

Within the context of the seminar, however, the nomad is born from a specific exercise in political analogy. The exercise begins with the innocence of a phenomenological axiom: "People and space mutually belong to each other." But this axiom is injected with a particular empirical content: "From the specific knowledge of a people about the nature of its space, we first experience how nature is revealed in this people. For a Slavic people, the nature of our German space would definitely be revealed differently from the way it is revealed to us; to Semitic nomads, it will perhaps never be revealed at all [*den semitischen Nomaden wird sie vielleicht überhaupt nie offenbar*]" (56). The unfortunate conclusion is that Semitic nomads are exceptions insofar as they belie the truths of phenomenology: nomads may not experience German space because they have no space that belongs properly to them at all. Outsiders to any *Umwelt*, it is their essential nature to remain wanderers and exemplars of a philosophical anomaly: every Dasein belongs properly to a space, *but not this one*. It is therefore unsurprising that they fail to comprehend the neo-romantic intuition of spatial belonging.[27] Indeed the protocols make it clear that this intuition can never be acquired through mere theory: "This way of being embedded in a people, situated in a people, this original participation in the knowledge of the people, cannot be taught; at most, it can be awakened from its slumber" (56).

The analogy connecting phenomenological spatiality to geopolitical space ultimately assumes a concrete and ideological purpose of justifying Germany's colonization of lands to the East, an effort that will presumably require farming (here dignified with a martial sobriquet, "rule over the soil." As in the 1929 letter warning of a *Verjudung* of the German spirit, Heidegger again contrasts the nomads to those fortunate enough to enjoy *Bodenständigkeit* or "rootedness in soil":

> Relatedness to space, that is, the mastering of space and becoming marked by space, belong together with the essence and the kind of Being of a people. So it is not right to see the sole ideal for a people in rootedness in the soil [*Bodenständigkeit*], in attachment, in settledness, which find their cultivation and realization in farming and which give the people a special endurance in its propagation, in its growth, in its health. It is no less necessary to rule over the soil and space, to work outwards into the wider expanse, to interact with the outside world. The concrete way in which a people effectively works in space and forms space necessarily includes both: rootedness in the soil and interaction. (55)

It is hardly necessary to observe that these encouragements to farming and settlement do not emerge with logical necessity from the phenomenology of space as adumbrated in *Being and Time*.

Method

All of the above exercises in political analogy should prompt us to ask whether something already built into the very method of existential phenomenology has *invited* such a transformation. In other words, is Heidegger's philosophy *especially* vulnerable to its political deployment? Is there something about his particular manner of thinking or method that already reveals its readiness or its *susceptibility*? The question is no doubt troubling especially for those who are invested in the endurance and promotion of a "Heideggerian method." Although I will refrain from offering any decisive answer to this question, it is worth noting that, *at least in this seminar*, the stratagem of political analogy already begins to work its effects at the level of phenomenological method itself.

To appreciate the extent of the contagion we might begin by looking more closely at the opening moments of the seminar when the rigorous practice of phenomenological inquiry is nearly sabotaged by two misguided participants: the first protocol (November 3) records the presence of "an older natural scientist" and "an older student of philosophy," both of whom express a misguided preference for beginning the phenomenological exercise with *concept* rather than *essence*. These men are "far too rash" and their speculations are "hasty" (16). Even more distressing is their penchant for "preconceived concepts and theories." The natural scientist is especially guilty insofar as he thinks of nature as "an exact lawfulness" (19). The protocol (written by Karl Siegel) complains that "a certain artificiality and affectation" took over the seminar (17). Some of the students betrayed "a hasty impatience" (*eine hastige Ungeduld*) and a "reflective adherence to principle" (18). But the attitude of these two gentlemen already commits a transgression against phenomenology, since this is a practice that demands one begin "naively and "naturally" or (as Husserl would have said) with one's attention directed squarely "to the things themselves." The two men in question are responsible for an initial disruption which effectively destroys the "innocence" of the phenomenological task: The simple "expression of what is given to us [*Aussagen dessen, was uns wie gegeben ist*]" (18).

Heidegger himself therefore feels compelled to intervene: these gentlemen are speaking "too philosophically" and their contributions are *too* "theoretical." The great challenge of the seminar will be "to take up a concrete and actual reflection [*als Aufforderung zur konkreten und wirklichen Aufnahme der Besinnung*]" (19). Abstraction must be avoided at all costs. If the seminar is to investigate the three phenomena—nature, history, and the state—precisely *as* they are given to us (which is to say, *qua* phenomena) then this will call for the naiveté of a phenomenological method that could take up any phenomenon at all. A welcome and familiar example presents itself: the chalk. Chalk is of course an obvious and reliable object to which any professor will turn when they need a handy illustration, and it is especially serviceable for phenomenological experimentation: Heidegger appeals to it in several places, including the 1935 *Introduction to Metaphysics*.[28] But here we can see how the everyday can take on the illumination of the miraculous: "Such a small and inconspicuous thing as a piece of chalk" presents the seminar with a tremendous challenge but also a pedagogical opportunity. For *just as* nature, history, and the state are "given to us as fields of Dasein" *so too is the chalk*. From this we come to the more striking insight that "*even the simple chalk stands in relation*" to nature, history, and the state (20; my emphasis).

At play in this opening session is an astonishing romanticism of the everyday. The preference for the concrete and the familiar is anticipated in *Being and Time* itself where Heidegger interrogates Dasein in its mode of "average everydayness" (*Alltäglichkeit*).[29] But in the protocols of the seminar we can see how this preference imposes a virtual ban on critical reflection, the errors of which are either "hasty" or "abstract." Haste is never wise for a philosopher, but it is especially bad when the ethos of the times favors profundity. (A philological note: even in contemporary German dictionaries one is still confronted with the injunction to avoid Jewish haste: "*nur keine jüdische Hast!*"). But for Heideggerian phenomenology in particular it is *abstraction* that must be avoided at all costs. In the seminar's first session the natural scientist commits the error of appealing to a "concept" of nature as an "exact lawfulness." But laws and precision are the stuff of modern mathematics, and so they fail to grasp nature as it is first unconcealed: that is, as *physis* (a theme explored in session three). The second transgressor is not a natural scientist but a philosopher, therefore accused of "philosophizing." Both men have committed the sin of abstraction that will serve throughout the seminar as the negative counterpoint to genuinely philosophical interrogation. This is also true of politics: the state cannot be "a sum of legal principles, or a constitution." Most of all it cannot be "an intellectual construct [*keine Konstruktion des Geistes*]" (55). But it is *also* true of the most fundamental themes in phenomenology: the Kantian and Newtonian concept of time "must lead into error and is *a violent abstraction* [*eine gewaltsame Abstraktion*]" (33, my emphasis).

We can therefore observe over the course of the entire seminar a quasi-logical train of argumentation that leads from methodology to political ideology. It begins with a primer in phenomenological method as devotion to the concretely given, and it therefore shuns two alternatives (conceptual epistemology and natural science) that would only lead students astray. It then inquires into the understanding of time and space as it is given in the very temporality of Dasein itself. This exposition leads to an affirmation of both historical time ("*history* is now the distinctive 'term' for human Being") and historical space (i.e. the space to which each people must belong) (37). The spatio-historical character of collective Dasein gains further specificity as the existence of a *people* who must *decide* upon its own historical existence or otherwise suffer an ignoble decline.

Throughout the seminar the political significance of its argument emerges chiefly through analogy. The leader understands the political *just as* Dasein understands Being. The people *belongs to* its geopolitical terrain *just as* Dasein belongs to its own region of space. Such analogies are deceptive because the comparative term belongs to the more "respectable" elements of Heidegger's work: after all, the proposition that the human being finds itself always already situated in a distinctive space appears to be little more than a formal discovery of phenomenology. It even recalls the exposition of existential space in *Being and Time* according to which Dasein always experiences space as a definitive *region* (*Ort*) or environment: Dasein establishes as a condition of its own being-in-the-world a kind of phenomenological intimacy that Heidegger calls *Ent-fernung* (the annulment of distance).[30] But this formal insight into the constitution of existential space serves as the license for a politics of colonization. In their final pages the protocols assume an overtly political meaning that is now unmistakable: it is necessary "to rule over the soil and space, to work outwards into the wider expanse, to interact with the outside world" (55).

A political susceptibility?

If one considers the terrific ease with which the seminar effects a constant movement from phenomenological inquiry to political ideology, one may feel tempted to ask if this movement is wholly accidental. Is there perhaps some *susceptibility* in Heidegger's philosophy that made this movement possible? Or is there even (to consider a graver possibility) a certain *anticipation* of the movement that is embedded already in the formal gestures of Heideggerian phenomenology itself? It is important to recognize that merely by raising this question we find ourselves in an unsettling proximity to a certain style of anti-intellectualism: to scrutinize a philosophy for its politics can too quickly turn into an exercise in *anti-philosophy* or the negation of philosophy in the name of political responsibility. While the risks in such an exercise are considerable, the question in itself cannot be deemed illegitimate: what is it that permits this seminar to adopt even the *pretense* that it serves as a forum for genuinely philosophical inquiry?

Such questions confront us with the possibility that Heideggerian phenomenology *as such* remains especially vulnerable to political analogy, precisely insofar as it prides itself on its precarious status as a philosophy that remains faithful to the non-conceptual and the concrete, a mode of thinking, in other words, that hovers *just above* the world it wants to describe. We should recall that antipathy for abstraction is itself an essential feature of the LTI. Klemperer observes that Nazism sustained a linguistic war on "the system" as anything "assembled . . . according to the dictates of reason." The disadvantage of a *system* from the National Socialist perspective is that "the word is used to refer almost exclusively to abstractions. The Kantian system is a logically structured network of ideas to grasp the world in its entirety; for Kant—for the professional, trained philosopher as it were—to philosophize means to think systematically. And it is this very way of thinking which the National Socialist rejects from the innermost core of his being. . . ."[31] This antipathy also extends to "intelligence" and "objectivity," both of which evoke a species of cool and distanced knowledge that is the very opposite of phenomenological insight. According to Klemperer the LTI therefore dislikes conceptuality and prefers intuition, or *Anschauen*, "a way of seeing which discerns more than simply the surface of a given object, which in a strange way also grasps its essence, its soul."[32]

In the lexicon of phenomenology, of course, the term "intuition" does not carry the sense of irrational or mystical insight that Klemperer hears in the LTI. On the contrary: phenomenology in its classical phase makes intuition the very ground of a "rigorous science." It is true that in Husserl's work we can already witness the philosophical attempt to draw near to what is given in nonrational intuition. But Husserlian phenomenology typically (though with Husserl qualifications are always in order) advertised itself as a *transcendental* phenomenology that required a principled *withdrawal* into essence via the method of *epoché*. An intuition for Husserlian phenomenology should always be a *pure* intuition (*reine Anschauung*). Heideggerian phenomenology, by contrast, *disallows* this withdrawal as a metaphysical error and wishes to draw *as near as possible* to the world about which it hopes to offer philosophical insight, without, however, plunging so completely into the world that its formal descriptions of existential modalities (care, language, history, and so forth) would dissolve into positivistic descriptions of the world that is merely there. It is almost as if the Heideggerian necessarily operated in a kind of limbo, between everydayness and abstraction, between the world as he found it and the world as it is seen with the ambiguous instrumentality of "formal indication."[33]

We know how Heidegger was riven with ambivalence about the very practice of "philosophy," a term he eventually disowned. The 1964 essay "The End of Philosophy and the Task of Thinking" announces the turn against the technical discipline of philosophy as if its abandonment were not an intellectual preference but the sign of a quasi-objective movement in world history. Implicit in this contrast—between "philosophy" and "thinking"—is a verdict *against* philosophy as *still-too-conceptual* and thus *still-unfaithful* to the world it means to describe. But this abandonment had been in preparation for many years. We know from memoirs that even before Heidegger had published any of his major works, students already revered him for his skill in thinking the concrete. It was Hannah Arendt who described this as a revolutionary capacity to use "think" as a *transitive verb*: "Heidegger never thinks 'about' something; he thinks something.

In this entirely uncontemplative activity, he penetrates to the depths, but not to discover, let alone bring to light, some ultimate, secure foundations which one could say had been undiscovered earlier in this manner. Rather, he persistently remains there, underground."[34]

The technical term for this capacity is *phenomenology*. It is a tool, however, that in the 1920s Heidegger takes up with the added proviso that it can only do its proper work within the bounds of the existential lifeworld. From this point forward the residence of the philosopher will not be the transcendental standpoint arrived at through bracketing but instead the native space to which the philosopher always-already belongs. As Heidegger explains in the famous 1921 letter to Löwith, the analytic of Dasein becomes a kind of existential autobiography:

> I work concretely and factically out of my "I am"—out of my spiritual and thoroughly factic heritage, my milieu, my life contexts, and whatever is available to me from these, as the vital experience in which I live. This facticity, as existentiell, is no mere "blind existence"—*this Dasein is one with existence*, which means that I live it, this "I must" of which one speaks.[35]

With this circular movement, authorized by the name of hermeneutics, Heidegger not only signals his leave-taking from the intellectualist ambitions of his teacher Husserl, he transforms phenomenology into a technique of worldly devotion. Like the tailor who cuts his cloth or the farmer who knows his field (both metaphors for the artisanal *mise-en-scène* Heidegger admired), the phenomenologist *just is* the philosophizing Dasein who throughout *Being and Time* remains attached to his workshop and remains always *as faithful as possible to* the things themselves (*die Sachen selbst*). The remarkable metaphors of intimacy in *Being and Time* culminate in the portrait of Dasein as a being whose very understanding is contingent upon the logic of what "belongs" (*gehört zu*) a given region or environment. This is true not only on the grand scale as a proprietary relation between distinct peoples and their environment (sea, mountains, or plains, as detailed in the 1933–4 Winter seminar). It is true already in the logical sense that it is only in virtue of belonging that *any object whatsoever* first earns its everyday intelligibility.

But this is a faith that also recognizes the meaning of any lapse. The famous "breakdown" of the hammer (in *Being and Time* section 16) serves as a cautionary tale about the dangers of conceptual distance. The Cartesian epistemologist who retreats too far for the sake of analysis gains conceptual clarity but loses felt contact with the world. From this inaugural moment in seventeenth-century natural-scientific metaphysics, humanity will commence its efforts in the mathematization and ontological deracination of an objective nature that will culminate with what Heidegger describes as a "loss" of existential space itself, or the *deworlding of the world* (*die Entweltlichung der Welt*).[36]

Phenomenology, in other words, is the name for Heidegger's attempt to undo this drama of metaphysical forgetting by recalling philosophy to the prelapsarian world, the world in which it was born and to which it claims an attachment. All of the themes associated with authenticity—the *eigenste* or ownmost understanding that remains for Dasein the only normative aspiration of its being—are strategies for recommending this restoration, and this remains true even if (or precisely *because*) Dasein cannot hope to evade the *uncanny* or not-at-home truth of its ungrounded condition.[37] It is this aspiration most of all that explains the charge that Heideggerianism is ultimately an Odyssey homeward.[38] We might even say that existential phenomenology was originally conceived as a philosophy *against* philosophy: a Wittgensteinian therapeutic for the pathology of reflective distance by which we have forgotten our native world and ensnared ourselves in the εἶδος or ἰδέα. This ambivalence concerning the purposes and very meaning of philosophy belongs to the deepest patterns of Heidegger's work. The broader condemnation of the entire metaphysical tradition as an *Irrweg* or path of error may strike some readers as a scandalous overstatement, but it is merely a radicalized repetition of the earlier phenomenologist's expression of discomfort at the classical attempt to draw back from reality for the sake of conceptual understanding. *Metaphysics* is merely the generic name in Heidegger's writing for the species of reflective distance whose modern supremacy he condemns.

But this means that his particular manner of philosophizing operates with a constant and constitutive risk of falling out of its own intellectual purgatory into the banality of the everyday. The appeal to everydayness is still an appeal to an abstraction—"everydayness" is after all still a *theme* or *category* as signaled by the suffix of abstract quality, *Alltäglichkeit*. But it is an abstraction that operates in an intimate conspiracy with the phenomena it wants to name. To be sure, it could be argued that every instance of figurative language carries the comparable risk that one could conflate metaphor and idea. But a philosophy that undertakes a war on abstraction renders this risk especially acute insofar as it eschews the unrealized idea and invites its appearance in concrete form. In Heidegger's own technical language we might call this the illicit movement from the ontological to the ontic. The Greek term is *bathos*, as theorized by Alexander Pope in his 1727 essay, "*Peri Bathous, Or the Art of Sinking in Poetry*.[39] But whereas

Pope wished to identify a comic effect, the bathetic in Heidegger is rarely amusing because it is a sinking into political barbarism.

Conclusion

The temptations of political analogy are temptations that might afflict any philosophy that is notoriously uncomfortable with its own status as philosophy. But it is only with *a political motive* that the analogies are realized. If we are trying to understand how Heidegger could have willfully committed his ideas to the bathos evident in the Winter 1933–4 seminar, we need to appreciate its peculiar vulnerability to gestures of political analogy. This is true not only of the Winter 1933–4 seminar. In the rectoral address of the previous spring, "The Self-Assertion of the German University," Heidegger catalogues the various misunderstandings of the term "spirit":

> For "spirit" is not empty cleverness, nor the noncommittal play of wit, nor the boundless drift of rational dissection, let alone world reason; spirit is the primordially attuned, knowing resoluteness toward the essence of Being. And the *spiritual world of* a people is not the superstructure of a culture any more than it is an armory filled with useful information and values; it is the power that most deeply preserves the people's earth- and blood-bound strengths as the power that most deeply arouses and most profoundly shakes the people's existence.[40]

The striking thing about this passage is not (as Derrida proposed) its appeal to "spirit" as such.[41] While it is obvious that the term is freighted with metaphysical significance, it is no less obvious that Heidegger feels authorized to use it only because he aims to dismantle the metaphysical meanings it has acquired in the course of history. Knowing its heritage, he hastens to provide an inventory of the many things spirit is *not*: it is not "empty cleverness," "wit," "rational dissection," or "world reason." (Needless to say this list runs together social physiognomy and high philosophy: who after all are the social types most often accused at the time of "empty cleverness"?) The consequence is a perfect specimen of bathos that embraces earth and blood and nationalistic belligerence as the only genuine manifestations of spirit. *Pace* Derrida, the rectoral address is not the occasion for a reprisal of "spirit" in the metaphysical sense. It is the more public occasion for a war on abstraction that Heidegger has been waging in the name of phenomenology since his earliest years.[42]

What conclusions might be drawn from the arguments above? It is my good fortune that I am not a Heideggerian, which means I feel no complicities, whether professional or doctrinal, that would oblige me to defend the pristine reputation of Heidegger's philosophy against its more zealous critics. Yet all the same I believe, for reasons of moral and intellectual principle having little to do with Heidegger, that we must continue to distinguish between philosophical argument and the politico-ideological ends to which such argument is deployed. That Heidegger may have betrayed this principle is to his eternal discredit, but his own failure to observe the boundary line between philosophy and ideology should not give us license to trespass the boundary ourselves. Animating this principle is a strong conviction that the life of the mind has its own standards of judgement that are not wholly commensurate to the standards by which we judge political action: if we find value in a certain philosophical perspective we may very well feel something like *regret* that the philosopher who developed this perspective was politically odious. But we would be rash to reject his perspective solely on these grounds.

The final and most troubling question is *where* the boundary between philosophy and ideology is properly to be drawn. If we attempt to cordon off a particular set of philosophical arguments and ideas as wholly free of ideological contamination we indulge a fantasy: the dream of sacred *contemplatio*, once associated with the Latin *templum* (a place of *ius augurium*, or divination with birds). Such a fantasy is merely the photographic negative of the polemicist's view that a given philosophy can never be anything *other than* ideology. To these extremes the only response is to draw the boundary *within* philosophy itself, recognizing the political deployment of ideas as a *potentiality* that inheres within thinking itself.[43] We should recall that during a 1936 meeting with Heidegger in Rome, his student Karl Löwith offered the opinion that "his taking the side of National Socialism was in agreement with the essence of his philosophy." Heidegger agreed "unreservedly" and added that "his idea of historicity [*Geschichtlichkeit*] was the foundation for his political involvement."[44] From this confession it would be wrong to conclude that the idea of historicity is merely a *non-philosophical fragment* of the LTI. It would be more consonant with our concepts of both philosophy and politics to conclude that historicity, like other ideas in Heidegger's work, remains open for interpretation both now and in the future. It is susceptible, in other words, to a range of political and ideological possibilities whose meanings are neither determined nor foreclosed by any distinct occasion of historical realization.

To see any given philosophical text as open rather than closed in its interpretative possibilities—and to see any ideological deployment under the aegis of susceptibility—permits us to avoid semantic determinism by appreciating all of the various ways such a text can be used. To speak of *susceptibility* does not imply that Heidegger's philosophy was somehow *already* and *nothing but* an erudite incitement to Nazism. Unlike scholars who wish to find a distinctive political attitude built-in to Heidegger's philosophy, it seems to me a matter of intellectual urgency that we deny the determinism this implies. That political analogies are *possible* does not make them *inevitable*. Nor are all political analogies illicit. They become illicit because of the interpretations they encourage and the policies they thereby help to promote. In its philosophical mode, Marxism, too, bears within it a concatenation of themes that have proven vulnerable to political analogy (e.g. the "dictatorship of the proletariat" or the necessitarian apology for "immiseration"). But it would be wrong to conclude that the philosophy as such must be judged only by each and every worldly movement it has inspired. Not every Marxist is responsible for the gulag, although anyone who endorses Marxism today should feel moved to explain why this affirmation is resistant to Stalinism.

One can still be a "Heideggerian" today, but this should allow space for a criticism of Heidegger's politics. We may find it instructive to revisit the question as to whether there is something distinctive about Heidegger's philosophy that made it especially vulnerable to such a trespass. But the question remains: should such a vulnerability move us to reject anything and everything that is found in Heidegger's corpus? The accumulation of facts has now reached the point that Heidegger may seem to have damned himself beyond any possible appeal. But if the life of the mind holds any promise, it is the hope that new insight may be derived even from what we thought was already understood. Strict determinism is refuted in the very instant of discovery. This is something Heidegger in his chauvinistic preference for "groundedness" did not understand: *ideas themselves are nomadic*. Uprooted from their land of origin, they escape the authoritarian determination of a unique realization in historical time that would contain all their possibilities. Heidegger may have believed he knew the full political implications of his work. But we can continue to sustain the hope of reading him otherwise, even while we condemn the man who willingly offered up his own ideas to the inferno.

3 WHO BELONGS? HEIDEGGER'S PHILOSOPHY OF THE *VOLK* IN 1933-4

Robert Bernasconi

I

It is clear that Heidegger was a committed Nazi during 1933-4, the period primarily under consideration here. But although there has been a great deal of debate about the relation of his politics to his philosophy, the discussion of his adherence to National Socialism has, with relatively few exceptions, tended to rest on the false unstated assumption that National Socialism was a largely uniform movement. As Christopher Hutton explains, there is a "considerable communication gap" between specialist studies on Nazi Germany and the wider academic public when it comes to exploring the competing understandings of German identity within National Socialism.[1] This communication gap is especially in evidence in the debate about Heidegger's Nazism. It is not enough to examine what Heidegger said in order to compare it either with our preconceived notions of National Socialism or even with his subsequent accounts of what he understood by the Nazi movement at that time. If we are to understand what Heidegger was saying and why he was saying it in the way he was, then at very least we need to have an understanding of the debates within the Nazi party so as to figure out his place in them. To be sure, because Heidegger's defense after the war partly rested on his claim that in company with many intellectuals he worked to transform some of the essential formulations of National Socialism (GA 16: 398), there is always a suspicion that asking "what kind of Nazi" he was is simply an exercise in apologetics.[2] But that would be a poor excuse for not pursuing the difficult scholarly task of trying to locate Heidegger within the ongoing debates among his contemporaries on the meaning of National Socialism so as to read him more rigorously. I will show that Heidegger's account of the *Volk* at the beginning of the Nazi period marks a decisive step in his philosophical itinerary and that it does so in an overdetermined political context. Understanding this step is crucial to the interpretation not just of his politics, but also of his philosophy, given—and I here confirm what others have long believed—they cannot always be neatly separated.

National Socialism was fractured from beginning to end but, because of the unique value that the Nazis placed on the unity of the German people, they can frequently be found in pursuit of biological community as well as psychic and spiritual conformity, or both, however those were to be understood. Frequently the emphasis was placed on the biological. As Alfred Rosenberg put it in 1934, the task of National Socialism was to turn the German nation into "one huge block of seventy millions suffused with the same blood,"[3] but whatever weight was placed on the biological, it was never all that mattered in a context of extreme antagonism with neighbor turning on neighbor. Appeals to unity were admissions of disunity, and by a remorseless logic that is not peculiar to National Socialism, but which that movement can be said to have taken to the limit, this led to a disciplining of the population and to violent purges not only against those whom they thought of as biologically alien, but also against those whom they recognized as like themselves in everything except ideology. The banning of all political parties with the exception of the Nazi Party on July 14, 1933 only served to internalize the strife for unity further. Divisions continued to multiply as individuals and factions fought for preeminence.

The universities were at the forefront of debates about the meaning of National Socialism and about the vexed question of the basis for claims about the unity of the German *Volk*. According to Heidegger himself, when he joined the Nazi Party and assumed the rectorship of Freiburg University, it was both to defend "the interest of the university" and to participate in the deepening and transformation of some of the positions of the Nazi movement (GA 16: 398). That is to say, he sought to establish a claim to leadership, initially within the reform of the universities, but soon more broadly. This put him in direct competition with other, more powerful figures who were also seeking to shape higher education in the new Germany, people like

Ernst Krieck, Alfred Baeumler, and Alfred Rosenberg.[4] They had at their disposal tools with which to exercise influence. Krieck had begun his own journal *Volk im Werden*, in 1933, in which he attacked Heidegger, albeit not as often as Heidegger maintained (GA 16: 391). In 1929 Rosenberg founded the Kampfbund für deutsche Kultur, which became increasingly established: for example, in 1932 Joseph Goebbels had written an essay under that very title promoting the idea of culture.[5] The philosopher Alfred Baeumler was a member of the Kampfbund für Deutsche Kultur from the start, and this helps to account for his influence. Within Rosenberg's bureau, known as the Rosenberg *Amt*, a number of ideologues engaged in an ongoing campaign to establish a notion of the *Volk* that was based in biology.[6] This was especially true of the division headed by Walter Gross, and it was in part on this basis that Gross in 1938 challenged Ludwig Ferdinand Clauss, who at one time rivaled Hans F. K. Günther for the title of the most popular race theorist in Nazi Germany. Clauss, who had been an assistant of Edmund Husserl at the same time as Heidegger, had a conception of race that, on phenomenological grounds, cut across any distinction between nature and culture and was based on the soul.[7] Heidegger would have been an even more appropriate target for Gross had he known and understood Heidegger's position on the *Volk*, given that Heidegger, even more than Clauss, tried to distance himself from *Rassenkunde* and from all biological conceptions of race strictly conceived.[8] But the fact that certain Nazis would have objected strenuously to his rejection of biologistic notions of race does not make him any less Nazi.[9] When Heidegger attacked the role of Jews in German universities, the objection was not a biological one, but the impact was nevertheless catastrophic for those thus targeted.[10]

The scholarly work which would establish in detail how Heidegger understood himself as opposing figures like Baeumler and the other ideologues mentioned above, while he at the same time proclaimed what he saw as, to use his famous phrase from 1935, "the inner truth and greatness of the movement" (GA 40: 208), still largely remains to be done.[11] Heidegger was fully aware that his conception of it was very different from that of many of his contemporaries, but he was hardly alone in that, given the plurality of views. In this paper I make a provisional attempt to show two largely unrecognized ways in which Heidegger's philosophical engagement with the question of the *Volk* in lectures, speeches, and seminars from the crucial years 1933 and 1934 was driven by the polemics of the time: His attacks on the Lamprecht Institute and on *Volkskunde*. In the course of doing so I show what a valuable document the reports of Heidegger's 1933–4 seminar "Nature, History, State" are to anyone attempting to address the question of the relation of Heidegger's philosophy to his politics. The seminar belongs to the semester prior to the lecture course now known under the title *Logic as the Question Concerning the Essence of Language*, and it shows very clearly the close relation of Heidegger's philosophical commitments to his political commitments.[12] These two texts should always be read in tandem because of their overlapping themes, even though much had changed in the break between the two semesters when they were held, not least the political shift that enabled Hitler to persuade top officials of the army and navy to support his assuming the Presidency of Germany, and, at a more personal level, Heidegger's resignation from the rectorship of Freiburg University.[13]

II

The importance of Heidegger's 1934 *Logic* for an understanding of Heidegger's concept of the *Volk* is not in dispute.[14] Heidegger himself chose to draw attention to the 1934 logic course in a letter he addressed to the Rector of Freiburg University in November 1945 as part of his self-defense after the war. He said in effect that every student with a head on his shoulders would have understood these lectures and their fundamental, presumably critical, intent (GA 16: 401). For good measure he suggested that the spies whose task it was to report back to Krieck and Baeumler about what he was saying in the lecture course also understood the intent of the lectures (GA 16: 402).

But what were the people who attended the course supposed to have understood? As I will show, his claim in 1945 that he had in this course rejected both any attempt to reduce language to a form of expression and any attempt to conceive the human being in biological and in that sense racial terms can be sustained, whereas his claim that in its place he advocated the idea of the essence of man as based in language as the fundamental actuality of spirit (*Geist*) has to be rejected (GA 16: 401). After the war's end Heidegger repeatedly suggested that he had appealed to spirit to counter the widespread focus on the racialized body, but the fact is that this was not the case in the logic course, although it is true of some of his more popular writings from this period and also true of *Introduction of Metaphysics*.[15] I take this as evidence that the 1934 course represents a more serious philosophical effort on his part to theorize what it meant to belong to a *Volk* along the lines already developed in *Being and Time*, where the notion of spirit was called into question (SZ 48, 117). Heidegger sought to show that *Being and Time*, which from the beginning tended to be read as an account of the individualization of Dasein on the basis of the account of being-toward-death, could accommodate belongingness to the *Volk*. To some commentators this constitutes prima facie evidence that in 1934 Heidegger distorted his philosophy to place it at the service of National Socialism, whereas others appeal to the single use of the word *Volk* in *Being and Time*, when he attempted to explain *Geschick* in terms of "the historicizing of the community, of a people" (SZ 384) as confirmation that the roots of his Nazism are already in evidence in 1927.[16] Because we now know a great deal more about what Heidegger was saying in this period, we can pass beyond these speculations, especially if our knowledge of the context informs us as to what to look for.

It should be noted at the outset that Heidegger lowers our expectations as to what we might find when, in this same self-serving letter to the Rector of Freiburg University from November 1945, at the very point where he appealed to the Logic lectures of 1934, he made only a limited claim on his own behalf. He suggested that it was unnecessary for him to attack Rosenberg's crude biologism because philosophical questioning was itself a form of opposition: "Given that the National Socialist worldview was becoming increasingly rigid and less inclined even to enter into a philosophical confrontation, the fact that I was active as a philosopher was resistance enough" (GA 16: 401). As an attempt to excuse himself, it is a model of self-deception. One can hardly count as an act of resistance an activity that one concedes is completely irrelevant to those one is allegedly resisting. And yet he seemed to be suggesting that it was his pursuit of philosophical questioning that made him suspect to the Nazi regime, rather than his isolated attacks on, for example, Rosenberg in his Hölderlin lectures (GA 39: 26) or Baeumler in his Nietzsche lectures (e.g. GA 43: 24–26).[17]

So how might we locate Heidegger's alleged philosophical resistance, for example in this 1934 lecture course or in the seminar "Nature, History, State," if it exists there at all? One is struck by Heidegger's reluctance— whether it be from prudence or cowardice—to name any specific targets in the 1934 course in spite of the fact that at every turn one gets the impression that it is, like many of his lecture courses, intended to be richly polemical. Just how polemical in tone Heidegger's 1934 logic course is can easily be illustrated by contrasting it with his lecture in November of the same year delivered under the title "The Present Situation and Future Task of German Philosophy." The latter presents many of the same ideas, albeit now integrated into a discussion of truth, while nevertheless omitting the negative polemics and replacing them only with an attack on the League of Nations that, of course, was orthodoxy to the Nazis (GA 16: 320). In other words, there is a rich dynamic to the lecture course that the subsequent lecture lacks. Nevertheless, in spite of the critical tone of *Logic*, Heidegger named only two specific targets there. He singled out Oswald Spengler's *Decline of the West* for criticism and at the same time criticized the widespread attempts to refute him. But given that he acknowledged that Spengler's standing in Germany itself was already in decline, it is clear that there was no pressing reason to make Spengler a major target of the lectures (GA 38: 92; L 78).[18] The other target that bears a proper name is the Lamprecht Institute, which he described as based on "a grotesque idea" (GA 38: 99; L 83).

What was the Lamprecht Institute? In 1909 Karl Lamprecht had opened the Königlich-Sächsischen Institut für Kultur- und Universalgeschichte at the University of Leipzig in order to promote his ideas. He had expounded these ideas in his multi-volume *Deutsche Geschichte* and in an essay on historical science where he tried to explain how psychology could be used in cultural history to penetrate the functional breadth of the soul of nations.[19] Even at that time Lamprecht was a hugely polarizing figure and many of the ideas associated with the Institute failed to attract much support beyond his immediate circle.[20] But he was not entirely forgotten, and in the summer of 1920 Heidegger referred to Lamprecht as one of the philosophers who had most influenced Spengler (GA 59: 16). Later in this essay I will follow the trail opened up by this remark about the grotesque idea behind the Lamprecht Institute in order to show where it leads us, but first I shall try to set the context for this remark in the lecture course by focusing on "Nature, History, State."

Although the protocols of "Nature, History, State" are difficult documents for the historian to assess, precisely because they are protocols, they offer a unique insight into how Heidegger positioned himself *vis-à-vis* his contemporaries in a way that the lecture course on logic does not.[21] He seems to have been less constrained in this less open setting and, in addition, one should not forget that the political situation was more fluid at this time, in late 1933 and into 1934. His attempt there to differentiate his position from that of Carl Schmitt is a clear example how philosophical and political debate were intertwined for him. He insisted that whereas Schmitt approached the political through the friend–enemy relation, which placed struggle in the sense of the possibility of war at its heart, Heidegger saw the political "as a way of Being of human beings and what makes the state possible" (46).

One of Heidegger's main preoccupations in the seminar "Nature, History, State" was to redefine the phrase "the Führer-state" (*Führerstaat*) (64). This is perhaps why in the seminar he passed from the state to the people, whereas in the subsequent lecture course the progression was from the people to the state. In any event, he insisted in the seminar that a Führer-state cannot be based on coercion, and even though at that time

Heidegger saw a role for political education, he rejected it in this context if it meant memorizing what one is supposed to think.[22] Political education, properly understood, was a way in which a people "becomes a people" (87 and GA 86: 177) and it can take place only through persuasion, which, it emerges, is the basis of what, at the end of the previous seminar, he called Führer-education (*Führerschulung*) (60). There is no mention of the Führer-state as such in *Logic*, but in both contexts he was clear that what was at issue was the "coming-to-be of the people," because for a state to endure it must be rooted in the being of the people (63).[23] Nevertheless, the relation of the state to the people is rendered more precise insofar as it is only in *Logic* that the historical aspect, already indicated in the title of the 1933–4 seminar, is fully developed. This is reflected in the fact that in the seminar he said that the state is grounded in the being of the *Volk* (74), whereas in the lecture course he explained that "the state is the historical being in the *Volk*" (GA 38: 165; L 136). This is again an ontological claim: *Volk* and *Staat* can only be understood as belonging to historical being (GA 38: 68, L 59).

In the next part of this paper I will seek to clarify the fundamental philosophical thrust of the 1934 logic lecture course when reread in the light of certain hints from "Nature, History, State" before focusing in the final part on the polemical component of Heidegger's account of the *Volk*.

III

As was so often the case in his courses, in *Logic* in 1934 Heidegger led his students down a path along which they were supposed to experience a transformation in relation to the question posed (GA 12: 149).[24] The fundamental transformation of the question here was one he frequently posed in his lectures and publications: the transformation was from the question of *what* "we" are to that of *who* "we" are. But on this occasion it was performed in the lecture hall. As he had already explained during the seminar in the previous semester, "original participation in the knowledge of the people cannot be taught; at most, it can be awakened from its slumber" (56). It was this transformation that he sought to enact during the 1934 lecture course when he brought the question closer to home by addressing the students directly about their political involvement (GA 38: 58; L 51). He described two students, one who became involved in politics to avoid studying and another who studied in order to avoid politics. It is noteworthy that in neither case was there a description of a "we" (GA 38: 50. L 44). Rather it seems that a "we" was formed among the people in the lecture-hall in their joint recognition of what was being described and they expressed their unity by stomping their feet on the floor. As usual, a "we" had been formed by isolating an "us" from a "them," but that was not Heidegger's point. He explained in a clear evocation of *Being and Time* that "we submitted ourselves to the moment" and that this led to a "quite other determination of the we" (GA 38: 57; L 50, translation corrected). They were not united by meeting some common criteria, although, of course, the fact that they were members of the same class and shared certain views about political involvement was a precondition of this transformation. All of that could be judged from the outside, whereas Heidegger was evoking the experience of community, the further conditions for which he went on to elaborate (GA 38: 51; 445). These could only be fully elaborated on the basis of an understanding of the being of historical Dasein, including the place of moods which Heidegger had brought to the fore in the lectures. He repeated the point at the end of the course when he claimed that in the process of asking the question of the essence of the human being, "we"—his student audience—had been changed (GA 38: 167; L 139).

The important lesson that Heidegger was trying to convey to his students was that science ultimately does not determine who does and does not belong to a people. Science might play a role in determining who is eligible to belong to a given *Volk* in the sense of establishing the necessary conditions of membership, and at times this might be conceived biologically, but it is through resoluteness that the belonging to historical being characteristic of *Volk* and the state was to be accomplished (GA 38: 68; L 59): "In resoluteness the human being is engaged in the future happening" (GA 38: 77; L 66, trans. modified). He insisted that each individual had to make the decision to belong singly (GA 38: 58; L 51). He was clear that only that individual himself or herself was in a position to ascertain what and how he or she had decided (GA 38: 58; L 51). In other words, he explicitly renounced any idea that what was specific to his account could be used by others as another way of determining who ultimately belonged to the *Volk* and who did not. As the example by which Heidegger transformed the students attending his course into a "we" shows, he was not focused on formal conditions of membership that on his account had the status of necessary but not sufficient conditions. That is why he insisted that what had happened in the lecture room had "nothing to do with science" (GA 38: 58; L 51). He meant that one could not leave to the scientists the decision as to who belongs to the *Volk*. It was a decision each individual had to make once they had met the other conditions.

By dethroning scientific approaches to the constitution of the *Volk*, he rejected the argument that descent (*Abstammung*) ultimately determines whether or not someone belongs to the *Volk*. Heidegger introduces that idea only to dismiss it (GA 38: 60; L 52).[25] Descent is not determinative because even if I meet the formal or preliminary conditions of membership, belonging is nevertheless ultimately a matter of my decision (GA 38: 60; L 50). In the lecture course contemporaneous with "Nature, History, State" Heidegger made the same point in a way that left unambiguous how his approach differed from those National Socialists who rooted everything in biology and he did so using the language of necessary and sufficient conditions that I employed above: "Today, there is much talk of *blood and soil* as forces that are frequently invoked. The literati, who are still around today, have seized upon these forces. Blood and soil are indeed powerful and necessary, but they are *not sufficient* conditions for the Dasein of a people."[26] So, for example, in "Nature, History, State" he denied that rootedness in the soil was sufficient to account for the way of Being of a people when there also must be interaction with the wider world (55). In *Logic* he went even further by arguing that the range of approaches that he was rejecting extended far beyond biology to any account of the "we" that relied on an external viewpoint. So he excluded any answer given in terms of "forms of life, races, cultures, and *Weltanschauung*" (GA 38: 32; L 30). That is to say, he rejected almost all of the dominant terms in which his contemporaries were addressing the question. This was because they all missed the human being in his or her being (GA 38: 60, 63, and 68; L 53, 55, and 59). It is this ontological point that explains the reference to bloodline in *Logic*; bloodline has to be understood in terms of moods, which in turn means one has to abandon any account in terms of a human subject. Moods share in our relation to things in the world (GA 38: 152; L 126). He also dismissed all attempts to circumscribe the "we" in terms of astronomical time, geographical place (GA 38: 56; L 49), characterology (see also GA 38: 99; L 83),[27] and skull measurements (GA 38: 54 and 63; L 48 and 53). Heidegger repeated this rejection of racially based accounts especially powerfully in 1937–8 when he attacked those who continued "to ramble on blissfully in the previous philosophy, that is, misuse it recklessly and mix it all up, provided we now only apply the racial to it and give the whole a correct political face" (GA 45: 143).[28]

In the 1934 course Heidegger saw liberalism as the enemy: "Our everyday mode of thinking is still stuck through and through in the foundations of liberalism that have not been overcome" (GA 38: 149; L 124). The attack on liberalism included explicitly all attempts to reduce the "we" to a plurality of individuals as in social contract theory. At their root lay Cartesianism.[29]

Heidegger's point was that he saw Cartesian subjectivity at work within much Nazi ideology. Later in the decade he took the point further when he characterized racial selection "as springing from the experience of Being as subjectivity" (GA 69: 70), but he had already made subjectivity and I-ness (*Ichheit*) the target of his polemic precisely in the context of the discussion of *Volk* in 1934. Both are "blasted" by temporality, that is to say, by the fundamental ontology to be found in *Being and Time* (GA 38: 163; L 135).[30] According to the account of Dasein's temporality given there, the past comes to us from out of the future. Or, as he said in 1934, "That which essences from earlier on determines itself from our future" (GA 38: 117; L 97). In other words, at this time Heidegger's "resistance," specifically as a philosopher, was to insist against the bulk of his contemporaries, especially among the Nazis, that any attempt to address the question of who we are in terms of a *Volk* would be inadequate unless it was accompanied by an effort to comprehend the human being as an historical being along the lines already developed in *Being and Time*.

The rejection of Cartesianism in *Being and Time* was conducted under the rubric of a destructuring of the history of ontology, where destructuring means tracing the categories we habitually take for granted back to the originary experiences that shaped them (SZ 22).[31] Given that in *Logic* "customary modes of thinking" are referred to originary experiences, as when he referred the widespread account of astronomical time to the experience of original temporality from which it arose, it seems that the same operation he had earlier called *Destruktion* was still taking place (GA 38: 131–2; L 109–10. Nevertheless, the word *Destruktion* is not used in *Logic*, and this raises the question of whether he was already on the way to transforming this approach or even abandoning it in favor of the overcoming (*Überwindung*) of metaphysics. In *Being and Time* he described the *Destruktion* of the tradition as directed negatively against the present and positively produced as a going back to the Greeks in order to go forward. Destructuring the history of ontology is directed against the tradition understood as what holds one back. (SZ 22). But in *Logic* the overcoming (*Überkommen*) of both genuine and non-genuine tradition is said to take place not under the guidance of the Greeks but in the name of "socialism," where the term "socialism" as the title for the formation of our historical being must enter the crucible of historical resoluteness (GA 38: 165; L 136). Socialism is not to be understood in terms of a changed economic mentality, a "dreary egalitarianism," or "an aimless common welfare." Rather socialism wills hierarchy, the dignity of labor, and the unconditional priority of service (GA 38: 165; L 136–7). The students attending the course would have been in no doubt that Heidegger meant

National Socialism. The hope that Heidegger still invested in National Socialism is apparent in this gesture, which also shows the extent to which he gave it extreme philosophical significance that went beyond its political significance.

In "Nature, History, State" Heidegger located the Führer-state at the completion of a historical development (64). I see no indication that Heidegger at that time was looking beyond that completion. Nevertheless, it is clear that a few months later, in the winter semester 1934–5, Heidegger was already questioning how that was to be understood. One sees it when he responded to Carl Schmitt's suggestion that the Hegelian state had on January 30, 1933 been replaced by another kind of state. Schmitt wrote: "One could say that on that day Hegel died."[32] Heidegger responded: "No! He has not yet 'lived'!" (GA 86: 85). Or, more precisely, Hegel first began to live at that time (GA 86: 606). Heidegger seems not just to have been saying that the theorization of the Nazi seizure of power that Schmitt and others attempted was philosophically inadequate. It implies that there was still a potential within the history of Western metaphysics that the Nazi movement was in a position to fulfill. The Nazi state was not at the completion of Western metaphysics, still less was it beyond it. It was located within the history of Western metaphysics and could be understood in its terms. Heidegger would never budge on that point, so that as he became disillusioned with National Socialism, he at the same time recognized the need to overcome Western metaphysics. He repeatedly came to say in a gesture that confirms the ineffectiveness of his form of resistance that the Nazi state belonged to the destiny of Western metaphysics. Strangely enough, Ernst Krieck in the early summer of 1934 criticized Heidegger for lacking a concept of destiny (*Schicksal*).[33] It is tempting to see this as betraying a thorough ignorance of the fifth chapter of the Second Divison of *Being and Time* or of the Rectoral Address (GA 16: 108–9), but it is possible that what Krieck meant by destiny was racial determinism, in which case he was correct.

In 1935 Heidegger would introduce the title "another beginning" (GA 40: 29; IM 41—trans. modified) for what in 1934 he referred to as an event that can "only be compared to the change at the beginning of the intellectual history of the western human being in general" (GA 38: 132; L 110). He did so in the context of a discussion of "our people" as "the most endangered people" and also "the metaphysical people" (GA 40: 42; IM 41). These two references suggest that the project that came to be known under the title of "the overcoming of metaphysics" was initially developed in this context of a questioning of the *Volk*, thereby making it harder to separate Heidegger's philosophy from the political context in which it was formed.

IV

Heidegger's questioning of the notion of the *Volk* has not always been well understood. Just as the young Heidegger had been faced with the manifold senses of Being, so the mature Heidegger was faced with the manifold senses of *Volk* found in the literature of the day. It is from his merely descriptive account of the linguistic usage of the day that Heidegger's harshest critics try to find something with which to compromise him, because they imagine that he is underwriting certain uses of these terms when he is in fact merely listing them.[34] The error can easily be demonstrated by observing the context in which Heidegger offers other uses of the word *Volk* that are incompatible with this one. Similarly, in the lecture course he is simply showing that there is no uniform notion of *Volk*, albeit this time employing a customary, almost hackneyed, way of organizing his presentation of these usages by dividing them between body, soul, and spirit (GA 38: 65–7; L 56–58). In the 1933–4 seminars he offered the warning: "We must above all guard ourselves against being overly impressed by the word '*Volk*'" (82). He was equally direct in the lecture course when he announced that the phrase "We are the *Volk*" is questionable as long as *Volk* is understood as body, soul, spirit (GA 38: 109; L 91). That blanket statement covered almost everyone writing about the *Volk* in Nazi Germany at that time and is a further indication of the fact that Heidegger was ready to move far from most of the dominant understandings of the term among his contemporaries in the effort to approach the *Volk* philosophically.

Although Heidegger renounced most of the ways his contemporaries thought about the *Volk*, he nevertheless had recourse to other words that were readily associated with National Socialism, albeit while trying to give them his own meaning. This was no doubt because, as I showed, at this time he still sought to put the framework developed in *Being and Time* at the service of National Socialism, at least as he conceived it. This happened most clearly when he introduced the terms "mandate," "mission," and "labor" as part of his attempt to reconceive temporality. He offered this set of equivalents: "mandate—future; endowment—mission—beenness; labor—present" (GA 38: 153; L 127). The mandate is the task; the mission is that which is handed down (GA 38: 155; L 128); but the most important of these words is "labor." Sometimes critics of Heidegger highlight a word for its Nazi resonances when the word is so widespread that the connection should not be drawn. On the surface the word "labor" seems to be like that, but I would argue that the context forces us to see him building a bridge to National Socialism.³⁵ Another instance of the same gesture of showing how *Being and Time* could readily accommodate the issues most dear to the Nazis was in the semester following the logic course, when he addressed care (*Sorge*) in a note written under the title "The Metaphysical Basic Power of the Coming State" (GA 86: 162).

Nevertheless, Heidegger never succeeded in convincing his contemporaries that his philosophy, at least insofar as it was known outside his close circle within Freiburg, could meet the demands of National Socialism. Oskar Becker had been one of Husserl's assistants in Freiburg at the same time as Clauss and Heidegger were, but even he engaged in an ongoing polemic that included the accusation that Heidegger lacked the resources to account for the notion of a *Volk*, or a race, or a state. It was at that time standard practice for academics to accuse their fellow academics of lacking a word or idea that was an important part of the Nazi vocabulary.³⁶ Nevertheless, in the heavily politically charged atmosphere of 1938 when the annexation of Austria and Czechoslovakia was a powerful issue, Becker's rejection of Heidegger's philosophy on the grounds that it was unable to take into consideration, as his philosophy could, the solitude of those who felt the emptiness of being away from the *Heimat* was especially vicious.³⁷ We now know that Heidegger had addressed "the great problem of those Germans who live outside the borders of the Reich" early in 1934 in "Nature, History, State," just as he had addressed the related notion of a people without space (52–6).³⁸ Nevertheless, whereas in 1934 he was still intent to show that his philosophy could be of value to the National Socialist movement, by 1938 he had renounced any hope of being taken seriously by the Nazi regime and he made no effort to respond to Becker.

Even though he had already resigned the rectorship by the time he delivered the lectures known as *Logic*, Heidegger still seems to have had some hope of influencing the direction in which Germany was going, and one way in which he sought to do so was by rejecting the regime's promotion of *Volkskunde*. It is important for my argument here that in "Nature, History, State" Heidegger dismissed *Volkskunde* as inadequate to the task of awakening a *Volk* from its slumber: "It is a peculiar mishmash of objects" that often has nothing to do with a specific people in its historical being (56). Given that the word *Volkskunde* does not appear anywhere in the summer 1934 course, not even when Heidegger was listing common uses of the word *Volk*, the fact that already in his seminar in February he had been dismissive of *Volkskunde* lends support to my claim that when the inquiry into the *Volk* passed into the discussion of lore (*Kunde*), *Volkskunde* was being evoked in order to be attacked discreetly.³⁹ Most people when they think of folklore in the German context would think of those things listed by Heidegger in his account of the determination of the *Volk* as soul: "folk songs, folk festivals and folk customs" in which "the emotional life of the *Volk* shows itself" (GA 38: 66; L 57), but political considerations, including race considered in terms of anatomical properties and language, were also considered part of *Volkskunde*.[40] It was already becoming clear in 1934 that Rosenberg's office was planning to use *Volkskunde* as an instrument of policy, particularly through the figure of Matthes Ziegler, the folklorist whom Rosenberg appointed director of the "Main Office for Weltanschauung" in April 1934.[41] Rosenberg was not personally active in *Volkskunde*, but it seems that he saw its potential as an instrument of control. When Heidegger was Rector he would have learned about the growing wars within the field of *Volkskunde*. John Meier, Professor at Freiburg University, had long been a leader in the so-called liberal tradition of *Volkskunde* and found himself under attack from Ziegler and the Amt Rosenberg.[42] Heidegger never seems to have reconciled himself to this development. He attacked *Volkskunde* in a number of places in the late 1930s, for example, when in "Die Bedrohung der Wissenschaft" he characterized it in terms of self-stupefaction and stupidity.[43]

However, in 1934 Heidegger had a more specific target in mind than *Volkskunde*, and he named it when he announced that in the nineteenth century it was claimed that historical research should be based in psychology, characterology, and sociology. That was the idea behind the foundation of the Lamprecht Institute in Leipzig and it is most likely what he meant by "the grotesque idea" that he referred to in *Logic*. On his understanding, those disciplines sought to reduce the understanding of history to the study of causal connections, a program foreign to his understanding of destiny (GA 38: 106–8; L 89–91). What Heidegger said about the Lamprecht Institute may be vague, but it was sufficiently specific to suggest that something determinative was meant when he said that "In spite of that [the foundation of the Lamprecht Institute], this grotesque idea [the claim that historical research should be based on psychology, characterology, sociology] could not last, although with a wider public, this position was still recently championed" (GA 38: 99; L 83). This mention of the revival of the ideas behind the Institute seems to be a reference to the revival of the Lamprecht Institute with the appointment late in 1933 of Hans Freyer to its Directorship. Freyer, who had been a student of Lamprecht at the University of Leipzig some 20 years earlier, had in the meanwhile established a reputation as a strong proponent of National Socialism.[44] His assumption of the Directorship to replace Walter Goetz, who was Lamprecht's immediate successor, was seen by many as a restoration of the Institute's original interdisciplinary vision, which Freyer hoped to bring about by highlighting "sociology."[45] Furthermore, Freyer leant heavily on the notion of "culture," and this can be seen as a continuation of Lamprecht's project.[46] Heidegger seems to have been as opposed to the enthusiasm for sociology and culture among some of his contemporaries as he was opposed to those among them who promoted biologistic notions of race. This is an indication of the degree to which Heidegger's position at this time was, in his terms, philosophical and, from our perspective, completely misconceived because it missed the political realities unfolding before him. In spite of his ambitions to transcend academia and have a broader impact, Heidegger seems to have been unable to leave behind academic politics, and it is hard not to see his polemic against Freyer and the Lamprecht Institute as in large part motivated by the kind of petty jealousy that is especially out of place in moments of political crisis.

The appointment of a successor to Goetz gave the Nazis in the Ministry of Education an opportunity to politicize the Institute. However, before long Freyer too would be subject to scrutiny; one of the accusations leveled against him was that he gave some of his students the impression that the Nazi leadership was not unified thereby confirming the extreme sensitivity of Nazi officials to any questioning of their unity, even though all attempts to enforce the impression of unity confirmed its absence.[47] Freyer had much in common with Heidegger. They both wanted to contribute to the ideological formation of the Third Reich and, in company with Carl Schmitt, they questioned the place of technology in modern society and employed the language of decision in a political context.[48] For example, in the context of a response to Eduard Spranger, Freyer saw technology as posing a problem for the unity of the *Volk*.[49] Indeed, some commentators have wanted to stress what Freyer and Heidegger have in common at the expense of their differences.[50] But if one looks at what Freyer says, for example, about race, then there is a clear contrast. According to Freyer, "The blood of the race is the holy material from which alone the structures of people can be shaped."[51] Heidegger never foregrounded race to the same degree. Equally striking are their contrasting educational views. Freyer was considered a rising star of the conservative movement, especially within educational circles, and in a series of essays in *Die Erziehung* he emphasized the need for the university to come under the rule of the state.[52] The rhetoric of Heidegger's "The Self-Assertion of the University" was significantly different, as the title already indicates.[53] And, most especially, Freyer engaged in practical political debate, of a kind absent from Heidegger.[54] Freyer's manifesto, *Revolution vom Rechts*, a prominent text of the time, had a very different tone and rhetoric from anything to be found in Heidegger. Even more than

Heidegger, and on a very different basis, Freyer insisted that "the People must be *exclusive*."[55]

If we now return to Heidegger's attack on *Volkskunde* in the knowledge that at the same time he was also opposing Freyer and the Lamprecht Institute, we can understand that Heidegger's attacks were in the service of his own kind of *Geschichtskunde*, historical lore. This was radically distinct from the kind of science of history promoted by Lamprecht and his school, which attempted to understand history on the basis of causal connections (GA 38: 106–8, L 89–91). For Heidegger, the lore of history is not an object of study. In it and through it "world rules" in the event of language (GA 38: 168; L 140). Heidegger was calling for a radical transformation away from *Volkskunde* toward lore. Lore announces. *Die Kunde kündet.* It announces itself as that which is concealed and is "given only to those who stand in resoluteness" (GA 38: 160–1; L 132–3). More specifically, the lore of history announces "the entire happening and the situation of its moment" (GA 38 159: L 132). This, Heidegger explained, happens in poetry. Indeed the essence of language announces itself (*kündet sich*) in "true poetry" (GA 38: 170; L 141). In this way the focus on language pointed the way to the lecture course for the following semester on Friedrich Hölderlin (GA 39).

At the end of the course on logic, when Heidegger tried to explain his claim that poetry brings the rule of Being to the original word, he could not resist attacking what should probably be identified as Rosenberg's advocacy of discipline (*Zucht*).[56] Heidegger wrote: "the Germans who talk so much today about discipline must learn what it means to preserve that which they already possess" (GA 38 170; L 142). In other words, the discipline of the Rosenberg Amt was to be replaced by dialogue with Hölderlin, who wrote in a letter to Böhlendorf: "We learn nothing with greater difficulty than the free use of the national."[57] This cannot be interpreted as a retreat from politics to poetry. Discrimination on the basis of language has long served as a useful tool in the hands of those committed to exclusion, and this was especially true for the Germans, in part because it was believed that the German language tied together the German people across a certain diaspora. And yet at the same time it was the attempt to employ language as a unifying force that fed anxiety in the face of those who spoke German but who—Jews or gypsies—nevertheless brought with them ideas thought of as alien to the German Volk.[58]

I have not in any way called into question the idea that the seminar "Nature, History, State" and the lecture course *Logic* are the work of someone committed to the National Socialist revolution. Instead, I have attempted, first, to begin the task of identifying some of the targets of Heidegger's polemics in the years 1933–4. He was clearly against Cartesianism and liberalism, but he was equally clearly against what was known to his contemporaries as *Rassenkunde* and *Volkskunde*. The fact that on the rare occasions when he chose to name publicly his opponents specifically he tended to limit himself to relatively powerless targets like Carl Schmitt, Oswald Spengler, the Lamprecht Institute, and Hans Freyer conforms with his claim after the end of the war that his main form of resistance was as a philosopher. This not only exhibits lack of courage on his part, it also shows a lack of understanding: it is clear, at least in retrospect, that his focus was misplaced. He was not alone in imagining a National Socialism that he wanted in place of the reality he was already witnessing, but it was the height of hubris on his part to imagine he could influence the ongoing policy debates among senior Nazis. Secondly, I have argued that the mere fact that Heidegger did not rely on a crude biological reductionism in order to establish who belonged to the *Volk*, as some of his critics maintain, did not somehow separate him from National Socialism, as some of his apologists maintain. It is true that there were Nazi ideologists around Rosenberg, like Walter Gross, who wanted to insist on a strictly biological conception of German identity, but when Heidegger conceived of *Blut und Boden* as necessary but not sufficient conditions of the existence of the German *Volk* he still gave those considerations a significant place, even though in using this language he was attempting to distance himself from racial science narrowly conceived. What is most sinister about Heidegger's approach is that the focus on decision and resoluteness placed him among those who sought to introduce new, more tenuous, standards by which to determine who did and did not belong to the *Volk*. As we saw, Heidegger acknowledged that someone's decision and resoluteness could not be determined from the outside (GA 38: 58; L 51), but he did not emphasize the point sufficiently if his intention was to reject this tendency of engaging in the question of who truly belonged to the German *Volk*, a tendency he himself indulged in when challenging the place of Jews within German philosophy departments. Heidegger had thus found his own way of contributing to the seductive but sinister logic by which attempts to unite a people only served to divide them further, and to the extent that he embraced National Socialism and was equipped to understand that Germany's new leaders lacked any sense of restraint, it is impossible to excuse him. Heidegger may have known better than most of his contemporaries the flaws of biologism, but he succumbed to a logic every bit as dangerous, a logic whose employment, in the wrong hands, could be even more arbitrary.

4 THE SEMINAR OF WINTER SEMESTER 1933–4 WITHIN HEIDEGGER'S THREE CONCEPTS OF THE POLITICAL

Theodore Kisiel

Heidegger's three concepts of the polis and the political[1]

The seminar entitled "On the Essence and Concept of Nature, History, and State," from its dating, clearly falls within the purview of Heidegger's metontological concept of the political. In the seminar, Heidegger develops his metontological concept of the political by way of a focus on the "ontological difference" between the people and the state. In point of fact, Heidegger's discussion of how a people authenticates itself by uncovering its historical self-identity already occurs *in ovo* in *Sein und Zeit* (SZ), in an application of his fundamental ontology in the direction of what he variously called a metontology, metaphysical ontic, and metaphysics of existence, where "the [ontic] question of ethics [and so of politics] can first be posed" (GA 26: 199/157)[2] along ontological lines. In SZ, this metontology is intertwined with the rhetorical concept of the political, where the authentic dimension of rhetoric as an unconcealing process is obscured by the all-pervasive predominance of the existential category of *das Man*, according to which I am one-like-many in an average being-with-one-another. The true bearer

Period		Basic text	Basic concepts
Phenomenological	1923–7	Aristotle, *Rhetoric*	Pathos, ethos, logos of doxic speech situation
Metontological	1927–34	Plato, *Politeia*	Leader of people, guardians of state, 3-leveled service
Archaic-Poietic	1934–54	Sophocles, *Antigone*	Pole-mos of thinker, poet, and statesman as pre-political

of the peculiar universal of averageness called the Anyone is our language, in the repetitive prevalence of "what one says" that circumscribes the self-evidence of public opinion. As many readers of SZ like Pierre Bourdieu have long suspected, *das Man*, the Anyone, *hoi polloi*, "the many" understood not as a loose sum of individuals but as a public kind of power of apathy and indifference built into the repeatability of language, is the base-line category or "existential" of Heidegger's properly political-rhetorical ontology. But what "many" have not noticed is that Heidegger also formally outlines a path out of the leveling, impersonal anonymity of the masses whereby a "being-with-one-another in the same world . . . in *communication* and in *struggle* [*Kampf*]" (SZ 384, my emphasis of these two rhetorical dimensions of political education) finds its way to an authentic grouping by actualizing the historical uniqueness and self-identity of its community. In the leveling of its essentially general—and so generic—state (SZ 300), the Anyone "itself" is not historical, just as the "masses" are rootless, homeless, and stateless, stripped of all uniqueness and credentials of historical identity. The everyday Dasein is infinitely scattered in the average with-world and in the multiplicity of the surrounding world (SZ 129, 389). The groupings of the Anyone are endlessly dispersed and manifold—businesses, circles, classes, professional associations, political parties, bowling clubs, robber bands—"such that no one stands with anyone else and no community stands with any other in the rooted unity of essential action. We are all servants of slogans, adherents to a program, but none is the custodian of the inner greatness of Dasein and its necessities. . . . The mystery is lacking in our Dasein" (GA 29/30: 244/163). The authentic grouping of being-with-one-another can never arise "from the ambiguous and jealous conspiracies and the garrulous factions of clans in the Anyone. . . . Authentic with-one-another first arises from the authentic self-being of resolute openness" (SZ 298). The passage to authentic co-existence "in the rooted unity of essential action" proves to be a historical rite of passage by way of a concerted historical action in first finding that one's own unique fate is inextricably rooted in the historical destiny of a unique historical people acting in community. "The fateful historical happening of unique Dasein as being-in-the-world is thereby a co-happening which is defined as *destiny*. This is how we define the happening of the community, of a people. . . . Only in communicating and in struggling does the power of destiny become free. Dasein's fateful destiny in and with its 'generation' constitutes its full and proper happening" (SZ 384–5).

It is noteworthy that the lecture course of WS 1933–4 once again gathers the existentials of SZ that are essential for the political maturation of a people, a We, in realizing its unique historical self-identity. "Man is a *self* . . . a being that in advance *decides about its own be-ing* [Sein], in this or that way. . . . Only because man is a *self* can he be an *I* and a *you* and a *we*. . . . This self-character of man is at once the ground for the fact that he has his *history*. . . . *Historicity* is a ground moment of his be-ing. This demands a completely new relationship of man to his history and to the question of his be-ing. Terminologically, I have designated this distinctive characteristic of man with the word '*care*' . . . this *fundamentally human way of be-ing* on the basis of which there are such things as resoluteness, readiness for service, struggle, mastery, action as an essential possibility" (GA 36/37: 215/163–4). "This care . . . designates the fundamental characteristic of the self, that its be-ing is an issue for it. How—this is left to the choice and mission of man. Only insofar as be-ing is care does a way of be-ing become possible such as resoluteness, labor, heroism, and so on. . . . Only on the basis of this be-ing (as care) is man a *historical* being. Care is the condition of possibility for man's ability to be a *political* being" (GA 36/37: 218/166–7). "In contrast [to categories], tradition, decision, struggle, insight,[3] are determinations that pertain to existence: *existential* concepts" (GA 36/37: 219/167). "Care is the *condition of possibility for resoluteness*, readiness, engagement, labor, mastery, heroism. . . . Care and historicity. Care as the condition of possibility of the political essence of man" (GA 36/37: 293/220).

"Who are we then? Do we know who we are? Who are we our*selves*? Are we in fact a community and a people?" This fateful question of definition of the historical uniqueness and self-identity of the community that is the German people is first posed by Heidegger in the microcosm of the university lecture hall toward the end of 1929 (GA 29/30: 103/69), with the world financial crisis in full swing, and finds its first public political denouement in the rectoral statement of the "Self-Assertion of the German

University" in 1933: "But do we know *who we ourselves are*, this corporate body of teachers and students of the highest school of the German people?" (RA 9/5, GA 16: 107).[4] The communal circle of the we becomes ever more comprehensive as Heidegger thinks more nationally: a teacher and his students engaged in their common study, the "fighting community" (*Kampfgemeinschaft* = struggle in common, a more benign translation) of the university, the German state-university system, the German people among the Occidental peoples, each struggling for its historical self-identity usually by way of statehood. In the logic course of SS 1934, the question "Who are we?" is answered by "We are a people" and the selfhood of a people is defined in terms of decision, mission and vocation, historical character, common tradition, and language, since this selfhood, the unique character proper to a people, is eventually the proper-dom of the properizing event of be-ing, *das Eigen–tum des Er–eignisses* (GA 65: 319–20). In the Hölderlin course of the next semester, the German people discover their original time of tradition in the poetic words "fatherland" and "home," the native senses of the "national." In SS 1935 German Dasein, the metaphysical people landlocked and squeezed in Europe's middle, is called upon to assume the mission of saving the West from its impending demise. In these contexts, Dasein no longer refers to the individual human situation, as in SZ, but to the unique historical situation of a people, German Dasein, Greek Dasein. For Heidegger and for Germany, it is now the "time of the we" (*Wirzeit*) of national socialism and not the time of the I characteristic of democratic liberalism (EM 53/74).[5] The characteristics of Dasein are thus transposed from the individual to the communal unit, the *polis*. Just as a generation is thoroughly temporal and historical and thus mortal, so is a people and a community. Like a mortal generation, a people also undergoes a rise, a peak, and a fall (GA 39: 51). Pushed to its extreme by "total" worldviews like capitalism and communism, the perspective of finite Dasein (erroneously) makes the people itself and not God "the aim and purpose of all history" (GA 65: 24, 40f.).

The content of Heidegger's middle concept of the political is first introduced in his Rectoral Address, where the Platonic *polis* of *paideia*, the "educational state" (*Erziehungsstaat*) outlined in Plato's *Republic*, is made the paradigm for the structure of the German university. For the German university is the institution of higher learning "that, grounded in science and by means of science, educates and disciplines the leaders and guardians of the destiny of the German people" (RA 10/6, GA 16: 108). But what is the destiny of the German people among the nations of the world? Nothing less than the development of the educational state itself as the highest expression of the German community and as a model for the rest of the world. To cite the opening pages of Paul Natorp's "war book," *Deutscher Weltberuf*: "To cultivate the new order of such a community: that is Germany's 'world-mission,' learned from the war; it is in the name of its culture for which it enters the lists against the 'equalizing and leveling "civilization"' that is now spanning the globe, in order to represent it as 'world culture'" (DWB 1, 2).[6]

Hence the provincial minister's complaint to Heidegger immediately following his Rectoral Address, that he was promoting "a kind of 'private national socialism' that circumvents the perspectives of the [Nazi] party program" (RA 30/23, GA 16: 381). But Heidegger's position was *hardly private, although it did in fact circumvent the strict party line.* Heidegger's brand of "national socialism" had been overtly part of the German public domain, from scholarly essays to the political tracts of right-wing political parties, at least since the emergence of the "Ideas of 1914" and the wide currency given to a uniquely "German socialism" of prominent figures like Natorp, Friedrich Naumann, and Werner Sombart. After Fritz Ringer,[7] Heidegger's more "private" brand might be called the "mandarin" socialism of an educational state that the social pedagogue Paul Natorp, by way of a hybridization of Plato with Pestalozzi and German idealism, had been promoting from the 1890s into the postwar years. It is this idealistic socialism centered in the moral and mental/spiritual will of the community that Heidegger seeks to promote in the "new German reality" of 1933, in his laudations of the national socialist "movement" and "revolution" during the rectoral period.

In the aftermath of the cultural propaganda wars that erupted shortly after the outbreak of the "Great War" in 1914, Paul Natorp defends the superior ideals of German culture over against the materialistic, utilitarian, libertarian, and plutocratic Western civilizations being increasingly leveled by technology. "The peculiarly German goal of 'culture' . . . wants to cultivate and develop humanity out of the inner roots of its inherent growth-potential, on the ancestral, religiously preserved, and faithfully prepared ground of a people's individuality. It is out of the genuinely German and humanized state that the human state is to grow, as the state of humanity's 'culture,' where only human beings dwell upon the earth. This is what we have been seeking: the *world mission* of the Germans" (DWB 2, 55–6). This home-grown community cultivated into a state is thus a moral-pedagogical totality that is at once a state of economy, a state of law, a state of education [*Wirtschaftsstaat, Rechtsstaat, Erziehungsstaat*], which do not constitute three competing and conflicting goals but instead three perspectives that together define the unified single possible goal of the state as the state of human culture, the genuinely human state (DWB 2, 195–6). The last and highest perspective is that of education. Humans do not work in order to work, let themselves be governed in order to be governed, "but in order to live the genuine human life of the spirit and the heart, for the sake of their humanity" (196). In order to develop the inherent strengths of a people and to attain its common goals, one requires not merely an economic and political, but a much more comprehensive and deeply grounded education, a "spiritual/ intellectual, moral, artistic, religious education of the entire nation" (197). The communism of the upper-class aristocracy of Plato's educational state is displaced by the *socialism of universal education* of a national community, as the "Swiss-German" Pestalozzi developed it, beginning with the working class, "out of the depths of the philosophy and religion of German idealism" (131–2). The idea of the state finds its high point in a social pedagogy grounded in a social economy and a social law, in a uniquely *German socialism* based on the Kantian categorical imperative that respects all persons as ends and resists treating them as means.[8] In this "kingdom of ends," education is the self-cultivated formation, that is, the shaping from within, of each individual and through it the internal shaping of the community itself into a genuine individuality, into a self-composed interiority.[9] In this communal individuality, the individual and the community are no longer separated, "but rather condition each other in freedom" (180). For freedom does not mean a lack of all restraining bonds, but rather internal self-binding and assumption of responsibility for the community and one's duty toward it (DWB 2, 132, 130). It is the freedom that Kant finds to be correlative with obligation and duty and regards as the sole transcendental fact of pure practical reason. German freedom is binding obligation (*Bindung*), and the individual's bonds in and with a community constitute a whole (*Bindungsganzes*) which is the human world (GA 26: 247/192).

"And where there is freedom, there is Germanness, there is a fatherland in the German sense, an internally grounded and free community of the free" (DWB 2, 110). This is the *German socialism* (in which "we will ourselves") that *Natorp in his social pedagogy makes into an ideal and an infinite task of the Germans*, years before August 1914 and the spontaneous unification of all Germans concentrated on the war effort in a solidarity that already in these war years was called a uniquely "German socialism" (Natorp, Naumann, Sombart) and even a "national socialism" (Plenge, from a more economic perspective). In the reciprocal relation between the individual and the community, German socialism is a social personalism whose motto is "all for one and one for all and yet each is entirely himself." It is precisely the opposite of Western individualism, whose commonality is regarded as a plurality of abstract atoms of equal and "private" individual persons (DWB 2, 20).

Heidegger's reception of the neo-Kantian Natorp's German socialism is, to be sure, not without qualification. We get a sense of this as well as a remarkable summation of Heidegger's motivations at this time from a revealing letter to Elisabeth Blochmann written exactly two months after the *Machtergreifung*, on March 30, 1933. Here, even before the very prospect of the rectorship that would empower him to implement his own long-incubating ideas on university reform for the Third Reich, Heidegger expresses his enthusiasm over the sudden surge of historical events on the political front, to the point of regarding it as an ontological *Ereignis* full of opportunity and potential, a veritable *kairos*:

> The current events have for me—precisely because so much remains obscure and uncontrolled—an extraordinarily concentrative power. It intensifies the will and the confidence to work in the service of a grand mission and to cooperate in the building of a world grounded in the people. For some time now, I have given up on the empty, superficial, unreal, thus nihilistic talk of mere "culture" and so-called "values" and have sought this new ground in Da-sein. We will find this ground and at the same time the calling of the German people in the history of the West only if we expose ourselves to be-ing itself in a new way and new appropriation [*Aneignung*]. I thereby experience the current events wholly out of the future. Only in this way can we develop a genuine involvement and that *in-stantiation* [*Inständigkeit*] in our history which is in fact the precondition for any effective action. . . . To be sure, we ought through misgivings neither to minimize the momentousness of today's events nor to take them as assurance that our people has thereby grasped its hidden commission—in which we believe—and has found the ultimately effective powers for its new course.[10]

Heidegger is thus already busy deconstructing neo-Kantian concepts like "culture" and "value," which he regards as "unreal" and "nihilistic," and at the same time reconstructing a *Kultur- und Erziehungspolitik* in terms of his own ontology of Da-sein and temporal-historical be-ing. This is clearly evident in the Rectoral Address, where the Da-sein of the German people is described in terms of the fateful communal decision that it must make over the critical historical situation in which it finds itself in Europe's middle. *A people deciding for the state appropriate to its be-ing*: this is the [met]*ontological essence of the political* for Heidegger during these trying times, which he is regarding not in terms of a calculative *Realpolitik* but as a potential *Bildungspolitik* to guide the self-determination of the university community on its way to reforming itself, indeed revolutionizing itself into and for the future "educational state," understood as a Teutonic *polis* of *paideia*.

The ontological deconstruction of the neo-Kantian concept of culture (*paideia*) into the ontological categories of Dasein is in full swing in the Rectoral Address. The traditional divisions of human "culture," deliberately listed in somewhat haphazard yet incomplete detail to exemplify the confusing variety of their division into "rigidly separate [scientific] specialties" (cf. Session 6) among the university faculties, and so "their endless and aimless dispersal into isolated fields and niches . . . such as: nature, history, language; people, custom, law, state; poetizing [art], thinking, believing; disease [medicine], madness [psychiatry], death; economy, technology," are instead re-identified as "world-shaping powers of human-historical Dasein" (RA 13–14/9, GA 16: 111). It is the task of the uni-versity, in its basic will to know (which Natorp likened to the Platonic *eros*), to bring this diversity of domains together under a single will to know, traditionally called science, which in turn creates the singular spiritual world of a historical people. This unifying science must be understood in the original Greek sense of philosophy, "not as a 'cultural asset' but as the innermost determining center of the entire Dasein of a people and its state" (12/7, GA 16:110). Science in this radical sense is the "passion to remain close to and pressed by beings as such," "the questioning stance that holds one's ground in the midst of the ever self-concealing beings as a whole" (12/8, GA 16:110), "*the questioning and exposed standing of one's ground in the midst of the uncertainty of beings as a whole*" (14/9, GA 16:111). This stormy questioning of the meaning of be-ing by and for Greek Dasein or German Dasein "will create for our people its world, a world of innermost and most extreme danger, that is, its truly spiritual world. . . . And the *spiritual world* of a people is not the superstructure of a culture, no more than it is an arsenal of useful information and values; it is the power that most deeply preserves the people's strengths tied to their earth and blood; as such it is the power that most deeply arouses and most profoundly moves the Dasein of a people" (14/9, GA 16:111–12). To counter the idealistic flight into superstructures which the term "spiritual" is prone to take, Heidegger must repeatedly emphasize that we are dealing with the *indigenous spirit of a native people ensconced in its unique historical infrastructure*, contrary to Natorp's quasi-cosmopolitan account of the situation. The "spiritual world" is in fact the thoroughly historical world of an earthbound historical people, which, like an individual life, comes into being, enters into its maturity, only to decline and pass away. In coming to its maturity, the Dasein of a people, like an individual Dasein, has its moments (*kairoi*) of crisis of self-definition, in which it must contextually "size up" its holistic situation in its historical sense (*Be-sinnung*) and direction, becoming responsive to the directive demands exacted by that unique situation in order to determine an appropriate course of action-in-crisis that would be true to its historical be-ing in context and direction. Aristotle called this responsiveness to the protopractical situation of action *phronesis*, and Heidegger, drawing on his analysis of Dasein's self-authentication in SZ, calls it *Ent-schlossenheit*, resolute openness, and equates it with "spirit" in this quasi-idealistic context of promoting "The Self-Determination of the German University." "Spirit is the originarily attuned, knowing resoluteness toward the essence of be-ing" which is "empowered by the deepest vocation and broadest obligation" (RA 14/9, GA 16:112) to be found in the Dasein of a people. In other contexts at this time, Heidegger describes resolute openness, again in quasi-idealistic terms, as the will to question, will to learn, and will to know. But to offset the activistic thrust of such formulations of willfulness, which are in keeping with the call for the "self-assertion of the university," it should be recalled that the "primal action" (*Urhandlung*), the action that underlies all actions, of the "virtue" of *phronesis*, resolute openness, is that of letting-be, *Gelassenheit*.

The Platonic-Teutonic educational state

And what resolute openness lets be in this context is the singular historical opening and unique "leeway of freedom" granted the German people to act historically, understood as the "space of play" (*Spielraum*) or leeway in which its indigenous "spiritual" powers are granted free play and full amplitude both on the domestic and larger European scene. This "temporal playing field" (*Zeit-Spiel-Raum*) of freedom is the educational state of national socialism, articulated "platonically" into the three levels of work service, defense service, and science service. Since this freedom that is granted to us from our historical opening is "of the essence of truth" (*Vom Wesen der Wahrheit*), Heidegger identifies such a state (and the university modeled after it) as the "place of truth" (*locus veritatis*) and the "clearing of be-ing," where the great powers of be-ing to which human being is exposed—nature, history, art, technology, economy, indeed the state itself—are gathered into their possibilities and bound into their limits (GA 16: 200f, 767f).

The Rectoral Address thus begins with the question of the essence of the university, which it provisionally grounds in the essence of science and eventually traces back to the originating ground of the "essence of truth," understood as the ever unique historical unconcealment of be-ing from which errant humans, individually and communally, must recover their equally unique historical opening, their "spiritual world." Noteworthy in the talk "On the Essence of Truth," which Heidegger delivered on several occasions in 1930–2, is the "German-conservative" emphasis on freedom as binding obligation, an emphasis that is muted in the published versions of the forties.[11] In the 1930 talk, the manifestive behavior operative within and through the truth of statements, in opening the leeway of a world, at once establishes a hold in the world. Thus, freedom as the letting-be of a world is sometimes described as letting oneself become bound, which in its binding obligation (*Bindung*) measures itself to the obligation (*Verbindlichkeit*) of the world. The world: a communal whole of binding obligations and playing field of freedom in the development of their possibilities, which constitutes the "cultivation of the world" (*Weltbildung*). "The two characters of any comportive behavior, manifestive opening and letting-itself-be-bound, are not at all double but one and the same." The note of necessity invested in such a freedom is in fact the state of "turning in the need" (*Not-wendigkeit*) between ex-sisting in the mystery and in-sisting in the errancy of untruth. "Freedom is nothing but the *need* that *must* take a first and last measure and *bind* itself to it."

The "Ideas of 1914"—"Socialism is freedom as binding obligation"—in their contrast with the "Ideas of 1789" are especially evident in Heidegger's notorious polemic in the Rectoral Address against academic freedom. Underlying the attack is the association of academic freedom with the "liberty" and "equality" of abstract individuals liberated from the old bonds of religion, natural necessities, and provincial communities, who then bind themselves artificially ("the social contract") in cosmopolitan "fraternity," the solidarity of which only thinly disguises liberalism's anarchy of "equal" individuals (GA 16: 290). Academic freedom is a purely negative "freedom from" abstracted from any binding context and all limitations, and thus is prone to arbitrary caprice, "arbitrariness of intentions and inclinations, lack of restraint in what was done and left undone." The German student body, on the other hand, in its resoluteness to will the essence of the new university, "through the new Student Law places itself under the law of its own essence and thereby first determines and defines this essence of being-students. To give the law to themselves is the highest freedom. [. . .] The concept of the freedom of the German student is now brought back to its truth. Henceforth the bond and service of the German student will unfold from this truth" (RA 15/10, GA 16:113).

This freedom of the German university students, preparing themselves to become the leaders and guardians of the nation, develops a triple bond (*Bindung*) of obligation to the educational state in its articulation into three services of equal rank and necessity.

1   The bond to the community of the people is cultivated by means of work service. "It obligates to help support the community by active participation in the struggles, strivings, and skills of all classes and elements of the people" (RA 15/10, GA 16: 113).

2   The bond to the honor and destiny of the nation among other nations is established through the defense service. It demands the readiness to give one's all, to make the ultimate sacrifice for one's nation, and to acquire the necessary military knowledge, skills, and discipline.

3   The bond to the spiritual mission of the German people is cultivated by the service to science, the knowledge service. Once again, it is the people who, especially in its various professions, wills to be a spiritual/intellectual people at the vanguard of the ever renewed struggle for its spiritual world. It does so "by putting its history into the openness of the overwhelming power [*Übermacht*] of all the world-shaping powers of Dasein," thereby becoming "exposed to the most extreme questionability of its Dasein" (RA 15/10, GA 16: 113). And extreme questions demand extreme answers. Therefore, such a people "demands of itself and for itself that its leaders and guardians attain the strictest clarity of the highest, broadest, and richest knowledge" (16/10, GA 16: 113). This extreme knowledge of the basic questions "is not the calm cognizance of essences and values in themselves; rather, it is the keenest threat to Dasein finding itself at the very center of the overwhelming power of beings. The very questionability of be-ing compels the people to work and struggle and forces it into its state, to which the professions belong" (16/11, GA 16: 114). "Because the statesman and the teacher, the doctor and the judge, the minister and the architect guide and *lead* the Dasein of a people in its state, because they *guard* and keep this Dasein keen in its fundamental relations to the world-shaping powers of human being, these professions and the education for them are the responsibility of the knowledge service" (16/10–11, GA 16: 114, my emphasis),

the service that has traditionally come to be expected from the university. But this does not mean that knowledge must serve the professions. On the contrary, "the professions [are called upon to] execute and administer this highest and essential knowledge of the people that concerns its entire Dasein" (16/11, GA 16: 114). This presumably applies especially to the statesman, who thereby assumes some of the traits and virtues of Plato's philosopher-ruler.

"These three bonds—*through* the people *to* the destiny of the state *in* its spiritual mission—are *equiprimordial* for German being. The three services that arise from it—work service, defense service, knowledge service—are equally necessary and of equal rank" (RA 16/11, GA 16: 114). To summarize the triple bond of obligation and service assumed by the German university student in the Third Reich:

Bond to	Service
Community of people	Work
Honor and destiny of nation	Defense
Spiritual mission of people	Knowledge

Political education

And clearly, the motivational preparation of the German university student for this manifold service to the people and the nation is the task of the German university. "The German university for us means the institution of higher learning that, grounded in science and by means of science, educates and disciplines the leaders and guardians of the destiny of the German people. The will to the essence of the German university is the will to science as will to the historical and spiritual mission of the German people as a people that knows itself in its state" (RA 10/6, GA 16: 108). Instilling a deep understanding and clear knowledge of the original and essential connection between the people and its state is precisely the task of political education, which in these days is assumed by the state university, which prepares the academic youth to become leaders of the people and guardians of its destiny as a state. From the above, it is clear that the new German university student is to engage in work service and defense service as well as in the main service of the university, the service of knowledge and science, which as the "work of the brain" does not differ in kind from, and so is no higher than, the two levels of the "work of the hand and fist." All work is intellectual or "spiritual," a knowledge-laden deed and action that incorporates a craft know-how and an ordered understanding of its place in the world. The new university now models itself after the *worker-state* projected by the National Socialist *German Workers* Party (GA 16: 239), thereby modifying the ideality of the university to accommodate a uniquely German folk ethos, its vaunted "work ethic." The new university student is now called upon to be exemplary in this work ethic, to which we might also add the prized German trait of *Gründlichkeit*, thoroughness, and even a related word then current in Nazi jargon, the "hardness" (*Härte*) needed to overcome almost insuperable obstacles. These traits carry over into the defense service and the knowledge service, which are after all "*equiprimordial* for German being" and "are equally necessary and of equal rank" (RA 16/11, GA 16: 114). Note that Heidegger's account of the knowledge service exposes Dasein to a situation of extreme questioning which dictates that it struggle mightily and even violently with the overwhelming power of be-ing: "The very questionability of be-ing compels the people to work and struggle and forces it into its state" (RA 16/11, GA 16: 114).

How is it that the state university must now assume the responsibility of politically educating the cadre of guardians needed for the furtherance of the state? Session 7 of the seminar traces Germany's political tradition back to the beginnings of the Holy Roman Empire, when "Otto the Great based his empire [*Reich*] on the prince-bishops by obligating them to political and military service and knowledge" (45, my trans.). The Second Reich took root when "Frederick the Great educated the Prussian nobility into guardians of his state. Bismarck oversaw this process of rooting his idea of the state in the firm, strong soil of political nobility," but the Second Reich went into demise after he left office. The historical pattern is clear on Germany's way of founding and sustaining a political tradition and its need to educate a political elite. But with the demise of the monarchy, this elite can no longer be the aristocratic nobility but rather falls to the "mandarin" class being educated by the university (cf. Note 7). Heidegger finds his model at a critical turning point in German history, at the turn from the eighteenth to the nineteenth century, when three great powers converged to work together in shaping Germany's destiny and articulating its historical identity and modern self-image: the new German poetry of Klopstock, Herder, Goethe, Schiller and the Romantics; the new German philosophy of Kant, Fichte, Schleiermacher, Schelling, and Hegel; the new German political will of the Prussian statesmen and soldiers, including Freiherr vom Stein, Hardenberg, Humboldt, Scharnhorst, Gneisenau, and von Clausewitz (GA 16: 291). The interplay of poets, thinkers, and statesmen now assumes center stage in Heidegger's model of Germany and German education and the shaping of Germany's identity. It might be noted that this is also the beginning of the tradition of bestowing seasoned German professors with the honorific title of *Geheimrat*, privy councilor, which became more than honorific for notables like Dilthey, Weber, and Scheler. (I am not aware of any instance of *Geheimrat* Husserl ever being consulted by German statesmen).

The Platonic basis woven into the metontological concept of the political indicates that the mantle of philosopher-ruler or supreme statesman of the national socialist worker state would fall upon Reichskanzler Adolf Hitler. Heidegger in 1933 in fact adjudged Hitler to be a *phronimos* or statesman capable of rising above narrow party interests to become a leader sensitive to the needs, desires, and tendencies of the German people as a whole. "Any statesman or leader *is* a leader . . . [insofar as] . . . he understands, considers, and actualizes, in the vital unfolding of his own being, what a people and state are" (45, translation amended). But Heidegger at once insisted that it is the people itself who must decide for a leader-state (*Führerstaat*) as the kind of state that is in keeping with the tradition of the previous two German Reichs and thus most appropriate for the German people. In short, the crux and core of Heidegger's metontological concept of the political is that the people itself *decide* on the kind of state most appropriate at this point in German history and at once *resolutely will to sustain and support* that state through its service and sacrifice. Hitler, in his very popular rise to power, thus cleverly devised a series of plebiscites (*Volksabstimmungen*), notably on the decision to withdraw from the League of Nations, along with the well-publicized public rallies (*Volksversammlungen*), to evoke a sense of public cooperation in at least some of the "state-founding deeds" of the new regime. But Heidegger sees the university as the ultimate educative force in convincing the people to decide for the leader-state at this crossroads in its history. He thus places his reformed state university in the service of the Third Reich precisely to fill the traditional role of educating a political elite, a cadre of guardians of the destiny of the nation who would be charged with awakening the German people to its grand historical mission, still by and large hidden from it, instilling in the heart and will of the people a clear knowledge of its mission. "The new university has to be the connecting link and bridge between the people and its leadership."[12] This awakening of the people to its mission constitutes the education and re-education of the people to becoming a unified people of and for the state. "The national socialist revolution is therefore not an external takeover of an existing state apparatus by a party become powerful enough to do so, but the internal re-education of an entire people to the task of willing its own unification and unity. [. . .] The basic character of the new spiritual and political movement which passes through the people is that of an education and *re-education of the people to the people through the state.* And when it is a matter of the deepest and broadest *education,* is this not the task of the highest school in the land? [. . .] *Education of the people through the state to the people—*that is the meaning of the national socialist movement, which is the essence of the new national education. *Such* an education in the highest knowledge is the task of the new university. Through this education the people comes to true self-responsibility" (GA 16: 302, 304, 307).

The disenchantment

Heidegger resigns his rectorship soon after the conclusion of this seminar of WS 1933–4, but continues to promote his national socialism of the educational state until mid-year in residual duties related to the rectorate, in introducing foreign students to the new German university and in evaluating the organization of a school for instructors. It gradually recedes into the background in favor of Heidegger's third concept of the political, the pre-political interplay between poets, thinkers, and statesmen. In the meantime, as his hoped-for educational state became more and more a totalitarian police state, plans were announced for a new "scientific university [*Hochschule*]," for the political education of the next generation of leaders under the auspices of the party and the leadership of Robert Ley, who was head of the German Labor Front, a *Hochschule* which the now mere Professor Heidegger regarded as a threat not only to the university but also to the very concept of science (10–11).[13] But it would take Hitler's announcement of the "Four Year Plan" in September 1936 and the impact that this "total mobilization" of the German military-industrial complex, tacitly in preparation for a total war in four years, would have on the universities before we find the first real evidence of wholesale, albeit (as usual) discreet, resistance to state policy and planning on the part of Heidegger. Consternation over the Four Year Plan, especially among the younger faculty at Freiburg, led to a series of working meetings among them, independent of the party-sanctioned discussions of the matter. Heidegger's notes for and from these working meetings turn again and again on the political constellations that relate science to the National Socialist "worldview" (and no longer to the "movement," as in 1933–5!).

Some choice examples from the intra-university debate, in Heidegger's own words: "There is not even a transformative will for this new organization [of science as a *spiritual/intellectual* power]. The farcical 550 jubilee celebration at Heidelberg University: forced and inflated without ground and background. And the Führer? Stays away! Instead, on August 16 [1936] he closes the Olympic games in Berlin; on the same day, he organizes the preparations for the Tokyo games! [. . .] The Olympic games are better suited for foreign propaganda. The sports greats from all lands are courted for their approval—one is more among one's own kind! 'University people' of the old style also know too much" (22). One of his greatest mistakes in the rectorate: "that I did not know that the ministry cannot be approached with creative projects and large goals" (24). Now that the "coarse and nonsensical and naive outburst of a 'new folkish science' has totally gone awry," the pendulum has swung the other way. In demanding undisturbed quiet for supra-temporal science, one finds a new common ground for compromise: from the side of science, one concedes that there is no such thing as pure theory, that there is room for a worldview. From the side of the folkish representatives, one concedes that one must concentrate work on the "matters themselves," but also that the demand for a worldview is indispensable. Both sides are now saying the same thing, but the compromise thereby diffuses all the forces of questioning that would bring us to "the moment of true inception and a real change" (24). What to do in this stalemate? Running away solves nothing. Best to remain and exploit the possibility of meeting like-minded individuals. "This not to prepare the university—now hopeless—but to preserve the *tradition*, to provide *role-models*, to inspire new demands in one or another individual—somewhere, sometime, for someone. This is neither 'escape' nor 'resignation' but the necessity that comes with the essential philosophical task of the second inception" (24–5). The university is at its end and so is science, "but this is precisely because philosophy has its second essential inception before itself. That what we have called science is running its course and technologizing itself, perhaps for a whole century, proves nothing to the contrary!" (26). In view of its uselessness, philosophy's positions and chairs are being reduced or cancelled. "*But with the abolition of philosophy, the Germans—and this with the intention of fulfilling their essence as a people!—are committing suicide in world history*" (27, my emphasis).

With this entry into the industrial arms race in preparation for total war, National Socialism, purportedly in search of geopolitical "living space" and scarce natural resources, has unequivocally placed itself on the same plane as capitalism and communism. The "movement" in search of its uniquely German roots has become, like them, a technological worldview. At this point, Heidegger abandons his fading hope in a difference in the decisions made by narrow-minded party functionaries and those by Hitler himself, the statesman whose originative deeds create a new state and a higher order. After he develops a more refined sense of the essence of technology as completed metaphysics, Heidegger will characterize Hitler as the supreme technician of a System as much being imposed upon him as manipulated by him, by way of a shrewd calculative thinking totally devoid of any vestige of the meditative thinking required of the statesman.[14]

"Early in 1938," Heidegger is purported to have already concluded that Adolf Hitler was "the robber and criminal of the century [*der Räuber und Verbrecher des Jahrhunderts*]."[15] In a discussion of Nietzsche's will to power at about the time of the outbreak of the Second World War, Heidegger observes that the *planetarische Hauptverbrecher* (global arch-criminals), whose "capacity for brutality" in their exercise of power is boundless, are an exclusive group whose number "can be counted on one hand" (GA 69: 78).

The archaic concept of the polis and the political

The transition from the second to the third concept of the political likewise shifts attention from a sole focus on the statesman, philosopher-ruler, or political leader of the *Führerstaat* to the ruler's reliance on the advice of the various "guardians," in founding dialogues that thus take place on a level that precedes purely political action. The shift constitutes a dilution and counter-thrust to the totalitarian direction that Nazism in fact took.

The regress to German-Greek Da-sein that founds the third concept of the political, the archaic (poietic, *seynsgeschichtlicher*) concept, is facilitated especially by Hölderlin's poetic German translations of Greek tragedy. It is a return to the great beginning and first inception of ontology in the Western language which, "next to German, is at once the most powerful and the most spiritual of languages (in regard to its possibilities of thought)" (EM 43/60). In the example that we shall now quickly track in its historical sense (*Be-sinnung*), it is a matter of restoring the originative power of one of the most influential words in the Greek language, *polis*, the root of the political, its politics, polity, policy, police, etc. in so many Western languages and overly exploited in the politicized time of 1935 (EM 102/141). In the context of the tragic fate of humanity drawn in the foreboding lines of the chorus of Theban elders in Sophocles' *Antigone*, Heidegger finds that *polis* is not merely a geographically located state (*Staat*) or city (*Stadt*) but, more basically, a historical site (*Stätte*: EM 156/220) virtually identical with the ontological site of Da-sein in which a unique humankind (e.g. Greek being-there, German being-here) "takes place" (*statt–findet, statt–hat*), is "granted stead" (*gestattet* = permitted), and in this "leeway" (*Spielraum*) of allotted time and historical place makes its unique "homestead" (*Heimstatt*) befitting its historical destiny.

> The *polis* is the site of history, the Here in which, out of which and for which history happens. To this site of history belong the gods, the temples, the priests, the celebrations, the games, the poets, the thinkers, the ruler, the council of elders, the assembly of the people, the armed forces, and the ships. All this does not first belong to the *polis*, is not first political, because it enters into a relationship with a statesman and a general and with the affairs of state. Rather, what we have named is political, that is, at the site of history, insofar as, for example, the poets are *only* poets, but then are actually poets, the thinkers are *only* thinkers, but then are actually thinkers, the priests are *only* priests, but then are actually priests, the rulers are *only* rulers, but then are actually rulers. *Are*: but this says, to use their power as violence-doers and to rise to eminent stature in historical be-ing as creators, as doers. Rising to a supreme stature at the site of history, they also become *apolis*, without city and site, alone, without a home, with no way out amidst beings as a whole, at the same time without statute and limit, without structure and fittingness, because they *as* creators must in each of their situations first ground all this. (EM 117/162–3)

Thus, the creators of the political are not only the politicians, but also the apolitical ones. Poets and thinkers, statesmen and priests are gathered together in unity and lonely, untimely, tragic, and contentious dialogue at this core of history, Da-sein. The very example, Heidegger's choice of Hölderlin's translation of Sophocles's *Antigone* itself illustrates this unity and peculiar interchange among the creators of the *polis*. To be truly political is to be at the site of history, Da-sein in its root facticity and possibility, which in each of its epochal instantiations is ours here-and-now. In each instantiation of Da–sein, "the human being is then related in an exceptional sense to this pole[16] [of the *pole-mos* of the *polis*], insofar as human beings, in understanding be-ing, stand in the middle of beings and here necessarily have a 'status' in each of their historical instantiations, a stance in their states and their circumstances. Such a 'status' is the 'State'" (GA 53: 100/81). Geopolitics is now to be regarded neither geographically nor metaphysically, but in its purity as a "site" within the *seynsgeschichtliche Urpolitik* of Da-sein as it instantiates itself in the epochal history of archaic be-ing, now on the verge of the revolution to a new and radically different inception. This "'politics' in the supreme and authentic sense" (GA 39: 214), what Nietzsche called "grand politics" that transcends the petty politics of narrow nationalisms, takes place at the supreme site of radical historical transition displayed by the Greek tragedy, which glosses the oxymoronic status of the tragic heroine (Antigone) as *hupsipolis apolis*, at once far beyond and without home and site, unhomely, lone-some, un-canny, singled out for lofty greatness by creating a new home for her people, as well as for the precipitous destruction which was also the fate of Heidegger's more contemporary heroes: Hölderlin, Nietzsche, van Gogh, and Schlageter. Throughout this "Greek-German mission of transmission [*Sendung*]" (GA 39: 151) across the history of be-ing by way of Hölderlin's translation of Sophoclean tragedy, Heidegger repeatedly alludes to the counter-essence of the tragic hero, his hubris in arrogating power (GA 53: 116/93), but without ever truly confronting the inhuman possibilities of this lonesome superiority and uncanny "greatness" that yields another kind of hero, or anti-hero (Creon, Hitler). The Greek-German mission focuses instead on a repetition of Hölderlin's transmission of a poetic sense of the "fatherland" and the "national" and "home" that Heidegger had originally hoped to find resonating in the folkish mythos of a uniquely German national socialism, guiding the decisions of its statesmen in the "land of poets and thinkers." Politics (or better, statesmanship) here finds its origins and inspiration in poetizing and thinking. "It is from these two prior activities that the Dasein of a people is made fully effective as a people through the state—politics" (GA 39: 51).

From this archaic vantage of Da-sein, Heidegger now criticizes the Nazi claim of the totalitarian character of the political (which he himself promoted in 1933!). "These [Nazi] enthusiasts are now suddenly discovering the 'political' everywhere. . . . But the *polis* cannot be defined 'politically.' The *polis*, and precisely it, is therefore not a 'political' concept. . . . Perhaps the name *polis* is precisely the word for that realm that constantly became questionable anew, remained worthy of question, and necessitated certain decisions whose truth on each occasion displaced the Greeks into the groundless or the inaccessible" (GA 53: 98–9/80). Aristotle saw clearly that man was a political animal because he was the animal possessed by speech. But he did not see the full uncanniness that membership in the *polis* brings, far outstripping the rhetorical as well as the political (GA 53: 102/83) of a people's state. Hölderlin's poetic words, "Since we are a conversation/ and can listen to one another" refer to the thoughtful dialogue among solitary creators (poets, thinkers, statesmen) at the very abysses of be-ing. Language here is the original institution of be-ing in the violent words of poetic origin and not just a means of communication for the sake of quick and easy agreement, rhetoric. The community of creators is a combative community of agonistic struggle over the extreme issues of archaic be-ing, *Seyn*. Hearing from one another, listening to one another, reciprocally involves radically placing each other in question over the radical issues at stake. Rapprochement here is contention, contestation, *pole-mos*, war, a war of agonistic spirits. Coming to an understanding is combat. "Conversation here is not communication, but the fundamental happening of radical exposure to the thick of beings" (GA 39: 73). It is precisely this pre-political *Geisterkrieg* between great and solitary individuals that Nietzsche called grand politics (*große Politik*) done in a grand style, and that Heidegger now turns to in order to launch a new and other beginning that would serve to arrest the "decline of the West."

The statesman is often left out in later accounts of this grand conversation between poets and thinkers since, in the language of the seminar (in its conclusion, 64), the Führer of the Third Reich broke with the tradition of the previous two Reichs by not remaining true to the grand tradition of leadership of the Prussian nobility, expressed succinctly in the maxim of the royal elector "spoken in the spirit of Luther": *Sic gesturus sum principatum, ut rem populi esse sciam, non meam privatam* (to assume the mantle of leadership is to understand that the affairs of the people are not my own private affair). It is the classic political problem with Plato's *Politeia* and its philosopher-rulers already expressed by the Roman Quintilian: "But who will guard the guardians?" Heidegger never publicly conceded the need for the political institution of "checks and balances" to guard against the errancy of absolutist arrogations of power. He continues to promote the still elitist pre-political *Geisterkrieg* of grand politics with great thinkers like Nietzsche in trying to come to terms with the planetary meaning of the Second World War. The upshot of this historical *Besinnung* in the spirit of Nietzsche is the call, not for democracy, which continues to be a "form of decadence of the state," but for a new "rank-order" of a ruling class of a kinder and gentler *Übermensch*, "poorer, simpler, gentler and harder, more reticent and self-sacrificing, slower in making resolutions and more sparing in speech," in short, a "Caesar with the soul of Christ"[17] rather than villainous natures like the Cesare Borgias of Western history that Nietzsche had earlier preferred. Is this not a continued expression of hope for enlightened despots who would exercise their will to power at least instinctively according to the meditative measures of the artist-tyrants and philosophical legislators that Nietzsche hoped would emerge? But is this "gentler and harder" guardianship adequate to the task of preventing the emergence of future "global arch-criminals"?

On the rhetorical-phenomenological concept of the political and its language

The seminar makes virtually a passing reference to the rhetorical sense of the political and the political power of speech in acknowledging the ancient Greeks as its source—with Thucydides as the prime example—and then bringing the discussion up to date by pointing to the power of the "speeches of the Führer" in acting like a "drummer" to forcefully drum his points across (62). But the topic of the context is persuasion "(1) through speech, and (2) through action" and the discussion quickly focuses on the latter and proclaims that a leader persuades especially by his deeds, clearly suggesting an admiration of Hitler as a man of action and doer of deeds, and an acknowledgment of the superior governing will of the Führer, his vaunted willpower as well as will to power, which at once grants him the right to rule. "The effective will is most urgently 'persuasive' in acts. The great effective actor is at the same time the 'powerful' one, the 'ruler,' whose Dasein and will becomes determinative—through 'persuasion,' that is, when one knows and recognizes the soaring will of the leader" (62).

So no attempt is made here to analyze the means of persuasion in the "speeches of the Führer" themselves. But another context suggests that Hitler had established himself as a master in not only reading, but also evoking and accentuating the fundamental moods (*Grundstimmungen*) of the German people to gain their active cooperation (*Zustimmung*) in the grand historical mission (*Be-stimmung, Sendung, Auftrag)* that he only gradually revealed to them (GA 38: 129–30/109–10).[18] And *pathos* is one of the three classical means of persuasion of Aristotle's *Rhetoric*, along with the demonstrative power of the words (*logos*) and the character (*ethos*) of the speaker himself, which is essentially coupled to his attunement to the deeper *ethos* (custom, usage, tradition) of the indigenous community to and for which he speaks and his capacity to draw on that *ethos* insightfully and wisely in appropriate speech situations in order to motivate that community to timely and appropriate action. For the final characteristics of the orator who would win our confidence and trust are the triad of *phronesis kai arete kai eunoia* (*Rhetoric* II, 1378a10), "good sense, goodness/excellence, good will," or, more idiomatically, "savvy, solid, and politic." More elaborately, our orator must be thoroughly familiar with the subject matter, trustworthy as a person, and well-disposed toward the audience.[19]

As to the deeper *ethos* of the community, Aristotle compiles and critiques a series of *gnomai* (maxims and proverbs, in *Rhetoric* II, 20–2) from which the native orator can draw to appeal to his native audience, a kind of "folk wisdom" built into the *doxa* of his native language. He also observes that the kind of demonstrations in the oratorical speech situation are not a matter of logical proof or scientific procedures. They are instead enthymemes, the abbreviated syllogisms of rhetoric, literally curt speech that goes directly "to the heart" (*en-thumos*): striking examples, memorable punch lines (what are currently called "sound bites"), emotionally charged but pithy tales ("the November betrayal," one of Hitler's favorites, the "stab in the back" that led to Germany's defeat in WWI), narrative "arguments" that hit home quickly and powerfully. Opinion formation is sometimes opinion creation, giving currency to a new view, which, however, is never out of keeping with the prevalent public opinion, *doxa*. The public speaker draws upon the way one on the average thinks about things, upon popular prejudices and suspicions, from which he selects the seldom stated major premises that found his abbreviated but striking conclusions about how things look and what seems to be the case, *doxa*. For the thinking of the crowd is short-winded, having absolutely no interest in the lengthy process of getting "at the things themselves." The Greeks, who loved to talk, had a strong sense of this most immediate phenomenon of speech, of being with one another in common gossip, chatter, and idle talk. The human being even for Aristotle is first of all not the rational animal, but rather the living being dwelling in ordinary language and idle talk, who has neither the time nor the inclination to speak primordially about the things themselves.

But getting "back to the things themselves" is precisely what Heidegger the phenomenologist is especially interested in. We therefore conclude with a deliberation on a rather unusual and little noted source of the language needed to get back to the matters themselves, or better, what truly matters itself, that is in fact alluded to in this seminar. In Session 8, the point is made that it is necessary for, say, an agrarian people that finds its sustenance in its rootedness in the soil, its *Bodenständigkeit*, to expand its space by interacting with the outside world, thereby expanding its homeland into the territory of the fatherland, the German state. Through rootedness and interaction, *Bodenständigkeit und Verkehr*, such a people achieves its fullness of being in the state. But years before *Bodenständigkeit* became tainted from its usage in Nazi propaganda, Heidegger was using it rather frequently in a very different sense.[20] In his course of SS 1924 on the *Basic Concepts of Aristotelian Philosophy*, Heidegger describes Aristotle's way of philosophical concept-formation through reshaping terms that are charged with a certain experiential meaning in his native language into his more philosophical terminology. The most telling example is Aristotle's word for being, *ousia*, which in the Greek language ordinarily means property, possessions and goods, real estate. This customary meaning is constantly present and simultaneously accompanies its terminological meaning. As property and possessions, the how of being here is being in its being-available. In living in the native language that imparts intelligibility to his world and all that is experienced within it, Aristotle draws on that natural intelligibility of experience to form his basic (i.e. root) concepts that accordingly remain indigenous (*bodenständig*) to that intelligible world wherein they are rooted and from which they are drawn (GA 18: 15/13, 18/15, 24/19, 40/29, 270/184, 340/229–30, 354/240). A decade later, Heidegger finds that same *Bodenständigkeit* of his native language operative in Hölderlin, the most German of poets thoroughly possessed, and even obsessed, by his native language, even as he eavesdrops in the conversation instituted by the early Greeks and translates their words into the Germanic world.[21]

Heidegger's and Hölderlin's *Bodenständigkeit* has little to do with Nazi *Bodenständigkeit* and a lot to do with getting at the roots of our native, indigenous, experiential language phenomenologically—getting back to the matters themselves. Even the 1933–4 seminar moves away from hard-core Nazi *Bodenständigkeit* by insisting on its essential linkage to interaction and thus moderating any attempt to over-exaggerate the indigenous, native, rooted elements of a people's way of being.

5 HEIDEGGER IN THE FOURSOME OF STRUGGLE, HISTORICITY, WILL, AND *GELASSENHEIT*

Slavoj Žižek

The time between *Being and Time* and the Nietzsche seminars of the late 1930s[1] is Heidegger's most productive period of inquiry when, upon becoming aware of the ultimate failure of the original *Being and Time* project, he was looking for a new beginning. With the conclusion of this work in the Nietzsche seminars, Heidegger established his "great narrative" of the history of the West as the history of the oblivion of Being, and it is only at this point that he historicized Will as the defining feature of modern subjectivity and its violent nihilism. (In his *Ereignis*-book written in the mid-1930s, which is usually taken as the beginning of his "mature" late thought,[2] Heidegger still speaks of the "will to *Ereignis*," an expression unthinkable a couple of years later.) It is against this background that accounts are usually given for Heidegger's Nazi engagement, which is most palpable in "On the Essence and Concept of Nature, History, and State," Heidegger's seminar of the Winter semester of 1933–4: he was still captured by the nihilist decisionism of Will.

The axiom of our reading is that a certain dimension which opened up another potential path got lost with the elaboration of what one is tempted to call Heidegger's late orthodoxy—it is thus urgent to return to Heidegger's texts between *Being and Time* and the Nietzsche seminars and treat them not just as works of passage, but as works containing a potential which became invisible with the establishment of Heidegger's orthodoxy. True, in some sense, these texts remain Heidegger's "lowest point," more or less coinciding with his Nazi engagement. However, our thesis is that these same texts open up possibilities which point in an entirely different dimension, towards a radical emancipatory politics. Although not pursued by Heidegger himself, these possibilities haunt his texts of the 1930s as an ominous spectral shadow. In the US presidential elections of 2000, Al Gore, who was generally taken as the next President, unexpectedly lost to Bush (as the result of the Florida mess); in the years after, Gore often ironically referred to himself as "the guy who was once the future US President"—a case of the future logged into the past, of something that was to-come and which unfortunately did not come. In the same way, Heidegger of the mid-1930s "was a future Communist": Heidegger's Nazi engagement was not a simple mistake, but a "right step in the wrong direction," that is, Heidegger cannot be simply dismissed as a German *Volks*-reactionary.[3]

Let us then take a closer look at "On the Essence and Concept of Nature, History, and State." His starting point is an immediate transposition of the ontological difference between an entity (*Seiendes*) and its Being (*Sein*) onto the relationship between a people and its state: the state is "a way of Being and a kind of Being of the people. The people is the entity [*Seiendes*] whose Being [*Sein*] is the state" (52). This gesture may appear problematic within Heidegger's own field: is "state" really a name for the Being of a people, for the ontological horizon of how a meaning of Being is disclosed to a people? Is the state not rather a set of ontic institutions and practices? If the state is the Being of a people, then "it is after all impossible to consider the people without a state—the entity without its Being, in a certain sense" (52). Does this mean that people who do not have a state are excluded from the history of Being? It is interesting to note here how, in contrast to the usual perception of him as an advocate of provincial life, Heidegger clearly opposes homeland as the provincial environs to fatherland:

The homeland is not to be confused with the fatherland. . . . We can speak of the state only when rootedness in the soil is combined with the will to expansion, or generally speaking, interaction. A homeland is something I have on the basis of my birth. There are quite particular relations between me and it in the sense of nature, in the sense of natural forces. Homeland expresses itself in rootedness in the soil and being bound to the earth. But nature works on the human being, roots him in the soil, only when nature belongs as an environment, so to speak, to the people whose member that human being is. The homeland becomes the way of Being of a people only when the homeland becomes expansive, when it interacts with the outside—when it becomes a state. For this reason, peoples or their subgroups who do not step out beyond their connection to the homeland into their authentic way of Being—into the state—are in constant danger of losing their peoplehood and perishing. This is also the great problem of those Germans who live outside the borders of the Reich: They do have a German homeland, but they do not belong to the state of the Germans, the Reich, so they are deprived of their authentic way of Being. (55–6)

Remember that these lines were delivered in 1934—do they not imply that the way to resolve this "great problem" is to *annex* to the Reich the homeland of the Germans living outside the German state, and thus to enable them to fully participate in their "authentic way of Being" (what Hitler was doing a couple of years later)? Heidegger then goes on with his analysis: what happens to a people (*Volk*) when it decides to form a state? "We must then ask what we understand by 'people,' for in the French Revolution they gave the same answer: the people" (38). (Note the negative tone of this specification: we should inquire further, since it is for sure that we don't mean "people" in the sense of the French Revolution.) In the "decision for a state," a people determines itself by way of deciding for a certain kind of state, or, to paraphrase the well-known proverb: tell me what kind of a state a people has, and I will tell you what kind of people it is. Humans have consciousness, they do not only interact with things like animals; they care about them, they knowingly relate to them. Members of a people thus know and care about their state, they will it. For a people, their state is not just an instrument of their welfare, but a thing that matters, a thing they love and are ready to sacrifice for, an object of their *erōs*. The constitution of a state is not just a matter of rational consideration and negotiation, of a social contract which regulates the welfare of the individuals, but a commitment to a vision of shared life.

If, then, the people is the entity which is in the mode and way of the state, we should further specify the question: "what character and form does the people give itself in the state, and what character and form does the state give to the people?" (38). Heidegger rejects the first answer, the shape of an organism, as missing the specifically human dimension; the same holds for the general answer—"order"—since any objects, books, stones can also be arranged in an order. "But what hits the mark is an order in the sense of mastery, rank, leadership and following. This leaves open the question of who is master" (38–9). In its authentic mode, the relationship of domination and following is grounded in a common will, in a commitment to a shared goal: "Only where the leader and the led bind themselves together to *one* fate and fight to actualize *one* idea does true order arise" (49). Without this shared commitment, which grounds the readiness to fight, domination turns into exploitation and order is enforced, externally imposed upon the people. This is what happens in the modern liberal epoch: state order is reduced to an abstract notion of order; the state becomes Hobbes's Leviathan imposed onto the people as the agent of absolute sovereignty which, instead of expressing the deepest will of the people, monopolizes all violence and acts as the force of law constraining the will of individuals. It is only after domination is reduced to sovereignty that the French Revolution becomes possible, in which sovereign power is transferred to the opposite pole of the social order, to the people: "Only on the basis of the notion of sovereignty as absolutism can we really understand and explain the essence of the French Revolution as an opposing phenomenon" (58).

In Germany itself, the living unity of the state and the people started to disintegrate with Bismarck: "We heard that a people, in addition to needing a leader, also needs a tradition that is carried on by a political nobility. The Second Reich fell prey to an irreparable collapse after Bismarck's death, and not only because Bismarck failed to create this political nobility. He was also incapable of regarding the proletariat as a phenomenon that was justified in itself, and of leading it back into the state by reaching out to it with understanding" (52). To the obvious counter-argument that, in Bismarck's Germany, the nobility continued to play a much larger public role than in other European states, and, furthermore, that Bismarck precisely did "reach out" to the proletariat with the first elements of the welfare state (retirement plans, etc.), Heidegger would have probably answered that Bismarck's Germany was a modern authoritarian-bureaucratic state *par excellence*. In absolutism as well as in liberal democracy, the unity of the will between the leader and the people is thus lost: the state moves between the two extremes, the sovereign absolute power experienced by the people as an external authority, and the service or instrument of civil society, fulfilling tasks necessary for the smooth social life in which individuals follow their interests. In both cases, the authentic people's will expressed by their leader is unthinkable: "The question of the consciousness of the will of the community is a problem in all democracies, a question that can really become fruitful only when the will of the leader and the will of the people are recognized in their essence. Our task today is to direct the fundamental attitude of our communal Being toward this actuality of people and leader in which both as a single actuality are not to be separated" (60).

What is there to add to these lines, spoken in 1934, which explain why Heidegger endorsed the Nazi takeover? Are we not getting here a rather simplistic conservative-authoritarian vision which is not even very original, since it fits perfectly the standard coordinates of the conservative-national reaction to the Weimar Republic? Indeed, the only open question here seems to be where, precisely, one should locate Heidegger on the spectrum delineated by the two extremes of direct Nazism and political naïveté: was Heidegger (as Emmanuel Faye claims) a full Nazi, did he directly "introduce Nazism into philosophy,"[4] or was he simply politically naïve and got caught in a political game with no direct foundation in his thought? I nonetheless propose to follow a different line: neither to assert a direct link between Heidegger's thought and Nazism, nor to emphasize the gap that divides them (i.e. to sacrifice Heidegger as a naïve or corrupted person in order to save his thought), but to transpose this gap into the heart of his thought himself, to demonstrate how the space for the Nazi engagement was opened up by the immanent failure or inconsistency of his thought, by the jumps and passages which are "illegitimate" in the very terms of this thought. In any serious philosophical analysis, external critique has to be grounded in immanent critique: one should show how Heidegger's external failure (Nazi engagement) reflects the fact that Heidegger fell short measured by his own aim and standards.

Such an immanent critique of Heidegger has a long history, beginning with Habermas's early attempt to think "Heidegger against Heidegger."[5] There are many pertinent attempts on this road—suffice it to mention Jean-Luc Nancy's observation that, already in *Being and Time*, Heidegger strangely leaves out the analytic of *Mitsein* as a dimension constitutive of *Dasein*.[6] Our starting point will be a different one, something that cannot but strike the eye of a reader of Heidegger's texts of the 1930s, especially of the seminar "On the Essence and Concept of Nature, History, and State": the preponderance of the topic of *Will*. The distinction between homeland and fatherland is that only the latter implies state, while the former is a mere "province," and this distinction relies on the fact that "province" stands for passive rootedness in a particular soil and set of customs, while state implies active will to expansion and confrontation with neighboring peoples (Session 8). The province thus lacks political will proper, in contrast to the state, which is grounded in political will (Session 9). Heidegger's (in) famous short text from 1934 "Why Do I Stay in the Provinces?" grounding his refusal to accept a university post in Berlin by a reference to a rather ridiculous figure of the "subject supposed to know," a simple farmer who just silently refused by shaking his head when Heidegger asked him for advice,[7] receives thus an unexpected prophetic dimension, pointing towards

Heidegger's later advocacy of the province as the site of authentic being over the state as the domain of the will to power and domination.

How, then, should we interpret this strange persistence of Will which continues to haunt Heidegger not only through the 1930s, but even later, when its overcoming becomes the very focus of his thought? In his detailed study on this topic, Bret Davis[8] proposes a twofold reading of this persistence: first, as a sign of "*Gelassenheit* as an unfinished project," an indication that Heidegger did not succeed in thoroughly "deconstructing" the Will, so that it is up to us, who continue in his path, to accomplish the job and draw all the consequences from *Gelassenheit*; second, as something that necessitates the distinction "between (1) what Heidegger calls 'the will' of subjectivity, a fundamental (dis)attunement that has risen up and prevailed in a particular epochal history of metaphysics, and (2) what we have (interpretively supplementing Heidegger) called 'ur-willing,' a non-historical dissonant excess which haunts the proper essence of non-willing" (HW 303). Recall how, in his reading of the fragment of Anaximander on order and disorder, Heidegger considers the possibility that an entity

> may even insist [*bestehen*] upon its while solely to remain more present, in the sense of perduring [*Beständigen*].That which lingers persists [*beharrt*] in its presencing. In this way it extricates itself from its transitory while. It strikes the wilful pose of persistence, no longer concerning itself with whatever else is present. It stiffens—as if this were the only way to linger—and aims solely for continuance and subsistence.[9]

Davis's thesis is that this "rebellious whiling" refers to a non-historical ur-willing, a willing which is not limited to the epoch of modern subjectivity and its will to power.[10] One should raise here a more fundamental question: Is Will the proper name for the "stuckness" which derails the natural flow? Is the Freudian drive (death drive) not a much more appropriate name? The standard philosophical critique of the Freudian drive is that it is another version of the post-Hegelian "will" first developed by the late Schelling and Schopenhauer and then reaching its highest formulation in Nietzsche. Is, however, the Freudian drive really a sub-species of Will?

While Will is the substance of life, its productive presence, which is in excess over its representations or images, drive is *a persistence which goes on even when the Will disappears or is suspended*: the insistence which persists even when it is deprived of its living support, the appearance which persists even when it is deprived of its substance. One has to be very precise here if we are not to confuse desire and drive: drive is not an infinite longing for the Thing which gets fixated onto a partial object—"drive" *is* this fixation itself in which resides the "death" dimension of every drive. Drive is not a universal thrust (towards the incestuous Thing) braked and broken up, it *is* this brake itself, a brake on instinct, its "stuckness," as Eric Santner would have put it.[11] The elementary matrix of drive is *not* that of transcending all particular objects towards the void of the Thing (which is then accessible only in its metonymic stand-in), but that of our libido getting "stuck" onto a particular object, condemned to circulate around it forever. The basic paradox here is that the specifically human dimension—drive as opposed to instinct—emerges precisely when what was originally a mere by-product is elevated into an autonomous aim: man is not more "reflexive"; on the contrary, man perceives as a direct goal what, for an animal, has no intrinsic value. In short, the zero-degree of "humanization" is not a further "mediation" of animal activity, its re-inscription as a subordinated moment of a higher totality (say, we eat and procreate in order to develop higher spiritual potentials), but the radical narrowing of focus, the elevation of a minor activity into an end-in-itself. We become "humans" when we get caught into a closed, self-propelling loop of repeating the same gesture and finding satisfaction in it. We all recall one of the archetypal scenes from cartoons: while dancing, the cat jumps up into the air and turns around its own axis; however, instead of falling back down towards the earth's surface in accordance with the normal laws of gravity, it remains for some time suspended in the air, turning around in the levitated position as if caught in a loop of time, repeating the same circular movement on and on. (One also finds the same shot in some musical comedies which make use of the elements of slapstick: when a dancer turns around in the air, s/he remains up there a little bit too long, as if, for a short period of time, s/he succeeded in suspending the law of gravity.[12] And, effectively, is such an effect not the ultimate goal of the art of dancing?) In such moments, the "normal" run of things, the "normal" process of being caught in the imbecilic inertia of material reality, is for a brief moment suspended; we enter the magical domain of a suspended animation, of a kind of ethereal rotation which, as it were, sustains itself, hanging in the air like Baron Munchhausen, who raised himself from the swamp by grabbing his own hair and pulling himself up. This rotary movement, in which the linear progress of time is suspended in a repetitive loop, is *drive* at its most elementary. This, again, is "humanization" at its zero-level: this self-propelling loop which suspends/disrupts linear temporal enchainment.

When one aims at designating the excess of drive, its too-muchness, one often resorts to the term "animality": what Gilles Deleuze called the "becoming-animal" (*le devenir-animal*) of a human being, which is rendered in an exemplary way in some of Kafka's stories. The paradox is that one uses the term "animality" for the very fundamental movement of overcoming animality, the working of animal instincts—drive is not instinct but its "denaturalization." There is, however, a deeper logic in this paradox: from within the established human universe of meaning, its own founding gesture is invisible, indiscernible from its opposite, so that it has to appear as its opposite.

For Heidegger, striving based on drive (*Trieb*) is animalistic, while human striving is higher because it takes the form of will and action: "An animal cannot act, because it cannot will." He also contrasts focused will to unfocused urge (*Drang*): "Urge does indeed aim at something, but this 'something' is, in contrast to willful striving, not sharply delineated, not clearly seen and recognized. Will aims at an individual thing, urge aims at a whole complex of possibilities" (58). Heidegger, then, misses two key facts: drive too is focused, indeed stuck on a particular object; and this very stuckness is distinctively human, not animal.

This, then, is—to put it in somewhat simplified terms—the basic difference between psychoanalysis and Christianity: while both agree that the life of the "human animal" is disrupted by the violent intrusion of a properly meta-physical "immortal" dimension, psychoanalysis identifies this dimension as that of (specifically (in)human) sexuality, of the "undead" drive as opposed to the animal instinct, while Christianity sees in sexuality the very force which drags humans toward animality and prevents access to immortality. Therein resides the unbearable "news" of psychoanalysis: not in emphasizing the role of sexuality as such, but in rendering visible the "meta-physical" dimension of human sexuality. The paradox of Christianity is that, in order to sustain its edifice, it has to violently suppress this meta-physical dimension of sexuality, to reduce it to animality. In other words, the "truth" of the Christian elevation of human spirituality is the violent de-spiritualization of the key dimension of being-human. Unfortunately, Hegel does the same in his theory of marriage—and Heidegger also:

> The Greeks had two words for what we call life: *bios* and *zōē*. They used *bios* in a twofold sense. First, in the sense of biology, the science of life. Here we think of the organic growth of the body, glandular activity, sexual difference, and the like. [. . .] Another sense of *bios* for the Greeks is the course of a life, the history of a life, more or less in the sense that the word "biography" still has for us today. *Bios* means here human history and existence—so there can be no *bios* of animals. *Bios*, as human *bios*, has the peculiar distinction of being able either to stand above the animal or to sink beneath it. [Session 8, 51]

If there is a lesson of psychoanalysis, it is that sexual difference belongs to the domain of *bios* as history, not to the domain of glandular activity, etc. Far from providing the natural foundation of human lives, sexuality is the very terrain where humans detach themselves from nature: the idea of sexual perversion or of a deadly sexual passion is totally foreign to the animal universe. Once we are within the human condition, sexuality is not only transformed/civilized, but, much more radically, *changed in its very substance*: it is no longer the instinctual drive to reproduce, but a drive that gets thwarted as to its natural goal (reproduction) and thereby explodes into an infinite, properly meta-physical, passion. The becoming-cultural of sexuality is thus not the becoming-cultural of nature, but the attempt to domesticate a properly un-natural excess of the meta-physical sexual passion.

The next, crucial, step is to see how this "stuckness" is not just our human deficiency due to our limitation or finitude, our inability to grasp pure Being from our partial perspective (where, then, the solution would have been a kind of Oriental self-effacement, immersion into the primordial Void): this "stuckness" bears witness to a strife in the very heart of Being itself. Gregory Fried[13] already did a lot of work in his deeply pertinent reading of Heidegger's entire opus through the interpretive lenses of his reference to Heraclitus' *polemos* (struggle—in German, *Krieg, Kampf,* or, predominantly in Heidegger, *Auseinandersetzung*) from the latter's famous fragment 53: "War is both father of all and king of all: it reveals the gods on the one hand and humans on the other, makes slaves on the one hand, the free on the other." It is not only that the stable identity of each entity is temporary, that they all sooner or later disappear, disintegrate, return back to the primordial chaos; their (temporary) identity itself emerges through struggle, that is, stable identity is something one should gain through the ordeal of struggle—and even "class struggle" is already here, in the guise of the struggle which "makes slaves on the one hand, the free on the other."

There is, however, one step more to be made with regard to *polemos*: it is easy to assert struggle as "father of all" and then to elevate this struggle itself into the highest harmony, in the sense that Being is the very hidden concord of the struggling poles, like a cosmic music in which the struggling opposite poles harmoniously echo each other. So, to put it in blunt and simplified terms, is this strife part of the Harmony itself, or is it a more radical discord, something which derails the very Harmony of Being? As Davis perspicuously notices, Heidegger remains here ambiguous and oscillates between the radically open "strife" of Being and its re-inscription into the teleological reversal of Danger into Saving.[14]

Here we arrive at a vertiginous question: what if there is *stricto sensu* no world, no disclosure of being, prior to "stuckness"? What if there is no *Gelassenheit* which is disturbed by the excess of willing, what if it is this very excess-stuckness which opens up the space for *Gelassenheit*?

The primordial fact is thus not the fugue of Being (or the inner peace of *Gelassenheit*), which can then be disturbed/perverted by the rise of ur-willing; the primordial fact is this ur-willing itself, its disturbance of the "natural" fugue. To put it in yet another way: in order for a human being to be able to withdraw itself from the full immersion into its life-environs into the inner peace of *Gelassenheit*, this immersion has first to be broken through the excessive "stuckness" of the drive. What if will is not just an irreducible obstacle, but a positive condition of *Gelassenheit*?

What we confront here is the problem of historicity at its most radical: a historicity which goes "all the way down" and cannot be reduced to the deployment/revelation in history of a non-historical Absolute.[15] In a way, the true *Kehre* from *Being and Time* to the late Heidegger is the shift from ahistorical formal-transcendental analysis to radical historicity.[16] This radical historicity reaches its definitive formulation with the shift from Being to *Ereignis*. This shift thoroughly undermines the idea of Being as a kind of super-subject of *history*, sending its messages/epochs to man. *Ereignis* means that Being is *nothing but* the *chiaroscuro* of these messages, *nothing but* the way it relates to man. Man is finite, and *Ereignis* also: the very structure of finitude, the play of Clearing/Concealment with nothing behind. "It" is just the impersonal it, a "there is." There is an un-historical dimension at work here, but what is un-historical is the very formal structure of historicity itself. It is this radical historicity that forever separates Heidegger from so-called Oriental thought: in spite of the similarity of *Gelassenheit* to nirvana, etc. the attainment of the zero-level of nirvana is meaningless within the horizon of Heidegger's thought—it would have meant something like doing away with all shadow of concealment.[17] Like Kafka's man from the country who learns that the Door of the Law is here for him only, *Dasein* has to experience how Being needs us, how our strife with Being is Being's strife with itself.

A closer analysis renders visible how this radical historicity resolves a deadlock which already haunts the analysis of *Dasein* in *Being and Time*, in which two couples echo in each other without fully overlapping. First, there is the opposition between *zuhanden* (ready-to-hand) and *vorhanden* (present-at-hand), between being engaged in the world and adopting towards it an attitude of a disengaged observer, which is an ontologically secondary mode (we assume theoretical distance when things malfunction, when our engagement ends in a deadlock). Then, we have the opposition between authentic *Dasein* and its *Verfallenheit* (fallenness) into *das Man*, between choosing one's project through assuming one's mortality and the non-authentic obedience to the anonymous "one does it." How, exactly, are these two couples related? Obviously, they form a kind of semiotic square whose terms are disposed along the two axes of authentic versus inauthentic and engagement-in-the-world versus withdrawal-from-the-world: there are two modes of engagement, authentic being-in-the-world and inauthentic *das Man*, and there are two modes of withdrawal, authentic assuming of one's mortality through anxiety and inauthentic distance of the subject towards the objectivized "reality." The catch is, of course, that the two inauthentic modes overlap (partially, at least): the inauthentic engagement is the one of technological manipulation in which the subject stands opposed to "external reality."

Heidegger sometimes hints at a link between *das Man* and the reduction of things to *vorhanden* objects of theory; this, however, implies a doubtful presupposition that our most common *Verfallenheit* into *das Man* is structured by the metaphysical categories—almost a kind of the Hegelian infinite judgment, a coincidence of the opposites: of the most vulgar and superficial following the predominant trend/ fashion of what "one" is supposed to do and think, and of the high speculative metaphysical effort of the greatest traditional Western thinkers from Plato to Hegel. The most succinct definition of modern technology is precisely that it paradoxically unites *Verfallenheit*, immersion into worldly affairs, the will to dominate, with a theoretical distance: objects of technology are not *zuhanden*, they are *vorhanden*, that is, technological Reason is theoretical, not practical.

The first task of *Being and Time* is to provide a phenomenological description of the "immediacy of everyday Dasein," not yet contaminated by the traditional metaphysical categorical apparatus: where metaphysics talks about objects endowed with properties, a phenomenology of everyday life sees things which are always-already ready-to-use, part of our engagement, components of a meaningful world-structure; where metaphysics talks about a subject who relates to the world, opposed to objects in the world, phenomenology sees a human being always-already in the world, engaged with things, etc. The idea here is that traditional metaphysics (which is to be "de(con)structed" by phenomenology) is a kind of secondary screen, an imposed network obfuscating, covering up, the true structure of everyday life. The task is thus to drop the metaphysical prejudices and describe phenomena the way they are in themselves; however, since, in our predominant philosophical attitude which is already deeply infected by metaphysics, such a pure phenomenological description is the most difficult task, it requires the hard work of getting rid of traditional metaphysics. Heidegger is looking for the conceptual apparatus that would sustain such a description in different sources, from the Paulinian early Christianity to the Aristotelian *phronesis*.

Heidegger's own life offers an ironic comment on this tension between the immediacy of everyday life and its metaphysical misreading: it seems that, in his last years, he returned to Catholicism, since he gave orders to be buried as a Catholic, with the Church funeral. So while, in his thought, he theorized about the immediacy of pre-metaphysical life, in his own everyday life, he remained faithful to Christianity which, in his theory, he dismissed as the result of the Roman misreading of the original Greek disclosure of Being, as the key step in the onto-theological forgetting of Being, that is, as a metaphysical-ontological screen obfuscating the immediacy of life. It is thus as if the terms changed places: his immediate life was metaphysically structured, his theory opened up the structure of the immediacy of everyday life.[18]

The problem with Heidegger here is that, paradoxically, he is not "subjectivist-decisionist" enough: his early "decisionism" is all too much the obverse of responding to—following—a pre-ordained Destiny. Radical "subjectivism" (the insistence on the decision—and responsibility for it—as absolutely mine) and universalism are not opposed, they are two aspects of the same position of singular universality; what they are both opposed to is the particular historical Destiny of a community (people). *This* is where the possibility of following Hitler enters: when we recognize in him not the voice of universal Reason, but the voice of a concrete historical Destiny of the German nation.

The big shift that gradually occurs from the late 1930s onwards resides in the radical historicization of this opposition between the universal and the concrete: traditional metaphysics is no longer a false screen covering up the structure of everyday life, but the elaboration of the epochal, historically-specific, fundamental "attunement" which provides the structure of our lives. All great metaphysics ultimately *is* a phenomenological ontology of the historical "immediacy of everyday Dasein": Aristotle provided the ontology that structured the everyday experience of Greek citizens; the philosophy of modern subjectivity provides the structure of willing, domination, and "inner experience," which is the structure of our daily lives in modern dynamic capitalist societies. Stepping out of metaphysics is thus no longer just destroying the obfuscating network and perceiving the true functioning of the extra-theoretical everyday life, but a matter of historical change in the fundamental attunement of the everyday life itself. The turn in philosophy from traditional metaphysics to post-metaphysical phenomenology is part of the world-historical turn (*Kehre*) in Being itself.

The naïve question is to be asked here with all force: how are figures like Meister Eckhart, Angelus Silesius, and Hölderlin, possible, how are their intimations of a non-metaphysical dimension (of *Gelassenheit*, of *ohne Warum*, of the essence of poetry) possible in the space of such radicalized historicity? Do they not suggest "the possibility of a non-historical excess to the history of metaphysics, an excess which both critically calls into question the seamless rule of its epochs and affirmatively suggests the possibility of participating in a transition to an other beginning beyond the closure of metaphysics in the technological will to will"?[19]

But if being is nothing but the movement of its revealing/disclosure, then the "forgetting of being" is also and above all self-relating, that is, the forgetting/withdrawal of this very historical play of revealing and withdrawal. And if we take this into account, then, as Davis writes, "the other beginning would not be a complete eradication of the problem of willing, but rather a vigilant opening to it, a watchful recognition of the finitude of our selves caught between this problem of willing and the possibility of non-willing."[20] To avoid paradoxes, we have to make a choice here: either we perceive the "impulse to persistence"[21] as a kind of eternal temptation of the human mind, akin to the Kantian "radical evil" as the tendency to the "fall" inscribed into the very human condition, or we fully assert this "fall" as the grounding gesture of being-human. With regard to politics, this changes everything.

The first change concerns the status of *polemos* as constitutive of politics. Does not Heidegger's idea that the order implied by state is the order of domination and servitude strangely recall the classical Marxist notion of the state as something that is strictly linked to class division? So when Heidegger, in his reading of Heraclitus's fragment 53, insists on how the "struggle meant here is originary struggle, for it allows those who struggle to originate as such in the first place,"[22] is, within the political, the name of this struggle constitutive of those who struggle, and not just a conflict between pre-existing social agents, not class struggle? Recall here the lesson of Louis Althusser: "class struggle" paradoxically *precedes* classes as determinate social groups, that is, every class position and determination is already an effect of the "class struggle." (This is the reason why "class struggle" is another name for the fact that "society doesn't exist"—it does not exist as a positive order of entities.) That is to say, one should always bear in mind that, for a true Marxist, "classes" are *not* categories of positive social reality, parts of the social body, but categories of the real of a political struggle which cuts across the entire social body, preventing its "totalization."

However, Heidegger ignores such a reading of *polemos* as the struggle between those who dominate and those who serve them: if homeland "becomes the way of Being of a people only when the homeland becomes *expansive*, when it *interacts with the outside*—when it becomes a state" (82; emphasis added), then it is clear that *polemos* is primarily the strife with the *external* enemy. No wonder that, when Heidegger elaborates the essence of the political, he sympathetically compares his notion of the political with two other notions: Bismarck's idea of politics as the art of the possible (not just opportunistic strategic calculation, but the leader's ability to grasp the "essential possibility" offered by a historical constellation and mobilizing the people for it), and Carl Schmitt's idea of the antagonistic relationship friend/enemy, that is, the tension with the *external* enemy, as the defining feature of the political.

However, do we here not directly contradict a text by Heidegger which not only also admits the internal enemy, but explicitly posits it as more dangerous than the external enemy? Here is the key passage:

> An enemy is each and every person who poses an essential threat to the Dasein of the people and its individual members. The enemy does not have to be external, and the external enemy is not even always the more dangerous one. And it can seem as if there were no enemy. Then it is a fundamental requirement to find the enemy, to expose the enemy to the light, or even first to make the enemy, so that this standing against the enemy may happen and so that Dasein may not lose its edge.

> The enemy can have attached itself to the innermost roots of the Dasein of a people and can set itself against this people's own essence and act against it. The struggle is all the fiercer and harder and tougher, for the least of it consists in coming to blows with one another; it is often far more difficult and wearisome to catch sight of the enemy as such, to bring the enemy into the open, to harbor no illusions about the enemy, to keep oneself ready for attack, to cultivate and intensify a constant readiness and to prepare the attack looking far ahead with the goal of total annihilation.[23]

First, one cannot but note the ominous implications of this passage—not only the mention of "total annihilation" of the enemy as the goal, but, maybe even more, the requirement to "find the enemy, to expose the enemy to the light, *or even first to make the enemy*, so that this standing against the enemy may happen and so that Dasein may not lose its edge" (italics mine). Does this not imply that, if there is no enemy out there to be discovered, we are justified in "making" (fabricating) it so that our people's movement will not "lose its edge," that is, so that it will be able to assert its will and program in contrast to the enemy? Did Hitler not do exactly this when he "made the enemy" out of Jews? Did Stalin not do exactly this in fabricating ever new enemy plots to sustain the unity of the Party?

However, it is much more important to bear in mind the radical difference between this mode of *polemos* and the authentic (not Stalinist) notion of class struggle. Even if, in Heidegger's *polemos*, the enemy is "internal," it remains a foreign intruder who penetrated the very heart of our people's Dasein, sapping its innermost possibilities, posing a threat to its unity. In other words, Heideggerian *polemos* relates to an enemy (in this case, the Jew) who is a threat to the hierarchic/organic unity of the leader and the people, while, from the Marxist perspective, *there is no such unity*, that is, every such unity is an ideological fake: *polemos* is the class antagonism which cuts across the very heart of a people.

Anti-Semitism "reifies" (embodies in a particular group of people) the inherent social antagonism: it treats Jewishness as the Thing which, from outside, intrudes into the social body and disturbs its balance. What happens in the passage from the position of strict class struggle to the Fascist anti-Semitism is not just a simple replacement of one figure of the enemy (bourgeoisie, the ruling class) with another (Jews); the logic of the struggle is totally different. In the class struggle, classes themselves are caught in the antagonism which is inherent to social structure, while the Jew is a foreign intruder which causes social antagonism, so that all we need in order to restore social harmony is to annihilate Jews. That is to say, in exactly the same way Freud's Wolfman as a child resuscitated the scene of the parental coitus in order to organize his infantile sexual theories, a Fascist anti-Semite elevates the Jew into the monstrous Thing that causes social decadence.

It is worthwhile to recall here Ernst Nolte's book on Heidegger: the merit of Nolte is to approach seriously the task of grasping Nazism as a feasible political project, of trying to re-create "the story the Nazis were telling themselves about themselves," which is a *sine qua non* of its effective criticism; the same has to be done for Stalinism. Nolte also formulated the basic terms and topics of the "revisionist" debate whose basic tenet is to "objectively compare" fascism and Communism: Fascism and even Nazism were ultimately a reaction to the Communist threat and a repetition of its worst practices (concentration camps, mass liquidations of political enemies): "Could it be the case that the National Socialists and Hitler carried out an 'Asiatic' deed [the Holocaust] only because they considered themselves and their kind to be potential or actual victims of a [Bolshevik] 'Asiatic' deed?

Didn't the 'Gulag Archipelago' precede Auschwitz?"[24] Reprehensible as it was, Nazism was thus temporally what appeared after Communism; it was also, with regard to its content, an excessive *reaction* to the Communist threat. Furthermore, all the horrors committed by Nazism merely copied the horrors already committed by Soviet Communism: the reign of the secret police, concentration camps, genocidal terror. . . . Nolte's conclusion is thus that Communism and Nazism share the same totalitarian form, and that the difference concerns only the empirical agents which fill in the same structural places ("Jews" instead of "class enemy," and so on and so forth). One should fully concede Nolte's central point: yes, Nazism was in fact a reaction to the Communist threat; it did indeed just replace class struggle with the struggle between Aryans and Jews—the problem, however, resides in this "just," which is by no means as innocent as it appears. We are dealing here with displacement (*Verschiebung*) in the Freudian sense of the term: Nazism displaces class struggle onto racial struggle and thereby obfuscates its true site. What changes in the passage from Communism to Nazism is the form, and it is in this change of the form that the Nazi ideological mystification resides: the political struggle is naturalized into the racial conflict, the (class) antagonism inherent to the social structure is reduced to the invasion of a foreign (Jewish) body which disturbs the harmony of the Aryan community. The difference between fascism and Communism is thus "formal-ontological": it is not (as Nolte claims) that we have in both cases the same formal antagonistic structure, where only the place of the Enemy is filled in with a different positive element (class, race). In the case of race, we are dealing with a positive naturalized element (the presupposed organic unity of Society is perturbed by the intrusion of the foreign body), while class antagonism is absolutely inherent to and constitutive of the social field—fascism thus obfuscates antagonism, translating it into a conflict of positive opposed terms.

Let us take Stalinism at its most brutal: the de-kulakization of the early 1930s. Stalin's slogan was that "kulaks as a class should be liquidated"— what does this mean? It can mean many things—from taking away their property (land), to forcibly removing them to other areas (say, from Ukraine to Siberia), or simply into gulag—but it did *not* mean simply to kill them all. The goal was to liquidate them *as a class*, not as individuals. Even when the countryside population was purposefully starved (millions of dead in Ukraine, again), the goal was not to kill them all, but to break their backbone, to brutally crush their resistance, to show them who was the master. The difference—minimal, but crucial—persists here with regard to the Nazi de-Judaization, where the ultimate goal effectively was to annihilate them as individuals, to make them disappear as a race. In this sense, then,

Ernst Nolte is right: Nazism *was* a repetition, a copy of Bolshevism—in Nietzsche's terms, it was a profoundly *re-active* phenomenon.

As in the case of sexual difference, then, Heidegger ignores the properly ontological status of class struggle: class struggle is a strife/antagonism which cannot be reduced to an ontic conflict, since it overdetermines the horizon of appearance of all ontic social entities. It is class struggle (social antagonism), not state, which is the mode of Being of a people—state is here to obfuscate this antagonism. Such a radicalized notion of *polemos* as class struggle brings us to the "question of the consciousness of the will of the community" as "a problem in all democracies" (60). Heidegger's idea of political commitment is the unity of people and their leader, who mobilizes them in a shared task of struggle against the (external) enemy, bringing them all together ("accepting" even the proletariat). If, however, we assert class struggle as the *polemos* constitutive of political life, then the problem of the common political will appears in a radically different way: how to build the collective will of the oppressed in the class struggle, the emancipatory will which brings the class *polemos* to its extreme. (And was this will not at work already in the Ancient Greek democracy, was it not operative at the very core of the Athenian *polis*?) This collective will is the crucial component of Communism that "seeks to enable the conversion of work into will. Communism aims to complete the transition, via the struggle of collective self-emancipation, from a suffered necessity to autonomous self-determination. It is the deliberate effort, on a world-historical scale, to universalize the material conditions under which free voluntary action might prevail over involuntary labor or passivity. Or rather: communism is the project through which voluntary action seeks to universalize the conditions for voluntary action."[25] The exemplary case of such activity is given by

> people like Robespierre, Toussaint L'Ouverture or John Brown: confronted with an indefensible institution like slavery, when the opportunity arose they resolved to work immediately and by all available means for its elimination. Che Guevara and Paulo Freire would do the same in the face of imperialism and oppression. Today Dr. Paul Farmer and his 'Partners in Health', in Haiti, Chile and elsewhere, adopt a somewhat similar approach when confronted by indefensible inequalities in the global provision of healthcare. In each case the basic logic is as simple as could be: an idea, like the idea of communism, or equality, or justice, commands that we should strive to realize it without compromises or delay, before the means of such realization have been recognized as feasible or legitimate, or even 'possible'. It is the deliberate

striking towards realization itself that will convert the impossible into the possible, and explode the parameters of the feasible.[26]

Such collective activity—which does not belong to the same space as technological *Gestell* (enframing)—realizes "this actuality of people and leader in which both as a single actuality are not to be separated" (85). Along these lines, Badiou recently[27] proposed a rehabilitation of the Communist-revolutionary "cult of personality": the real of a Truth-Event is inscribed into the space of symbolic fiction through a proper name (of a leader)— Lenin, Stalin, Mao, Che Guevara. . . . Far from signaling the corruption of a revolutionary process, the celebration of the leader's proper name is immanent to the process: to put it in somewhat crude terms, without the mobilizing role of a proper name, the political movement remains caught within the positive order of Being rendered by the conceptual categories— it is only through the intervention of a proper name that the dimension of "demanding the impossible," of changing the very contours of what appears as possible, arises.

What if this "essential possibility" of Communism, ignored by Heidegger himself,[28] and not his continuing hidden fidelity to Fascism, is the truth of his ill-famed doubt about democracy from his posthumously published *Spiegel* interview: "How can any political system be coordinated to the technological age, and which political system would that be? I know of no answer to this question. I am not convinced that it is democracy."[29] How are we to read this statement? The obvious way seems to be that, for Heidegger, a more adequate political response to the technological age than liberal democracy is probably a kind of "totalitarian" socio-political mobilization in the Nazi or Soviet style; the no less obvious counter-argument to such a position is that it ignores how liberal-democratic freedom and individualist hedonism mobilizes individuals much more effectively, turning them into workaholics: "One can wonder as to whether Heidegger was right to suggest, as he did in the *Der Spiegel* interview, that democracy is perhaps not the most adequate response to technology. With the collapse of fascism and of soviet communism, the liberal model has proven to be the most effective and powerful vehicle of the global spread of technology, which has become increasingly indistinguishable from the forces of Capital."[30] But it would also be easy to reply that the rise of the so-called "capitalism with Asian values" in the last decade unexpectedly justifies Heidegger's doubt— this is what is so unsettling about today's China: the suspicion that its authoritarian capitalism is not merely a remainder of our past, the repetition of the process of capitalist accumulation which, in Europe, went on from the sixteenth to the eighteenth century, but a sign of the future. What if it signals that democracy, as we understand it, is no longer a condition and motive force of economic development, but its obstacle?

But what if we take the risk of reading Heidegger's statement on democracy in a different way: the problem he is struggling with is not simply which political order *fits* best the global spread of modern technology; it is, rather, if anything can be done, at the level of political activity, to *counter* the danger to being-human that lurks in modern technology. It never entered Heidegger's mind to propose—say, in a liberal mode—that the failure of the Nazi engagement is merely the failure of a certain kind of engagement which conferred on the political the task of carrying out "a project of onto-destinal significance," so that the lesson of this failure is simply that we should endorse a more *modest* political engagement. Therein resides the limitation of what one may call "liberal Heideggerians" (from Hubert Dreyfus to John Caputo): from the failure of Heidegger's political engagement, they draw the conclusion that one should renounce the prospect of a political engagement with destinal ontological pretensions and engage in "merely ontic," modest, pragmatic politics, leaving destinal questions to poets and thinkers.

The answer of traditional Heideggerians to such a reading would have been, of course, that, in advocating the Communist radicalization of Heidegger's politics, we are falling into the worst trap of the modern subjectivist decisionism of Will, replacing one (Fascist) totalitarianism with its Left mirror-image which is in a way even worse, since, in its "internationalism," it endeavors to erase the last traces of "provincial" homeland, that is, to render people literally rootless (a feature it shares with capitalist liberalism). However, the core of the problem does not reside here, it rather concerns the sphere of capitalist economic life: crazy, tasteless even, as it may sound, the problem with Hitler was that *he was not violent enough*, that his violence was not "essential" enough. Hitler did *not* really act, all his actions were fundamentally *reactions*, that is, he acted so that nothing would really change, he staged a big spectacle of pseudo-Revolution so that the capitalist order could survive. Hannah Arendt was right when (implicitly against Heidegger) she pointed out that Fascism, although a reaction to bourgeois banality, remains its inherent negation, that is, within the horizon of bourgeois society: the true problem of Nazism is not that it "went too far" in its subjectivist-nihilist hubris of exerting total power, but that it did *not* go far enough, that its violence was an impotent acting out which, ultimately, remained in the service of the very order it despised. Hitler's grand gestures of despising the bourgeois self-complacency, etc. were ultimately in the service of enabling this complacency to continue: far from effectively disturbing the much despised "decadent" bourgeois order, far from awakening the Germans from the immersion into its complacency, Nazism was a dream which enabled them to go on.

The fact remains that, as we tried to indicate apropos the status of *polemos* and collective will, Heidegger does not follow his own logic to the end when he endorses the Fascist compromise. To put it in the terms of the well-known metaphor, Fascism wants to throw out the dirty water (of liberal-democratic individualism that comes with capitalism) and keep the baby (of capitalist relations), and the way it tries to do this is, again, to throw out the dirty water (of a radical *polemos* which cuts across the entire social body) and keep the baby (of corporatist unity of the people). What one should do is the exact opposite: throw out both babies (capitalist relations as well as their corporatist pacification) and keep the dirty water of radical struggle. The paradox is thus that, in order to save Heidegger from Nazism, we need *more* will and struggle and *less Gelassenheit*.[31] This, then, is our true choice when we are reading Heidegger's "pro-Nazi" seminars from 1933–4: do we engage in sanctimonious criticism and gloat in the *Besserwisserei* of our later historical position, or do we focus on the missed potentials in these seminars, raising the difficult question of how to resuscitate them in our era when, after the big failure of the twentieth century Communist project, the problems to which Communism tried to answer (radical social conflicts, collective will) are still here.

NOTES

Introduction

1 The official documents and speeches produced by Heidegger as rector have been published in Martin Heidegger, *Reden und andere Zeugnisse eines Lebensweges*, ed. Hermann Heidegger, *Gesamtausgabe* (henceforth GA) vol. 16 (Frankfurt am Main: Vittorio Klostermann, 2000) and in Alfred Denker and Holger Zaborowski, eds, *Heidegger und der Nationalsozialismus I: Dokumente, Heidegger-Jahrbuch* IV (Freiburg: Karl Alber, 2009). The two lecture courses that he delivered in 1933–4 have been published as *Sein und Wahrheit*, ed. Hartmut Tietjen (GA 36/37, 2001), translated by Gregory Fried and Richard Polt as *Being and Truth* (Bloomington: Indiana University Press, 2010).

2 *Heidegger: The Introduction of Nazism into Philosophy in Light of the Unpublished Seminars of 1933–1935*, trans. Michael B. Smith (New Haven: Yale University Press, 2009). Faye's book was originally published in French in 2005. His interpretation of the seminar, in the context of Heidegger's other writings and activities of the time, takes it as evidence of the irredeemably Nazistic character of Heidegger's lifelong views, which in Faye's opinion do not even merit the title of philosophy.

3 "'Über Wesen und Begriff von Natur, Geschichte und Staat': Übung aus dem Wintersemester 1933/34," in Denker and Zaborowski, eds, *Heidegger und der Nationalsozialismus I*, 53–88.

4 *Seminare: Hegel—Schelling*, ed. Peter Trawny, GA 86 (2011), 898.

5 *Sein und Zeit* (Tübingen: Niemeyer, 1953), 384; *Being and Time*, trans. John Macquarrie and Edward Robinson (New York: Harper & Row, 1962), 436; *Being and Time*, trans. Joan Stambaugh, revised by Dennis J. Schmidt (Albany: SUNY, 2010), 366. It is possible to read *Being and Time* as an essentially political work in an ontological guise. See Johannes Fritsche, *Historical Destiny and National Socialism in Heidegger's "Being and Time"* (Berkeley: University of California Press, 1999) and William H. F. Altman, *Martin Heidegger and the First World War: "Being and Time" as Funeral Oration* (Lanham, MD: Lexington Books, 2012).

6 The Rectoral Address and some political texts of the period are translated in Richard Wolin, ed., *The Heidegger Controversy: A Critical Reader*, 2nd edn (Cambridge: MIT Press, 1993).

7 *Being and Truth*, 73.

8 E. G. Kolbenheyer, *Lebenswert und Lebenswirkung der Dichtkunst in einem Volke* (Munich: Albert Langen-Georg Müller, 1935). Kolbenheyer argues that literature must contribute to the "self-assertion of a people" (5), for each people must form its specific "life-domain" (7) based on communal realities that "constitute the sense and value of our existence" (16). Art must be judged in terms of whether it supports the "struggle for existence" of the nation to which the artist owes his life (20). The "struggle of life against inferior humanity" requires us to suppress "devastating art" (21).

9 *Logik als die Frage nach dem Wesen der Sprache*, ed. Günter Seubold (GA 38, 1998); *Logic as the Question Concerning the Essence of Language*, trans. Wanda Torres Gregory and Yvonne Unna (Albany: SUNY Press, 2009).

10 Peter Trawny, Marcia Sá Cavalcante Schuback, and Michael Marder, eds, *Heidegger on Hegel's "Philosophy of Right": The 1934–5 Seminar and Interpretative Essays* (London: Bloomsbury, 2014). The German text is included in GA 86.

11 *Hölderlins Hymnen "Germanien" und "Der Rhein,"* ed. Susanne Ziegler (GA 39, 1980), 290–4.

12 *Einführung in die Metaphysik* (Tübingen: Niemeyer, 1953), 152; *Introduction to Metaphysics*, trans. Gregory Fried and Richard Polt, 2nd edn (New Haven: Yale University Press, 2014).

13 The original lecture courses on Nietzsche are *Der Wille zur Macht als Kunst*, ed. Bernd Heimbüchel (GA 43, 1985); *Nietzsches metaphysische Grundstellung im abendländischen Denken: Die ewige Wiederkehr des Gleichen*, ed. Marion Heinz (GA 44, 1986); *Nietzsches Lehre vom Willen zur Macht als Erkenntnis*, ed. Eberhard Hanser (GA 47, 1989); and *Nietzsche: Der europäische Nihilismus*, ed. Petra Jaeger (GA 48, 1986). The version of these and related texts published in 1961 can be found in *Nietzsche I*, ed. Brigitte Schillbach (GA 6.1, 1996) and *Nietzsche II*, ed. Brigitte Schillbach (GA 6.2, 1997); these volumes have been translated as *Nietzsche*, 4 vols, ed. David Farrell Krell (New York: Harper & Row, 1979–87). For examples of the depoliticization of the Nietzsche lectures in their postwar form, see the Appendix to Gregory Fried, *Heidegger's Polemos: From Being to Politics* (New Haven: Yale University Press, 2000).

14 *Zu Ernst Jünger*, ed. Peter Trawny (GA 90, 2004).

15 Richard Polt, "Beyond Struggle and Power: Heidegger's Secret Resistance," *Interpretation* 35:1 (Fall 2007): 11–40.

16 "Evening Conversation: In a Prisoner of War Camp in Russia, between a Younger and an Older Man," in *Country Path Conversations*, trans. Bret W. Davis (Bloomington: Indiana University Press, 2010).

17 *Bremen and Freiburg Lectures: Insight Into That Which Is and Basic Principles of Thinking,* trans. Andrew J. Mitchell (Bloomington: Indiana University Press, 2012), 27.

18 *Introduction to Metaphysics,* German p. 22.

19 Ibid., German p. 127. On this theme cf. Richard Capobianco, *Engaging Heidegger* (Toronto: University of Toronto Press, 2010), Chapter 3. Capobianco shows that Heidegger's later work emphasizes home over homelessness.

20 Heidegger's statement is a mild version of a cliché that Schmitt was to express with full anti-Jewish venom during the war: "The real misunderstanding of the Jewish people with respect to everything that concerns soil, land, and territory is grounded in its style of political existence. The relation of a people to a soil formed by its own work of settlement and culture and to the concrete forms of power that arise from this is incomprehensible to the mind of the Jew. He does not, moreover, even wish to understand this, but rather only to dominate these relations conceptually in order to set his own concepts in their place. 'Comprendre c'est détruire,' as a French Jew once betrayed of himself. These Jewish authors have of course as little created the hitherto existing spatial theories as they have created anything else. But they were, here as elsewhere, an important fermenting agent in the dissolution of concrete, spatially determined orders": Carl Schmitt, "The *Großraum* Order" (1941), in *Writings on War,* trans. and ed. Timothy Nunan (Cambridge: Polity, 2011), 121–2, translation modified.

Session 1

1 The original consists of 19 unnumbered pages in Latin script. The protocol was written by Karl Siegel. [Notes are by editors Alfred Denker and Holger Zaborowski, except translators' notes, which are enclosed in brackets.]

2 [*Dasein*, literally "Being there," usually means "existence" in general. In Heidegger it refers to the distinctively human way of Being. We follow most translators in leaving the word in German.]

Session 2

1 The original consists of eight unnumbered pages in German script. The protocol was written by Wolfgang Feuerschutze.

Session 3

1 The original consists of ten unnumbered pages in German script. The protocol was written by Marliese Kremer (?).

Session 4

1 The original consists of seven numbered pages in German script. The protocol was written by Fritz Kaulbach.
2 [Cf. *Critique of Pure Reason*, A33/B49. Kant writes "all [*alle*] intuitions," not "alone [*allein*] intuitions"; the *allein* is found only in the text edited by Benno Erdmann (Leipzig: Leopold Voss, 1878).]
3 [Perhaps a reference to Heidegger's contemporaneous lecture course "On the Essence of Truth," where earlier in the semester he had argued, "The animal does not speak because it cannot speak. And it cannot because it does not need to speak . . . . it is not *compelled by need*": *Being and Truth*, trans. Gregory Fried and Richard Polt (Bloomington: Indiana University Press, 2010), 80.]

Session 5

1 The original consists of 14 unnumbered pages in German script. The author is not indicated.

Session 6

1 The original consists of six pages in Roman script. The protocol was written by Ital Gelzer.
2 [Reading *Verengungen,* with Klaus Stichweh's transcription, for *Abweichungen* in the *Heidegger-Jahrbuch* text. We have relied on the Stichweh transcription as well as Marion Heinz's reading of the original manuscript to correct some passages in the *Heidegger-Jahrbuch* text in the remainder of this session.]

3   [Reading *begrenzten* for *bevorzugten.*]
4   [Reading *daß "politisch" gleichgesetzt werden konnte etwa mit "gerissen,"
    und Politiker einen bedeutete, der verstand, mit parlamentarischen Kniffen
    etwas anzudrehen.*]
5   [Reading *Mensch* for *Kampf.*]
6   [Reading *und das um so ausgesprochener, je mehr sie durch gewaltige
    Leistungen erweitert wurden und somit eben spezialisiert wurden. In den
    Folgezeiten aber ließ man die sämtlichen Kulturgebeite nur immer weiter
    ins Unübersehbare auseinanderwachsen.*]
7   [Reading *naive* for *gewisse.*]
8   [Reading *nur die verstehen, welche den Stellungsbefehl erhalten, und auch
    etwas anderes als die bloße Summe.*]

Session 7

1   The original consists of 12 2/3 pages in Latin script. The protocol was
    written by Ingeborg Schroth.
2   The last three words were added in pencil by Heidegger.
3   The last five words were added in pencil by Heidegger.
4   [Roman consul in 503 BC. According to Livy's history of Rome (2.32),
    Menenius calmed a plebeian rebellion by citing Aesop's fable in which
    the members of the body rebel against the belly, but then realize they
    are starving. See also Shakespeare, *Coriolanus* 1.1; Marx, *Capital*, vol. I,
    chap. 14, sec. 5.]

Session 8

1   The original consists of 21 unnumbered pages in Latin script. The
    protocol was written by Helmut Ibach.

Session 9

1   The original consists of ten numbered pages in Latin script. The protocol
    was written by Emil Schill.

Session 10

1 The original consists of 12 numbered pages in Latin script. The author is not indicated.

2 [Hitler was known as "the drummer" (*der Trommler*) in the early years of the Nazi party.]

3 [Jean Bodin, 1529/30–96.]

4 The reference is to the Great Elector Friedrich Wilhelm I of Brandenburg (1620–88). The sentence quoted was inscribed over the portal of the royal palace in Berlin. Cf. G. Oestreich, "Calvinismus, Neustoizismus und Preußentum," in Otto Büsch and Wolfgang Neugebauer, eds, *Moderne Preußische Geschichte 1648–1947: Eine Anthologie* (Berlin: Walter de Gruyter, 1981), 1268–93, 1283.

1. *Volk* and *Führer*

1 *Heidegger, l'introduction du nazisme dans la philosophie. Autour des séminaires inédits de 1933–1935* (Paris: Albin Michel, 2005). I will cite the English translation by Michael B. Smith (New Haven: Yale University Press, 2009). For the debate around Faye's book, cf. Jürg Altwegg, "Wirkt sein Gift bis heute? Frankreich debattiert über Heidegger als Hitlers Philosoph," *Frankfurter Allgemeine Zeitung*, May 21, 2005, 31; Emmanuel Faye, "Der Nationalsozialismus in die Philosophie: Sein, Geschichtlichkeit, Technik und Vernichtung in Heideggers Werk," in Hans J. Sandkühler, ed., *Vergessen? Verdrängt? Erinnert? Philosophie im Nationalsozialismus* (Bremen: University of Bremen, 2008), 53–73; Emmanuel Faye, "Wie die Nazi-Ideologie in die Philosophie einzog," *Zeit Online* 34/2005 (www.zeit.de/2005/34/AntwortHeidegger, accessed April 16, 2009); Anton M. Fischer, *Martin Heidegger: Der gottlose Priester, Psychogramm eines Denkers* (Zürich: Rüffer und Rub, 2008); Kurt Flasch, "Er war ein nationalsozialistischer Philosoph," *Süddeutsche Zeitung*, May 14, 2005, 16; Hassan Givsan, *Heidegger – das Denken der Inhumanität: Eine ontologische Auseinandersetzung mit Heideggers Denken* (Würzburg: Königshauser & Neumann, 1998); Walter Hanser, "Eine Wurzelbehandlung," *Junge Welt*, May 27, 2005, 12; Reinhard Linde, *Bin ich, wenn ich nicht denke? Studien zur Entkräftung, Wirkung und Struktur totalitären Denkens* (Herbolzheim: Centaurus, 2003); Reinhard Linde, "Devil's Power's Origin: Zur Problematik der 'Einführung des Nazismus in die Philosophie' durch Heidegger,"

Aufklärung und Kritik 2/2008, 175–92; Gabriele Meierding, "Die Sucht nach Größe," *Spiegel Online*, November 6, 2005 (www.spiegel.de/kultur/ literatur/0,1518,383197,00.html, accessed April 16, 2009); Thomas Meyer, "Denker für Hitler?" *Zeit Online* 30/2005 (www.zeit.de/2005/30/ Heidegger, accessed April 16, 2009); Henning Ritter, "Aus dem eigenen Dasein sprach schon das deutsche," *Frankfurter Allgemeine Zeitung*, October 29, 2005, 45; Bernhard H. F. Taureck, "Martin Heidegger und das Ende einer Hermeneutik der Unschuldigsprechung," *Freitext: Kultur- und Gesellschaftsmagazin*, April 2006, 41; Dieter Thomä, "Alle zwanzig Jahre wieder: Eine neue französische Debatte über Heidegger und den Nationalsozialismus," *Neue Zürcher Zeitung*, June 30, 2005; Robin Celikates, "Heidegger and National Socialism: New Contributions to an Old Debate," *H-Net Reviews in the Humanities and Social Sciences*, March 2006.

2 Faye, *Heidegger*, xxiv. On the various interpretations of Heidegger's engagement in National Socialism, see Thomä's concise survey in Dieter Thomä, ed., *Heidegger-Handbuch: Leben – Werk – Wirkung* (Stuttgart/ Weimar: J. B. Metzler, 2003), 141–62, 159ff. Cf. also Marion Heinz and Goran Gretić, eds, *Philosophie und Zeitgeist im Nationalsozialismus* (Würzburg: Königshausen & Neumann, 2006): on Heidegger, see Marion Heinz, "Die Politisierung der Philosophie: Heideggers Vorlesung 'Welt, Endlichkeit, Einsamkeit' (WS 1929/30)," 269–90; Theodore Kisiel, "The Essential Flaw in Heidegger's 'Private National Socialism,'" 291–311; Beate Obst, "Heideggers seynsgeschichtlicher Antikommunismus," 313–26.

3 Heidegger's papers continue to be only partially available for research: texts that have already appeared in print may be used without further ado; in order to inspect other manuscripts one needs special permission from the administrator of his *Nachlass*, who must also agree to any use of these manuscripts with the purpose of publication. When I was visiting the Marbach Literary Archive in May 1999, I was mistakenly handed a folder containing the protocols of the seminar on *Nature, History, and State*. This is notable because until then, this folder was completely unknown to scholarship. In the reading room I began to prepare a handwritten copy of the text—a photocopy could not be made. Shortly thereafter I sent a typed version of this copy to my colleagues Theodore Kisiel and Alfred Denker. As far as I know, my partial copy was then supplemented by Klaus Stichweh, and this completed text circulated among a few scholars. It was difficult to publish about this seminar in Germany for legal reasons. It is all the more gratifying that the text could finally appear in 2009.

4 Cf. Faye, *Heidegger*, xxiv–xxv.

5 Ibid., 113.

6 This makes it clear that the *bios politikos* can no longer be taken as the *entelecheia* of the human being qua rational animal, and that the character of political community can no longer be defined on the basis of this human essence. If Heidegger substitutes his concept of temporal Dasein for the concept of the rational animal, this replacement of *essentia* by temporal existence permeates the essence of the political community in which Dasein is supposed to be fulfilled. Just as individual existence in *Being and Time* comes to a resolution by taking over itself in its past on the basis of its future, resolving on particular possibilities of existence in the moment of vision, now we must decide on the essence of the political community as *telos* of Dasein on the basis of the historical moment that is grounded in future and past.

7 Faye notes that Heidegger's reflections on political history rely on Stadelmann: Faye, *Heidegger*, 123–8.

8 Herbert Marcuse, "The Struggle Against Liberalism in the Totalitarian View of the State," in *Negations: Essays in Critical Theory* (Boston: Beacon Press, 1968). Cf. Sabine Doyé, "Deutsche Philosophie und Zeitgeschichte," in Heinz and Gretić, eds, *Philosophie und Zeitgeist im Nationalsozialismus*, 215–31.

9 Heidegger himself distinguishes himself in this seminar from Carl Schmitt's understanding of the political on the basis of the friend-enemy relationship with the following remark: "a decisive aspect of this view is that the political unit does not have to be identical with state and people" (Session 8, 46).

10 Faye, *Heidegger*, xxv.

11 See Marion Heinz, "'Schaffen.' Revolution der Philosophie. Zu Heideggers Nietzsche-Interpretation (1936/37)," in Alfred Denker and Holger Zaborowski, eds, *Heidegger und Nietzsche*, Heidegger-Jahrbuch 2 (Freiburg/Munich: Karl Alber, 2005), 174–92; Heinz, "Politisierung der Philosophie," in Heinz and Gretić, *Philosophie und Zeitgeist im Nationalsozialismus*, 269–90.

12 See Heidegger's lecture course of 1937 *Nietzsches metaphysische Grundstellung im abendländischen Denken: Die ewige Wiederkehr des Gleichen*, ed. Marion Heinz, *Gesamtausgabe* vol. 44 (Frankfurt am Main: Vittorio Klostermann, 1986). A translation of the postwar edited version of the text is available as *Nietzsche*, vol. 2, *The Eternal Recurrence of the Same*, trans. David Farrell Krell (San Francisco: Harper & Row, 1984).

13 [*Wende der Not*: a play on *Notwendigkeit*, "necessity." See Nietzsche, *Thus Spoke Zarathustra*, Part III, "On the Great Longing." Cf. Heidegger, *Nietzsche*, vol. 2, 207. —Translators]

2. Heidegger in purgatory

1 See, for example, Heidegger's postwar exchange with Herbert Marcuse, available in translation in Richard Wolin, *The Heidegger Controversy: A Critical Reader* (Cambridge: MIT Press, 1993), 152–64.

2 On the distinction between positive and negative implication, see Julian Young, *Heidegger, Nazism, Philosophy* (Cambridge, UK: Cambridge University Press, 1997).

3 A noteworthy example is Hannah Arendt, whose portrait, "Martin Heidegger at Eighty," combines an admiring encomium to Heidegger as a teacher with a highly ambivalent assessment of Heidegger as an other-worldly Platonist whose absorption with philosophical matters distorted his understanding of this-worldly political events. For a summary of this verdict, see Dana R. Villa, *Arendt and Heidegger: The Fate of the Political* (Princeton: Princeton University Press, 1995), esp. 230 and ff.

4 Victor Klemperer, *LTI-Lingua Tertii Imperii: Notizbuch eines Philologen*, 2nd edn (originally published in 1947) (Berlin: Aufbau Verlag, 1949); in English as *The Language of the Third Reich: LTI-Lingua Tertii Imperii: A Philologist's Notebook*, trans. Martin Brady (London: Continuum Press, 2006); also see Anke Sißmeier, *Der Eingriff in die sprachliche Alltagswelt . . . Propagandistische Sprache im Nationalsozialismus als erfolgsorientierte Kommunikationsform* (GRIN Verlag, 2003).

5 Hereafter cited with reference to the pagination of the translation in this volume.

6 See Richard Wolin, *The Politics of Being: The Political Thought of Martin Heidegger* (New York: Columbia University Press, 1992), 5.

7 Quoted from Thomas Sheehan, "Heidegger and the Nazis," *The New York Review of Books* 35:10 (June 16, 1988), who takes this from Guido Schneeberger, *Nachlese zu Heidegger: Dokumente zu seinem Leben und Denken* (Bern, 1962), 137.

8 See Heidegger's claim from his 1966 interview with *Der Spiegel*, where he says: "My judgement was this: insofar as I could judge things, only one possibility was left, and that was to attempt to stem the coming development by means of constructive powers which were still viable." Quoted from "Nur noch ein Gott kann uns retten: Der Philosoph Martin Heidegger über sich und sein Denken," in *Der Spiegel*, as translated in English as "'Only a God Can Save Us': *Der Spiegel's* Interview with Martin Heidegger (1966)," in Wolin, *The Heidegger Controversy*, 91–116; quote from 92.

9 As quoted by Hugo Ott, *Zeitschrift des Breisgau-Geschichtsvereins* (1984), 116; cited by Thomas Sheehan, "Heidegger and the Nazis."

10 Martin Heidegger, "German Men and Women!" in Wolin, *The Heidegger Controversy*, 47.

11 Ibid.

12 Martin Heidegger, *Being and Time*, trans. John Macquarrie and Edward Robinson (New York: Harper and Row, 1962), hereafter abbreviated as BT. German citations from Martin Heidegger, *Sein und Zeit* (Tübingen: Niemeyer, 1967), hereafter abbreviated as SZ. Quoted here from BT, 32; SZ, 12.

13 BT, 191–2; SZ, 150–1.

14 See my remarks on these statements, above.

15 Note that the last three words "and brings about" were added in pencil by Heidegger when he read the student's protocol.

16 Heidegger's original phrase was: "Bildung ist ganz gleichgültig, sehen Sie nur seine wunderbaren Hände an!" As quoted by Karl Jaspers, *Philosophische Autobiographie. Erweiterte Neuausgabe* (Munich: Piper, 1977), 101.

17 For *Zuhandenheit* see esp. the section on "Involvement and Significance" in BT, 114–22; SZ, 76–83.

18 See the account of the guardians in Plato, *Republic* 371e and ff.

19 Karl Jaspers, *Notizen zu Martin Heidegger*, ed. Hans Saner (Munich: Piper, 1978), 183.

20 Martin Heidegger, "The Self Assertion of the German University," in Günther Neske and Emil Kettering, eds, *Martin Heidegger and National Socialism: Questions and Answers* (New York: Paragon House, 1990), 5–15.

21 For Heidegger's ambition to transform education, see Iain Thomson, *Heidegger on Ontotheology: Technology and the Politics of Education* (Cambridge: Cambridge University Press, 2005).

22 See esp. BT, 135–48; SZ, 102–13.

23 See, for example, BT, 91–5; SZ, 63–6.

24 For the text and analysis, see Ulrich Sieg, "Die Verjudung des deutschen Geistes," *Die Zeit*, December 22, 1989, Feuilleton, 52.

25 Klemperer, *The Language of the Third Reich*, 166.

26 Klemperer, *The Language of the Third Reich*, 167, my emphasis.

27 It is worth noting that such a view of intuitive belonging ignores Heidegger's own philosophical view that collective identification is conditional not merely upon thrownness (*Geworfenheit*) but *also* upon projection (*Entwurf*). Because Dasein is a being that necessarily takes a stand on its own existence, its communal-historical being is available only insofar as it has resolved upon the heritage into which it is thrown. The seminar betrays this requirement and endorses a portrait of Dasein that is far too passive and objectivistic. On the requirement of resoluteness, see, for example, BT, 438; SZ, 386.

28 See Graham Parkes, "Thoughts on the Way: *Being and Time* via Lao-Chuang," in *Heidegger and Asian Thought*, ed. Graham Parkes (Honolulu: University of Hawaii Press, 1987), 105–44.

29 BT, 16.

30 BT, §23, 138ff.; SZ 104ff.

31 Klemperer, *The Language of the Third Reich*, 92.

32 Ibid.

33 On the method of formal indication, see, for example, Heidegger's nuanced effort to explain how the first-person pronoun "I" can be used even in an ontological inquiry that purports to work out its meanings *prior* to any metaphysical commitments regarding the ontic self: BT, 151–2; SZ, 116–7.

34 Hannah Arendt, "Martin Heidegger at Eighty," *The New York Review of Books*, October 21, 1971.

35 Heidegger, "Letter to Karl Löwith on His Philosophical Identity" (August 19, 1921), in Theodore Kisiel and Thomas Sheehan, eds, *Becoming Heidegger: On the Trail of his Early Occasional Writings* (Evanston: Northwestern University Press, 2007), 99–102; quote from 99–100; my emphasis on "this Dasein is one with existence."

36 For Heidegger's idea of "deworlding", see my essay "Science, Realism, and the Unworlding of the World," in Mark Wrathall and Hubert Dreyfus, eds, *A Companion to Phenomenology and Existentialism* (Oxford: Blackwell, 2006), 425–44.

37 On the themes of homelessness and homecoming, see Richard Capobianco, *Engaging Heidegger* (Toronto: University of Toronto Press, 2010), esp. 52ff.

38 Emmanuel Levinas, *Totality and Infinity: An Essay on Exteriority*, trans. Alphonso Lingis (Pittsburgh: Duquesne University Press, 1969); see, for example, the remark on philosophy as an adventure homeward like that of Ulysses, "Preface," 27.

39 Alexander Pope, "*Peri Bathous*, or, The Art of Sinking in Poetry," in *The Works of Alexander Pope*, ed. John Wilson Croker, vol. 10. (London: John Murray, 1886), 344–409.

40 Heidegger, "The Self Assertion of the German University," 4.

41 Jacques Derrida, *Of Spirit: Heidegger and the Question*, trans. Geoffrey Bennington and Rachel Bowlby (Chicago: University of Chicago Press, 1991).

42 For another contemporary illustration of this interrogation of "spirit" see the summer semester 1933 lecture course, "The Fundamental Question of Philosophy," in *Being and Truth*, trans. Gregory Fried and Richard Polt (Bloomington: Indiana University Press, 2010), esp. 3–6.

43 For more on this theme, see my critical review of Emmanuel Faye, *Heidegger: The Introduction of Nazism into Philosophy in Light of the Unpublished Seminars of 1933–35*, trans. Michael B. Smith (New

Haven: Yale University Press, 2009), published online in *Notre Dame Philosophical Reviews*, March 12, 2010, http://ndpr.nd.edu/news/24316/

44 Karl Löwith, "My Last Meeting with Heidegger in Rome," in Wolin, *The Heidegger Controversy*.

3. Who belongs? Heidegger's philosophy of the *Volk* in 1933–4

1 Christopher M. Hutton, *Race and the Third Reich: Linguistics, Racial Anthropology and Genetics in the Dialectic of Volk* (Cambridge: Polity Press, 2005), 3. This book should be required reading for anyone writing on Heidegger and the *Volk*.

2 See Charles Bambach, *Heidegger's Roots* (Ithaca: Cornell University Press, 2003), xv.

3 Alfred Rosenberg, *Krisis und Neubau Europas* (Berlin: Jünker und Dünnhaupt, 1934). Quoted in Aurel Kolnai, *The War Against the West* (New York: Viking Press, 1938), 522.

4 The rivalry between Krieck and Heidegger should not be underemphasized. See Gerhard Ritter, "Die Universität Freiburg im Hitlerreich," in *Die Freibürger Philosophische Fakultät 1920–1960* (Freiburg: Karl Alber, 2006), 782.

5 Joseph Goebbels, "Fighting League for German Culture," in *The Weimar Sourcebook*, eds, Anton Kaess et al. (Berkeley: University of California Press, 1995), 143.

6 On the Rosenberg Amt, see Reinhard Bollmus, *Das Amt Rosenberg und seine Gegner. Zum Machtkampf im nationalsozialistischen Herrschaftssystem* (Stuttgart: Deutsche Verlag, 1970). As soon as Walter Gross was appointed to the dictatorship of the Office of Racial Policy (Rassenpolitisches Amt des NSDAP) he placed Heidegger under scrutiny. Erich Jaensch obliged with a vicious report. See Hugo Ott, *Martin Heidegger. Unterwegs zu seiner Biographie* (Frankfurt: Campus, 1988), 240–6; trans. Alan Blunden, *Martin Heidegger: A Political Life* (New York: Basic Books, 1993), 253–360. See also Michael Grüttner's correction of Ott in "Das Scheitern der Vordenker," in *Geschichte und Emanzipation. Festschrift fur Reinhard Rürup*, eds, M. Grüttner et al. (Frankfurt: Campus, 1999), 460–1.

7 See Peter Weingart, *Doppel-Leben* (Frankfurt: Campus, 1995), 137–48. Also Robert Bernasconi, "Ludwig Ferdinand Clauss and Racialization" in Lester Embree and Thomas Nenon, eds, *Husserl's Ideen* (Dordrecht: Springer, 2013), 55–70. For Walter Gross's racial views, see, for example,

Heilig is das Blut. Eine Rundfunkrede (Berlin: Vom Rassenpolitischen Amt, 1935).

8   Although there are one or two places where Heidegger appears to accept the term *Rasse*, it is not the biological conception of some of his contemporaries. On Heidegger's relation to the biological in this context see Robert Bernasconi, "Heidegger's Alleged Challenge to the Nazi Concepts of Race," in James E. Faulconer and Mark A. Wrathall, eds, *Appropriating Heidegger* (Cambridge: Cambridge University Press, 2000), 50–67. See also Sonia Sikka, "Heidegger and Race," in *Race and Racism in Continental Philosophy*, ed. Robert Bernasconi with Sybol Cook (Bloomington: Indiana University Press, 2003), 74–97.

9   The reduction of National Socialism to biological or somatic racism is attacked by Wolfgang Fritz Haug, *Die Faschisierung des bürgerlichen Subjekts* (Hamburg: Argument, 1987), 55–69.

10 Ulrich Sieg, "'Die Verjudung des deutschen Geistes.' Ein unbekannter Brief Heideggers," *Die Zeit*, December 22, 1989, 50.

11 Translated by Gregory Fried and Richard Polt as *Introduction to Metaphysics* (New Haven: Yale University Press, 2000), 213. Henceforth IM. On the meaning of this phrase and its textual history, see Theodore Kisiel, "Heidegger's Philosophical Politics in the Third Reich," in Richard Polt and Gregory Fried, eds, *A Companion to Heidegger's "Introduction to Metaphysics"* (New Haven: Yale University Press, 2001), 241–2. Frank Edler's work on Heidegger's relation to Baeumler is a fine example of the kind of close reading we need more of: Frank H. W. Edler, "Alfred Baeumler on Hölderlin and the Greeks: Reflections on the Heidegger-Baeumler Relationship," www.janushead.org/jhspg99/edler.cfm, accessed December 4, 2012.

12 Translated by Wanda Torres Gregory and Yvonne Unna as *Logic as the Question Concerning the Essence of Language* (Albany: State University of New York Press, 2009). Henceforth L.

13 Of course, Hitler did not in fact assume the Presidency until Hindenburg died on August 2, 1934.

14 Emmanuel Faye describes it as "the text in which the control axis of Heidegger's doctrine—namely, his idea of the people—appears the most clearly," *Heidegger. L'introduction du nazisme dans la philosophie* (Paris: Albin Michel, 2005), 164; trans. Michael B. Smith, *Heidegger. The Introduction of Nazism into Philosophy* (New Haven: Yale University Press, 2009), 99. Nevertheless, Faye devotes only four pages to the course and by mining the work for incriminating quotations fundamentally misreads it, as will be clear from a comparison between his discussion and mine here. Most of the mere three pages Holger Zaborowski dedicates to this course in a book of almost 800 pages seem designed to answer Faye, but by failing to offer his own reading the critique is incomplete: *"Eine Frage von Irre und Schuld?"* Martin

Heidegger und der Nationalsozialismus (Frankfurt am Main: Fischer, 2010), 467–9. The most sustained treatment is by Bernard Radloff in *Heidegger and the Question of National Socialism* (Toronto: University of Toronto Press, 2007), 173–209. He provides a good summary of the ideas of some Nazi theorists with whom Heidegger can be compared (111–72), but this is then left behind when he begins his dense account of Heidegger's own ideas.

15 For more on this complex issue which Jacques Derrida brought to the fore, see Bernasconi, "Heidegger's Alleged Challenge to the Nazi Concepts of Race," 55–6.

16 Perhaps the most extreme proponent of this view is Johannes Fritsche. See his *Historical Destiny and National Socialism in Heidegger's Being and Time* (Berkeley: University of California Press, 1999), pp. 126–42, and "Heidegger's *Being and Time* and National Socialism," *Philosophy Today* 56:3 (2012), 255–84.

17 On Heidegger's relation to Baeumler's account of Nietzsche, see my essay "Heidegger, Nietzsche, National Socialism" in Eric Nelson and François Raffoul, eds, *The Bloomsbury Companion to Heidegger* (London: Bloomsbury, 2013), 47–53.

18 Oswald Spengler, *Der Untergang des Abendlandes* (Vienna and Leipzig: Wilhelm Braumüller, 1918 and Munich: Oskar Beck, 1922).

19 Karl Lamprecht, *Moderne Geschichtswissenschaft* (Freiburg: Hermann Heyfelder, 1905), 85; trans. E. A. Andrews, *What is History?* (London: Macmillan, 1905), 150–1. See also Karl J. Weintraub, *Visions of Culture* (Chicago: University of Chicago Press, 1966), 166–7.

20 Roger Chickering, *Karl Lamprecht* (Atlantic Highlands, NJ: Humanities Press, 1993), 352–66.

21 It should also be noted that there are even more problems with the editing of Heidegger's 1934 *Logic* course than is usual for volumes of the *Gesamtausgabe*. At the time that the *Gesamtausgabe* volume was prepared Heidegger's own notes for the lectures could not be located. I am grateful to Richard Polt for providing me with a copy of Silvio Vietta's essay which includes a brief comparison between organization of the lectures as published and of the manuscript which had been found in the possession of members of his family: "Wandel unseres Daseins. Eine Unbekannte Vorlesung Martin Heideggers von 1934," *Frankfurter Allgemeine*, November 9, 2006. The text subsequently appeared in an auction catalogue but was withdrawn before the sale and, so far as I know, its current location is unknown.

22 In a speech to German scholars in November 1933 Heidegger called for a "folkish science" (*völkische Wissenschaft*) (GA 16; 191). He associated it with courage for "a total transformation of our German existence" that would happen though decision and responsibility (GA 16: 191–2). See the insightful comments by James Phillips on Heidegger's subsequent withdrawal from this phrase early in his book, although I am less convinced about what he has to say about it later in the book: *Heidegger's Volk: Between National Socialism and Poetry* (Stanford: Stanford University Press, 2005), 3–4 and 111–2.

23 One should beware any temptation to understand the fact that, for Heidegger the *Volk* is always to come, as a form of resistance to Nazi ideas of the *Volk*, which are often assumed to be backward looking and more essentialist than that. For many prominent Nazis, including Rosenberg, the *Volk* was also in the process of becoming, just as for Baeumler in an essay from 1934 it was futural: Alfred Rosenberg, "Die Volkwerdung der Deutschen," *Nationalsozialistische Monatshefte*, 4 Jg., Heft 39, June 1933, 241–4; Alfred Baeumler, "Der politische Volksbegriff," in *Politik und Erziehung* (Berlin: Junker und Dünnhaupt, 1939), 48.

24 Translated by Peter D. Hertz as *On the Way to Language* (New York: Harper & Row, 1971), 57.

25 Although Heidegger dismissed the idea, he did not do so as forcefully as Hans Freyer did in *Soziologie als Wirklichkeitswissenschaft* (Leipzig: B.G. Teubner, 1930), 252.

26 Translated by Gregory Fried and Richard Polt as *Being and Truth* (Bloomington: Indiana University Press, 2010), 201. The phrase *Blut und Boden* was already formulated in the nineteenth century, but it gathered new momentum in 1930 with Richard Walther Darré's *Neuadel aus Blut und Boden* (Munich: J.F. Lehmann, 1930). See especially p. 68, where the close proximity of the two terms is made clear. Darré represents a clear example of the biological conception of the *Volk* that Heidegger was opposing. See also R. Walter Darré, *Das Bauerntum als Lebensquell der Nordischen Rasse* (Munich: J.F. Lehmann, 1929), esp. 353–423. The extent to which *Blut und Boden* was part of the ideology of *Volkskunde* is clarified by Wolfgang Emmerich, *Zur Kritik der Volkstumideologie* (Frankfurt: Suhrkamp, 1971), 122–31.

27 This is most likely a reference to Ludwig Klages. See *Der Geist als Widersacher der Seele* (Bonn: Bouvier, 1969), 395–412. The book was originally published in 1929. On Klages' reputation during the Third Reich, see Tobias Schneider, "Ideologische Grabenkämpfe," *Vierteljahrshefte Zeitgeschichte* 49:2 (2001), 275–94. See also GA 67: 122.

28 Translated by Richard Rojcewicz and André Schuwer as *Basic Questions of Philosophy* (Bloomington: Indiana University Press, 1984), 124.

29 Franz Böhm is often cited as someone offering a parallel attempt to break from Cartesianism, but Böhm's embrace of race and breeding would have been seen by Heidegger as still under the sway of Cartesianism in spite of its author's intentions: *Anti-Cartesianismus. Deutsche Philosophie in Widerstand* (Leipzig: Felix Meiner, 1938), 245.

30 Heidegger had not yet drawn the distinction we find at GA 48: 212 between *Subjektivität* and *Ichheit*. Both terms are used interchangeably at GA 38: 163; L 135. However, it should be noted that Emmanuel Faye, who drew attention to this distinction, misinterpreted its significance, as part of a more systemic distortion of these texts, by insisting that the first term is used "positively" whereas the second is used "negatively." See Emmanuel Faye, "Subjectivity and Race in Heidegger," *Philosophy Today* 55:3 (Fall 2011), 271.

31 For my understanding of the difference between these two approaches, see Robert Bernasconi, *The Question of Language in Heidegger's History of Being* (Atlantic Highlands, NJ: Humanities Press, 1985), 87–9.

32 Carl Schmitt, *Staat, Bewegung, Volk* (Hamburg: Hanseatische Verlagsanstalt, 1935), 32.

33 Ernst Krieck, "Germanischer Mythos und Heideggersche Philosophie," *Volk im Werden* 2:3 (1934), 249.

34 Faye could not be clearer. Or more wrong. He falsely claims that when Heidegger says in the seminar that in the term *Volksgesundheit*, public health, "one also now feels the tie of the unity of blood and stock, the race" (43; see also GA 38: 61; L 53–4), he is underwriting this as the meaning of the *Volk*. Faye, *Heidegger. L'introduction du nazisme dans la philosophie*, 190–201; *Heidegger: The Introduction of Nazism into Philosophy*, 115–21.

35 The significance of Heidegger's adoption of the language of labor (*Arbeit*) from National Socialism at this time should not be underestimated. See Christopher Rickey, *Revolutionary Saints: Heidegger, National Socialism, and Antinomian Politics* (University Park. PA: Penn State University Press, 2002), 201–8.

36 Claudia Koonz, *The Nazi Conscience* (Cambridge, MA: Harvard University Press, 2003), 196.

37 Oskar Becker, "Nordische Metaphysik," *Rasse: Die Monatsschrift der Nordischen Metaphysik* 5 (1938), 88. See Robert Bernasconi, "Race and Earth in Heidegger's Thinking During the Late 1930s," *Southern Journal of Philosophy* 48:1 (March 2010), 53–4.

38 See Hans Grimm, *Volk ohne Raum* (Munich: Albert Langen, 1926). This novel drawing extensively on the author's time in South Africa was heavily influential.

39 Already since the 1920s Heidegger had appealed to the word *Kunde* in a positive sense. Indeed he used it in his translation of *hermeneia* from at least 1923 to 1959 (GA 63: 10 and GA 12: 122). Wanda Torres Gregory and Yvonne Unna's translation of *Kunde* as lore is inspired, whereas the French translation of it by Frédéric Bernard as *la mise au fait* is misguided. See *La logique comme question en quête de la pleine essence du langage* (Paris: Gallimard, 1998), passim.

40 Karl von Spiess, *Deutsche Volkskunde als Erchliesserin deutscher Kultur* (Berlin: Herbert Stubenrauch, 1934), esp. 31. For the broader political

sense of *Volkskunde*, see Karl von Spiess and Edmund Mudrak, *Deutsche Volkskunde als politische Wissenschaft* (Berlin: Herbert Stubenrauch, 1938). See also Rolf Wilhelm Brednich, "Volkskunde—die völkische Wissenschaft von Blut und Boden," in *Die Universität unter dem Nationalsozialismus*, ed., Heinrich Becker (Munich: K.G. Saur, 1987), 313–20.

41 Hannjost Lixfeld, *Folklore and Fascism: The Reich Institute for German Volkskunde* (Bloomington: Indiana University Press, 1994), 32; Bernard Mees, *The Science of the Swastika* (Budapest: Central European Press, 2008), 228–33.

42 Anka Oesterle, "Letzte Autonomieversuche: Der Volkskundler John Meier. Strategie and Taktik des Verbandes deutscher Vereine für Volkskunde 1933–1945," in *Die Freibürger Universität in der Zeit des Nationalsozialismus*, eds, E. John et al. (Freiburg: Ploetz, 1991), 151–62, and "The Office of Ancestral Inheritance and Folklore Scholarship," in *The Nazification of an Academic Discipline*, eds, James R. Dow and Hannjost Lixfeld (Bloomington: Indiana University Press, 1994), 189–205; Hannjost Lixfeld, *Folklore and Fascism*, 22–5; see also Hannjost Lixfeld, "Die Deutsche Forschungsgemeinschaft und die Dachverbände der deutschen Volkskunde im Dritten Reich," in Helge Gerndt (ed.), *Volkskunde und Nationalsozialismus* (Munich: Münchner Vereinigung für Volkskunde, 1989), 69–82.

43 Martin Heidegger, "Die Bedrohung der Wissenschaft," in Dietrich Papenfuss and Otto Pöggeler, eds, *Zur philosophischen Aktualität Heideggers*, vol. 1 (Frankfurt: Klostermann, 1990), 23. See also GA 46: 60 and 281 as well as GA 52: 132.

44 Jerry Z. Muller, *The Other God That Failed: Hans Freyer and the Deradicalization of German Conservatism* (Princeton: Princeton University Press, 1987), 237–45. For an appreciation of Freyer's relation to Lamprecht, see Roger Chickering, "Comment: Hans Freyer," in *Paths of Continuity*, eds, H. Lehmann and James Van Horn Melton (Cambridge: Cambridge University Press, 1994), 231–7.

45 Freyer's role as one of the leading spokespersons of sociology is apparent in *Soziologie als Wirklichkeitswissenschaft* and *Einleitung in die Soziologie* (Leipzig: Quelle und Meyer, 1931). Heidegger rejected sociology at GA 38: 68; L 59.

46 Hans Freyer, "Ethische Normen und Politik," Kant-Studien 35 (1930), 196 and 114, and "Typen und Stufen der Kultur," in *Handwörterbuch der Soziologie*, ed., Alfred Vierkandt (Stuttgart: Ferdinand Enke, 1931), 294–308 with its numerous references to Lamprecht. See also Elfriede Üner, *Soziologie als "geistige Bewegung." Hans Freyers System der Soziologie und die "Leipziger Schule"* (Weinheim: VCH, Acta Humaniora, 1992), 153–65.

47 Muller, *The Other God That Failed*, 286.

48 Hans Freyer, "Die Universität als hohe Schule des Staates," *Die Erziehung* 7 (1932), 674. Also Hans Freyer, *Der Staat* (Leipzig: Fritz Rechfelden, 1925), 153.

49 Hans Freyer, "Zur Philosophie der Technik," *Blätter für deutsche Philosophie* 3 (1927–8), 201. For more on technology, see Hans Freyer, *Die Bewertung der Wirtschaft*, 141–2 and Jeffrey Herf, *Reactionary Modernism* (Cambridge: Cambridge University Press, 1986), 121–9.

50 Georg Lukács, *Die Zerstörung der Vernunft*, Werke 9 (Berlin-Spandau: Hermann Luchterhand, 1962), 564; trans. Peter Palmer, *The Destruction of Reason* (Atlantic Highlands: Humanities Press, 1981), 648. Radloff, *Heidegger and the Question of National Socialism*, 132.

51 Hans Freyer, *Der Staat* (Leipzig: Fritz Rechfelden, 1925), 153.

52 Hans Freyer, "Die geistige Gestalt der Gegenwart und die Volkshochschule," *Die Erziehung* 4 (1929), 283–300; "Zur Bildungskrise der Gegenwart," *Die Erziehung* 6 (1931), 597–626; "Die Universität als hohe Schule des Staates," *Die Erziehung* 7 (1932), 520–37 and 669–89.

53 See Volker Böhnigk, *Kulturanthropologie als Rassenlehre* (Würzburg: Königshausen und Neumann, 2002), 143–4.

54 Hans Freyer, "Arbeitslager und Arbeitsdienst," *Studentwerk*, May/June 1932. Reprinted in *Gespräch und Aktion in Gruppe und Gesellschaft 1919–1969*, eds, Walter Grieff, R. Rudolf Jentsch, and Hans Richter (Frankfurt: dipa, 1970), 148–55.

55 Hans Freyer, *Revolution von Rechts* (Jena: Eugen Diederich, 1931), 63.

56 For example, Rosenberg, *Der Mythus des 20. Jahrunderts*, 485; trans. *The Myth of the Twentieth Century*, 335. The linguistic distance between the idea of "discipline" and "breeding" is misleading because it conceals the easy transference between *Zucht* and *Züchtung* in German. Discussions of *Zucht* can very easily be exclusively about breeding programs. See, for example, Georg Usadel, *Zucht und Ordnung* (Hamburg: Hanseatische Verlagsanstalt, 1935), 15.

57 Hölderlin to Böhlendorf, December 4, 1801. Frequently cited by Heidegger, for example, at GA 39: 290; GA 52: 131; and GA 53: 168.

58 Christopher M. Hutton, *Linguistics and the Third Reich* (London: Routledge, 1998), 1–5.

4. The seminar of winter semester 1933–4 within Heidegger's three concepts of the political

1 This schema (revised) as well as a detailed account of Heidegger's three concepts of the political is to be found in Theodore Kisiel, "In the Middle of Heidegger's Three Concepts of the Political," in François Raffoul and David Pettigrew, eds, *Heidegger and Practical Philosophy* (Albany: SUNY Press, 2002), 135–57. The present essay incorporates portions of Theodore Kisiel, "On the Purported Platonism of Heidegger's Rectoral Address," in Catalin Partenie and Tom Rockmore, eds, *Heidegger and Plato: Toward Dialogue* (Evanston: Northwestern University Press, 2005) and "The Essential Flaw in Heidegger's 'Private National Socialism,'" in Marion Heinz and Goran Gretić, eds, *Philosophie und Zeitgeist im Nationalsozialismus* (Würzburg: Königshausen & Neumann, 2006).

2 This essay will use the following conventions to refer to Heidegger's collected works (*Gesamtausgabe*), published by Vittorio Klostermann (Frankfurt am Main); when a translation exists, it will be listed after the German edition: GA 16 = *Reden und andere Zeugnisse eines Lebensweges, 1910–1976*, ed. Hermann Heidegger (2000); GA 18 = *Grundbegriffe der aristotelischen Philosophie*, ed. Mark Michalski (2002), *Basic Concepts of Aristotelian Philosophy*, trans. Robert D. Metcalf and Mark Basil Tanzer (Bloomington: Indiana University Press, 2009); GA 26 = *Metaphysische Anfangsgründe der Logik im Ausgang von Leibniz*, ed. Klaus Held (1978), *The Metaphysical Foundations of Logic*, trans. Michael Heim (Bloomington: Indiana University Press, 1984); GA 29/30 = *Die Grundbegriffe der Metaphysik: Welt, Endlichkeit, Einsamkeit*, ed. Friedrich-Wilhelm von Herrmann (1983), *The Fundamental Concepts of Metaphysics: World, Finitude, Solitude*, trans. William McNeill and Nicholas Walker (Bloomington: Indiana University Press, 1995); GA 36/37 = *Sein und Wahrheit*, ed. Hartmut Tietjen (2001), *Being and Truth*, trans. Gregory Fried and Richard Polt (Bloomington: Indiana University Press, 2010); GA 38 = *Logik als die Frage nach dem Wesen der Sprache*, ed. Günther Seubold (1998), *Logic as the Question Concerning the Essence of Language*, trans. Wanda Torres Gregory and Yvonne Unna (Albany: SUNY Press, 2009); GA 39 = *Hölderlins Hymnen "Germanien" und "Der Rhein,"* ed. Susanne Ziegler (1980), *Hölderlin's Hymns "Germanien" and "Der Rhein,"* trans. William McNeill (Bloomington: Indiana University Press, forthcoming); GA 53 = *Hölderlins Hymne "Der Ister,"* ed. Walter Biemel (1994), *Hölderlin's Hymn "The Ister,"* trans. William McNeill and Julia Davis (Bloomington: Indiana University Press, 1996); GA 65 = *Beiträge zur Philosophie (vom Ereignis)*, ed. Friedrich-Wilhelm von Herrmann (1989), *Contributions to Philosophy (Of the Event)*, trans. Richard Rojcewicz and Daniela Vallega-Neu (Bloomington: Indiana University Press, 2012); GA 69 = *Die Geschichte des Seyns*, ed. Peter Trawny (1998).

3 Instead of "insight", Arnold Bergstraesser's transcript here names "state" as an existential concept.

4 RA (Rectoral Address) = Martin Heidegger, *Die Selbstbehauptung der deutschen Universität* (1933; 9–19) and *Das Rektorat 1933/35: Tatsachen und Gedanken* (1945; 21–43), ed. Hermann Heidegger (Frankfurt: Klostermann, 1983). English translation by Lisa Harries, "The Self-Assertion of the German University" (5–13) and "The Rectorate 1933/34: Facts and Thoughts" (15–32), in Gunther Neske and Emil Kettering, eds, *Martin Heidegger and National Socialism: Questions and Answers* (New York: Paragon, 1990). In GA 16, 107–17 and 372–94.

5 EM = Martin Heidegger, *Einführung in die Metaphysik* (Tübingen: Niemeyer, 1953), English translation by Gregory Fried and Richard Polt, *Introduction to Metaphysics* (New Haven: Yale UP, 2000).

6 DWB 1 & 2 = Paul Natorp, *Deutscher Weltberuf. Geschichtsphilosophische Richtlinien*. First Book: *Die Weltalter des Geistes*; Second Book: *Die Seele des Deutschen* (Jena: Eugen Diederichs, 1918).

7 Fritz K. Ringer, *The Decline of the German Mandarins: The German Academic Community, 1890–1933* (Cambridge: Harvard UP, 1969). Ringer defines the mandarins "as a *social and cultural elite which owes its status primarily to educational qualifications, rather than to hereditary rights or wealth*" (5, my emphasis). They include doctors, lawyers, ministers, government officials, gymnasium teachers, and university professors, precisely the "professions" that Heidegger identifies in the Rectoral Address as the "leaders and guardians of the state."

8 Paul Natorp, *Gesammelte Abhandlungen zur Sozialpädagogik. Erste Abteilung: Historisches* (Stuttgart: Fr. Frommanns Verlag [E. Hauff], 1907), 23–4, 36, 70, 282.The first essay in the collection is "Platos Staat und die Idee der *Sozialpädagogik*," 1–36.

9 Ibid. 132, 95.

10 Martin Heidegger/Elisabeth Blochmann, *Briefwechsel 1918–1969*, Joachim W. Storck (ed.) (Marbach am Neckar: Deutsche Schillergesellschaft, 1989), 60. Translated by Frank W. H. Edler in "Selected Letters from the Heidegger-Blochmann Correspondence," *Graduate Faculty Philosophy Journal* 14/2–15/1 (1991): 557–77, esp. 570–1.

11 The most accessible transcript of these unpublished talks, the one delivered by Heidegger in Freiburg on December 11, 1930, is to be found in the Helene Weiss Archive at Stanford University.

12 Guido Schneeberger, *Nachlese zu Heidegger. Dokumente zu seinem Leben und Denken* (Bern: private circulation, 1962), 214. Comments made on February 21, 1934.

13 Martin Heidegger, "Die Bedrohung der Wissenschaft: Arbeitskreis von Dozenten der naturwissenschaftlichen und medizinischen Fakultät (November 1937)—(Auszüge)," in D. Papenfuss and O. Pöggeler, eds., *Zur philosophischen Aktualität Heideggers*, vol. 1; *Philosophie und Politik* (Frankfurt: Klostermann, 1991), 5–27. Page references here are mostly to a set of loose "notes on the working circle" that was held *privatissime* since the Fall of 1936, which the editor (Hartmut Tietjen) has entitled "Philosophie, Wissenschaft und Weltanschauung" (14–27).

14 Martin Heidegger, "Überwindung der Metaphysik," *Vorträge und Aufsätze* (Pfullingen: Neske, 1954), 71–99, esp. 94 and 96. English translation by Joan Stambaugh in Martin Heidegger, *The End of Philosophy* (New York: Harper & Row, 1973), pp 84–110, esp. 105 and 107; reproduced in the Wolin edition, *The Heidegger Controversy*, "Overcoming Metaphysics (1936–1946)," 67–90, esp. 85 and 87; references are to no. XXVI of this collection of notes, a note that was written not earlier than late 1942.

15 Silvio Vietta, *Heideggers Kritik am Nationalsozialismus und an der Technik* (Tübingen: Niemeyer, 1989), 47, cites a diary notation of the pedagogue Heribert Heinrich on a "private" conversation in which Heidegger observes that "most Germans came to see Adolf Hitler as the robber and criminal of the century only with the catastrophe at Stalingrad and the disaster of the air war." But for Heidegger, "1938 was a turning point in my life. 1938! That was even before Hitler's great triumphs!" beginning with the *Anschluß* of Austria.

16 "The *polis* is *polos*, that is, the pole, the vortex in which and around which everything revolves. In both words, *the* essential is named, what in the second verse of the chorus the verb *pelein* says: constancy and change" (GA 53: 100/81).

17 Martin Heidegger, *Was heißt Denken?* (Tübingen: Niemeyer, 1954), 67. English translation by Fred D. Wieck and J. Glenn Gray, *What is Called Thinking?* (New York: Harper & Row, 1968), 69. One aphorism (No. 983) in the published version of *Wille zur Macht* speaks of "the Roman Caesar with the soul of Christ."

18 In the recent film "The King's Speech," the stuttering King George VI, in viewing a newsreel of a Hitler speech with his children, one of whom asks, "What is he saying?," replies: "I don't know, but he seems to be saying it rather well." This is a step back from the usual Western parodies of Hitler speaking, as in Chaplin's "Modern Times."

19 Moving from the Athenian democracy of Aristotle's time to our own democratic *polis*, it is worthy of note that all of the rights and freedoms granted by our Bill of Rights are more or less "rhetorical" in nature: freedom of speech, of the press, of religion, of assembly, and the right to petition the government to redress our grievances.

20 Cf. Charles Bambach, *Heidegger's Roots: Nietzsche, National Socialism, and the Greeks* (Ithaca and London: Cornell UP, 2003). In this most thoroughgoing account of *Bodenständigkeit* in Heidegger's sense and in the NS sense, Bambach nowhere notes its relationship to a native or indigenous language.

21   Cf. Theodore Kisiel, "The Siting of Hölderlin's 'Geheimes Deutschland'
      in Heidegger's Poetizing of the Political," *Heidegger-Jahrbuch* 5 (2009),
      145–54, esp. 152.

5 Heidegger in the foursome of struggle, historicity, will, and *Gelassenheit*

1   See Martin Heidegger, *Nietzsche*, 2 vols. (New York: HarperOne, 1991).
2   See Martin Heidegger, *Contributions to Philosophy (From Enowning)*
     (Bloomington: Indiana University Press, 2000), 40; *Contributions to
     Philosophy (Of the Event)* (Bloomington: Indiana University Press,
     2012), 46.
3   Even at the superficial political level, Heidegger followed with great
     sympathy the student revolt of the late 1960s (as told to me by Wolfgang
     Schirmacher, who visited Heidegger in 1968 as part of a student
     delegation). After World War II, he more or less consistently voted for
     the Social Democrats or SPD; this was reported to me by Karl-Heinz
     Volkmann-Schluck when he visited Slovenia in the early 1970s, and is
     confirmed by Heidegger's letter to his wife of November 11, 1966. "Let's
     hope the SPD & FDP stick together so the conservatives don't make any
     headway": *Letters to His Wife*, ed. Gertrud Heidegger, trans. R. D. V.
     Glasgow (Cambridge: Polity, 2008), 299.
4   See Emmanuel Faye, *Heidegger, l'introduction du nazisme dans la
     philosophie* (Paris: Albin Michel, 2005); *Heidegger: The Introduction
     of Nazism into Philosophy in Light of the Unpublished Seminars of
     1933–1935*, trans. Michael B. Smith (New Haven: Yale University
     Press, 2009).
5   See Jürgen Habermas, "Mit Heidegger gegen Heidegger denken. Zur
     Veröffentlichung von Vorlesungen aus dem Jahre 1935," *Frankfurter
     Allgemeine Zeitung*, 25.7.1953, published as "Martin Heidegger: Zur
     Veröffentlichung von Vorlesungen aus dem Jahre 1935," in J. Habermas,
     Philosophisch-politische Profile (Frankfurt am Main: Suhrkamp, 1971),
     67–75.
6   See Jean-Luc Nancy, *Être singulier pluriel* (Paris: Galilée, 1996).
7   "Why Do I Stay in the Provinces?" trans. Thomas Sheehan, in Manfred
     Stassen, ed., *Martin Heidegger: Philosophical and Political Writings*
     (London: Continuum, 2003), 18.
8   See Bret W. Davis, *Heidegger and the Will* (Evanston: Northwestern
     University Press, 2007).

9 Martin Heidegger, *Holzwege, Gesamtausgabe,* vol. 5 (Frankfurt: Klostermann, 1977), 355.

10 For a closer analysis of the vicissitudes of Will in Heidegger's development, see Chapter 3 of Slavoj Žižek, *In Defense of Lost Causes* (London: Verso, 2008).

11 See Eric Santner, *On the Psychotheology of Everyday Life* (Chicago: University of Chicago Press, 2001).

12 Michael Jordan was also known as "Air Jordan" because his jumps seemed to defy the laws of gravity.

13 See Gregory Fried, *Heidegger's Polemos: From Being to Politics* (New Haven: Yale University Press, 2000).

14 Davis, *Heidegger and the Will,* 294.

15 Heidegger's relation to Schelling and Hegel is crucial here. See Slavoj Žižek, *Less Than Nothing: Hegel and the Shadow of Dialectical Materialism* (London: Verso, 2012), 887–90.

16 Attentive interpreters noticed the multiplicity of meanings of Heidegger's *Kehre.* The three main ones are: 1 the shift in Heidegger's thought from Being to *Ereignis*; 2 the shift in the world-history of Being from technology to *Ereignis*; 3 the strife in *Ereignis* itself between *Ereignis* and its *Unwesen, Ent-eignis.*

17 When Heidegger speaks of the "concealment of concealment itself" or "oblivion of oblivion," one should not reduce it to a double movement of first forgetting Being in our immersion in beings and then forgetting this forgetting itself: Forgetting *is* always also a forgetting of forgetting itself, otherwise it is not forgetting at all—in this sense, as Heidegger put it, it is not only that Being withdraws itself, but Being is *nothing but* its own withdrawal. (Furthermore, concealment is a concealment of concealment in a much more literal way: what is concealed is not Being in its purity but the fact that concealment is part of Being itself.)

18 Of great interest here are Heidegger's attempts to "repeat" Kant. See Žižek, *Less Than Nothing,* 894.

19 Davis, *Heidegger and the Will,* 145.

20 Ibid., 279.

21 Ibid., 286.

22 Heidegger, *Introduction to Metaphysics,* trans. Gregory Fried and Richard Polt (New Haven: Yale University Press, 2000), 47.

23 Heidegger, *Being and Truth,* trans. Gregory Fried and Richard Polt (Bloomington: Indiana University Press, 2010), 73.

24 Ernst Nolte, *Martin Heidegger—Politik und Geschichte im Leben und Denken* (Berlin: Propyläen, 1992), 277.

25 Peter Hallward, "Communism of the Intellect, Communism of the Will," in *The Idea of Communism* (London: Verso, 2010), 117.

26 Ibid., 112.

27 At his intervention at the conference "On the Idea of Communism," organized by the School of Law, Birkbeck College, London, on March 13–15, 2009.

28 Heidegger's qualifications of Soviet Communism as "metaphysically the same" as Americanism, that is, as another version of the total technological mobilization, are well known: for example, *Introduction to Metaphysics*, 40, 48.

29 "Only a God Can Save Us: *Der Spiegel's* interview with Martin Heidegger," in Richard Wolin, ed., *The Heidegger Controversy*, (Cambridge: MIT Press, 1993), 55.

30 Miguel de Beistegui, *Heidegger and the Political* (London: Routledge, 1998), 116.

31 Against Davis's sympathies for Zen Buddhism, one should bear in mind that Japanese militarism perfectly fitted Zen warriors who killed with *Gelassenheit*.

INDEX

of the leader 9–10, 49, 81, 84, 147
of the people 9, 48–9, 60, 61, 63,
    78, 91, 154
political 167
to power 6, 143, 146–7
and subjectivity 151, 156, 169
transformation of 84
and unwillingness 62
wish (*Wunsch*) 4, 48, 58–9, 61, 78
Wittgenstein, Ludwig 104

work 132–3, 135, 137–9, 167
    see also labor
world (*Welt*) 104, 129, 133–4, 181
World War I 62, 131, 148
World War II 146, 192

Ziegler, Matthes 122
zōē 51–2, 158
zōon logon echon 52
zōon politikon 41, 72